Jonathan Bazzi (they/them) ~~was~~ born in Milan in 1985. They grew up in Rozzano, on the extreme southern outskirts of the city. They studied philosophy and graduated with a thesis on symbolic theology in the work of Edith Stein. Jonathan has collaborated with various newspapers and magazines, including *Gay.it*, *Vice*, *The Vision*, and *Il Fatto.it*. *Fever* is their first novel.

Alice Whitmore (she/her) is a writer and literary translator living on Eastern Maar country. Her translation of Mariana Dimópulos's *Imminence* was awarded the 2021 NSW Premier's Translation Prize.

FEVER

JONATHAN BAZZI

Translated by Alice Whitmore

SCRIBE
Melbourne • London

Scribe Publications
18–20 Edward St, Brunswick, Victoria 3056, Australia
2 John St, Clerkenwell, London, WC1N 2ES, United Kingdom
3754 Pleasant Ave, Suite 100, Minneapolis, Minnesota 55409, USA

First published in Italian as *Febbre*
Published by Scribe 2022

Typeset in Adobe Caslon Pro by the publishers

Printed and bound in the UK by CPI Group (UK) Ltd, Croydon CR0 4YY

Scribe is committed to the sustainable use of natural resources and the use of paper products made responsibly from those resources.

978 1 950354 96 2 (US edition)
978 1 922310 90 3 (Australian edition)
978 1 913348 83 0 (UK edition)
978 1 922586 39 1 (ebook)

Catalogue records for this book are available from the National Library of Australia and the British Library.

Questo libro e' stato tradotto grazie ad un contributo alla traduzione assegnato dal Ministero degli Affari Esteri e della Cooperazione Internazionale Italiano.

This book has been translated thanks to a contribution to the translation assigned by the Italian Ministry of Foreign Affairs and International Cooperation.

This project has been assisted by the Australian Government through the Australia Council, its arts funding and advisory body.

scribepublications.com
scribepublications.com.au
scribepublications.co.uk

For the invisible children

In every love relationship, even the most passionate and impulsive, some blows must be held back; I mean, some words must not be spoken, some thoughts must not be expressed, some questions must not be asked.

Elsa Morante, *House of Liars*

I am writing with my burnt hand about the nature of fire.

Ingeborg Bachmann

Three years ago the fever came over me and never left

Three years ago the fever came over me and never left.

11 January, 2016.

Almost thirty-one years old.

I get home from university; it's lunchtime, but I'm not hungry.

What's wrong?

I don't feel so good, I think I might be coming down with a fever.

I lie down on the couch, but I can't focus on my book.

The fever sets in.

It doesn't go away.

One week, two weeks.

A month.

Thirty-eight, thirty-eight point five, then it goes down slightly.

Thirty-seven point four, thirty-seven point three. The fever doesn't break.

The mercury must be stuck.

I cool it down.

It climbs back up.

Each time I remove the thermometer from my armpit, I hope to see that the fever has subsided. But it never has. The mercury sits at a little over thirty-seven degrees, right on the edge, at the turning point — the boundary between what I was and what I've become.

I get home from university and take my temperature. I take it again, and again, I take it incessantly.

My mother calls me. She starts calling every three hours.

So, is that fever still hanging around?

Yes, mamma, it's still here.

So strange — take your temperature again later.

And again. Never stop taking it.

Soon she's asking me for an update every two hours.

Paracetamol doesn't help; my temperature falls briefly, then rises again.

Three days, five, ten.

I go to work even though I don't feel like it; for the past four years (or is it five?) I've been teaching yoga at different gyms across Milan. I enjoyed it at first, but not anymore. I've been forced to teach too many classes, at all times of day, all over the city. Health clubs, dance schools, gyms. The quality of the venues varies, but more often than not they're dumps. Still, teaching has kept me afloat through university. I accept every job, every substitution, even when I really don't want to.

If I don't go to work, I won't get paid. I have to go, fever or no fever.

I'm a freelancer, so I don't have a contract. No sick leave, no holiday pay. Tomorrow I have an early class, I have to leave the house at seven. I thought I would have been feeling a bit better by now. It's too late to call in sick. The guy in charge of scheduling classes is new, he's been laying off a bunch of people. Sucking up to management: calling instructors, threatening them, reducing their hours. In Milan there are now more yoga instructors than there are students — the teacher-training business has really taken off — so, if he wanted to, he could replace any one of us at a moment's notice.

★

I sweat so much at night. When I wake up the bed is drenched. A black stain on the blue sheets, in the shape of my sleeping body. A black me-shaped stain.

Even the pillow is soaked with sweat. I wet one side; I turn it over and wet the other side.

I get up and change. I go through three T-shirts a night. This is how it will be from now on: at night, my body dissolves into a pool of water. My body surrenders to this mad fever, which rises and falls according to its own rhythms.

I wake up, take a shower, accidentally fall back to sleep on the couch.

I sweat some more, I wake up, I leave the house just after seven, running late, bathed in sweat.

Milan in January; it must be two degrees. The icy air creeps inside my coat, freezes the sweat on my skin. I want to turn around and go back inside. I brace against the cold, pull up my hood, protecting my head. I walk slowly, enveloped in my layers of fabric and sweat. One foot after the other.

I speed up, then slow back down.

I have to figure out what's wrong with me.

Street, crossing, then Metro. I need to sit down.

My body stalls. I can't do this.

I deepen my breaths, breathing right into the bottom of my rib cage — I *have* to do this.

I make it to the gym, change, join the class. Everyone is waiting for me; I'm at least fifteen minutes late. The class only goes for fifty minutes. No doubt someone has already complained.

I apologise, I admit it, I tell them the truth: I'm not feeling well.

3

We thought you weren't going to show up.

I smile. *What the fuck do you want from me?*

The older women who come to my classes are used to seeing me move easily from one pose to the next. Flexible, strong, like an athlete. *What's wrong with him? What's happened to him?* I apologise at first, but then I stop. What's the point?

Four days into the fever, my mother starts losing her mind. She heard about a girl — she tells me over the phone — who started out like me, with a mild but persistent fever. One week later she was dead.

Acute meningitis.

Go to the doctor, what are you waiting for? For it to be too late?

She calls me nonstop. When she's not calling, she's texting me. If I don't respond immediately she sends another, then another, dozens and dozens of text messages; she transmits her fear to me through the phone's electromagnetic field, until her fear is my fear.

Go and see a doctor.

I don't even have a doctor. I had one, until the end of last year. One of those temporary doctors they assign to you if you're a student, or if you're residing somewhere different from where you usually live. After a year the arrangement expires, and I never got around to renewing mine.

My mother is right — I have to do something.

I try getting in touch with a new doctor, one recommended by my friend Gianfranco. He's young, I think he's gay. He's on Facebook and Instagram. He's into art history — he posts more photos of paintings than anything else. He studies Traditional

Chinese Medicine, acupuncture. He posts vegan recipes. I write to him on Messenger.

Hi, can I bother you for a minute?

Of course, no problem at all.

I don't have a GP at the moment. I'm from outside Milan, but I've lived here for a few years now. I haven't changed my residency details yet. A friend of mine suggested I get in touch with you, for a medical opinion.

Go ahead.

I've had a fever for several days. It goes up and down, but I don't have any other symptoms.

Cough, sore throat?

No, everything else is fine.

Are you urinating normally? Normal bowel movements?

Yes.

Can you come in tomorrow morning? I can make time to see you, even though you're not my patient.

Okay.

If we need to, I might send you to the local health department afterwards. I'll be at the clinic between 10 and 12:30. Come in, we can have a chat and see if we can't send you home with some peace of mind.

Mamma and I are alone when they come to scare us

Mamma and I are alone when they come to scare us.

I'm one and a half; we've been living in the one-bedroom apartment at 10 Hyacinth Street for just a few months.

We're home alone because papà is at work.

At around four in the morning, mamma wakes up. There are noises, banging sounds. It's been raining since last night. Mamma thinks: *it must be the rain, or a branch in the wind.*

But no, it's not the rain, or the wind.

Mamma gets up, goes to the kitchen, where the sound is coming from.

I'm still asleep in the cot next to papà and mamma's bed. *You didn't notice a thing.* Bee mobile hanging over my head, little zoo of stuffed animals sitting quietly, everything in its place. You didn't notice a thing — cover it up, minimise; our life, your life, is a perfectly normal life.

The shutters on the glass doors that open out to the kitchen balcony are rolled down; whenever papà leaves he shuts and locks them, for security. Mamma doesn't turn on the kitchen light; she doesn't have to. The streetlamp in front of the apartment we were allocated a few months ago by the city council — on the second of eight floors, the first door to the right when you come up the stairs — illuminates the facade of our building, and our balcony.

In the light from the Hyacinth Street streetlamp mamma can

see a pair of hands reaching underneath the shutter, trying to force it open. The hands pull upwards, but the harder they pull, the harder the locks jam the shutter into place.

Mamma feels her legs buckle.

Dear god, I beg you, please make the locks hold.

Give me time to call someone.

My mother is in the kitchen doorway, watching the shutter that's about to give.

The hands persist, they refuse to quit — they have a mission to complete. They pull fiercely against the shutter that is meant to protect us. The hands are hairy, a man's hands. The hands of the man who is trying to break into our house. Nails edged with black dirt, calloused fingers straining: the hands of an ogre, a criminal, a rapist?

Mamma flicks the switch beside the door; the kitchen fills with light, but the man doesn't go away. He's not scared of being seen. If he's not a burglar, then what does he want from us?

One of the locks fails and goes flying. It hits the glass door. The man seems encouraged by the sound of the impact. He shakes the shutter even harder.

Help, mamma, what do we do?

Mamma realises the man isn't going to leave. Ready for anything, nothing to lose.

She turns, reaches for the telephone in the hallway. She calls her father-in-law, nonno Pier, who lives nearby.

Why don't you escape, mamma? Why don't you run and ask the neighbours for help?

Mamma is afraid there might be someone on the stairs; she's afraid the man on the balcony hasn't come alone. How many of them are there? A gang? An army? There's no hope for the two of us: a nineteen-year-old girl and her eighteen-month-old baby. Trapped in the tiny home the council gave to us as though we were grown-ups, as though we were adults. What have we done? Why have you come for us?

Mamma dials quickly — my grandparents' number.

She knows it by heart.

Signor Pierluigi?

Signor Pierluigi, can you hear me?

It's Tina. Signor Pierluigi, please come to the apartment, someone's trying to break in.

Nonna Nuccia calls papà. Nonno Pier throws his shoes on and runs downstairs. He cuts through the parking garage and courtyard, crosses the few streets that separate us. Azalea Street, Begonia Street, Narcissus Street, Rhododendron Street. Nonno sprints to our house as fast as he can, he is coming to save us.

While nonno is still on his way, the man on the balcony gives up and flees.

Did he hear mamma making the phone call?

Nonno arrives, then papà.

My father — twenty-two years old — has already figured out what's happened. He heads straight for Carmelo's apartment, on the ground floor.

Do whatever the hell you want with *your* life, but don't you dare fuck with my family.

Papà is confident: he tells mamma nobody was actually trying to break into the apartment. They just wanted to scare us. They wanted us to know who's in charge. Carmelo is the resident mob boss of Hyacinth Street — he and his people carry weapons, run a black market. They knocked out all the interior walls in the basement of our building to use it as a warehouse for stolen goods. Our basement doesn't belong to us; along with the basements of just about every other building in the street, it belongs to the petty criminals of Rozzano.

People complain, but nobody does anything.

You try standing up to those thugs …

One of these days I'll report them to the carabinieri — the promise is made constantly, unanimously. People complain about the basements and all the rest of it, but things can only change if someone dies. And when they do change, it's not always for the better. A new order is simply established, a new hierarchy. A new mob boss comes along.

It's still drizzling outside. When nonno and papà arrive, they roll up the kitchen shutter and find the man's footprints. The balcony has no tiles; while he's saving up the money to fix it, papà has laid a sheet of plastic over the bare cement.

The man left his muddy footprints on the plastic.

He almost broke in once, he can easily try again. Mamma knows this; she says it to my father.

Roberto, I refuse to stay here alone. What is this awful place they've made us live in?

Tina, calm down, I'll figure it out.

Everything's going to be fine. I promise.

How are you feeling?

How are you feeling?

Weak, floppy, like I've got the flu.

I give the same three or four adjectives to anyone who asks. Loose, vague, inept descriptions.

That's it, I've made up my mind: I'm going to the doctor.

I take the Metro towards Sesto to visit my new doctor in his clinic, nestled between Viale Monza and Via Padova. I wait on a grey, Sixties-style felt chair. The doctor is busy at the front desk with a young African girl who doesn't speak good Italian. She has a gynaecological problem. The doctor is booking her in with a specialist.

Do you understand what I'm saying?

The specialist can see you tomorrow, okay?

Do you know how to get there?

The girl collects her things and leaves.

Next patient, please.

As I enter the room, my new doctor tells me I'm dehydrated. He asks me to sit down on the examination table, looks at my eyes, my skin. See how dry your lips are? Have you been drinking enough water? Try making some infusions — ginger, turmeric.

I've had a fever for a week. I have no other symptoms.

No sniffle, no sore throat.

Your body needs to heal on its own, he says. I'm not going to prescribe antibiotics.

He recommends supplements, echinacea, a multivitamin, probiotics for my gut. I buy them all at the pharmacy. They're bound to make me feel better. When I get home, I take a photo of the little collection of bottles lined up in front of the kitchen window, bathed in clean white light.

Natural therapies — this will heal me.

Wrong. Nothing changes.

The fever remains.

Thirty-seven point three, thirty-seven point four.

My temperature doesn't skyrocket, but it doesn't go down either.

It stays where it is, morning to evening.

I check it over and over again. *Have you taken your temperature?* Bed, couch, then bed again. My mother calls me — I can't bear to tell her that the fever hasn't subsided. That it's still here, just as bad as before. It's not a flu, I have to admit that now. At least, not a normal flu.

I start looking up symptoms and causes on the internet. What is this mysterious sickness?

I leave home as little as possible. I drag myself to my yoga classes, and occasionally to the supermarket, when I have absolutely no other choice. The rest of the time I lie on the couch, looking up diagnoses online. I have to find answers. I need to understand what is happening to me.

Low-grade fever, it's called. Turns out there's a special name for it. I google: *fever that won't go away; constant low fever.* I search again and again. I scan websites, forums, online consultations with doctors. *Persistent low-grade fever; mild fever for two weeks.* For some people the fever never goes away, it's a kind of syndrome. I read accounts from people who've had what I have, or who still have it. *Fever of Unknown Origin (FUO)*. There are much more severe cases, too. People who fall seriously ill.

I'm scared, I'm starting to get really scared.

Hidden abscesses, infections, thyroid problems, tumours.

11 January, 2016. I got home from university, and the fever set in.

I walked home that day, even though I'd already been feeling unwell in class. The university is a ten-minute walk from home. I didn't take the Metro — a decision I soon regretted.

Lunchtime: I should eat something but I'm not hungry. In the Political Philosophy class I just started taking, the professor used the example of the Siege of Melos to illustrate the theory that power relations are the only relevant factor in world politics. I try to read over my notes, but my eyes are burning. I can't do it. I have a fever, and it's never going away.

I stop attending my university classes. I stop going the very next day. I drop out and never go back.

I'll never graduate.

Monday, 11 January. It was my boyfriend Marius's birthday on the eighth. We've lived together for three years. Me, Marius, and the two Devon Rex cats I got with my ex: Blueberry and Mashed Potatoes (I wanted to call them Rosaspina and Léon, my ex wanted to call them Poor Thing and Unfortunately, so we compromised). On the Saturday night, to celebrate Marius's birthday, we went out dancing with his friends. Or rather, we went to a couple of local bars for drinks and then went to a club. I wasn't feeling sick, maybe a little tired. Nothing out of the ordinary. In the bathroom of the club one of Marius's friends looked at me and said, laughing: you don't look healthy, I think you've got HIV. I think *you've* got HIV, I replied. All the HIV-positive people I know are total sluts, like you.

The thing is, I've always had a weary, drained look — ever since I was a kid, people have been telling me I look sick.

You've got bags under your eyes, you're so pale, go outside and get some sun.

Have you been eating properly?

I have a video from the night of Marius's birthday: in one of the bars we visited before we went out dancing, I filmed myself stuffing a wad of cling wrap into my mouth. I was drunk. I uploaded the video to Instagram, in reverse: it looks like a large flower made of crushed glass is sprouting from my mouth. The swollen, shiny ball grows long and thin, emerging from the bud of my lips. My eyes are wide, my skin flushed, the phone's flash lighting up my face.

Two more days pass.

I go back to see my new doctor.

The clinic is empty; it just opened, so they don't have many patients yet. I take advantage of the doctor's availability, and his eagerness to please.

I walk in, sit down.

So, how's it going?

The fever hasn't gone away. It goes up and down, but it hasn't gone away.

He plays it down, thinks maybe I'm just not looking after myself — it's probably a flu, it's the season for it, after all.

Have you been taking your supplements? It could be glandular fever. Symptoms include low-grade fever and night sweats, and you're experiencing both. We'll need to do some blood tests. The results will help us understand what kind of infection you've got — whether it's viral, as I suspect, or bacterial.

I go in for my tests the next day. My friend Alessandro comes with me. Alessandro and I met at university; he graduated with a degree in art history and recently started working at a couple of auction houses. He has an obsession with Renaissance marriage chests, the kind used to store the bride's trousseau. He lives in Bergamo with his boyfriend, but he's made a special trip to Milan to accompany me to the hospital. He stays at my apartment the night before, and early in the morning we head to the Policlinico. It's in the centre of town, Via Sforza, just behind La Statale, the university I'm still enrolled in.

We leave home at around seven. It's not far from my apartment, in Porta Venezia, to the hospital, but I tire quickly. Each step is an effort. I walk in silence — sooner or later this will be over. Surely. But when?

We stop at a café.

I'm wearing my usual brown puffer jacket. Marius gave it to me last year, because I didn't own anything warm enough for the winter. Since we've been together I've practically stopped buying clothes — I just wear his. I like them, and he likes being my stylist. Being with Marius has definitely improved my fashion sense. I no longer dress like a library mouse slash Swiss goatherd. I don't even have a separate wardrobe anymore — Marius and I share everything. We are one; even our clothes are one.

I wait for Alessandro to finish his breakfast. He eats a brioche, drinks a soy cappuccino. I have to fast until my blood sample is taken. He pays and we leave. We walk a little more, take a bus, exchange as few words as possible, then, finally, we're here.

At the hospital, standing in line at the co-pay desk, I come back to life — it's as if the chaos flicks a switch inside me. To distract myself from the boredom of waiting, I take a selfie and post it to Instagram; surrounded by all the screens and monitors, I look like a tv news reporter.

I hear snatches of the conversations happening around me.

I lose myself in the snippets of phrases and the refrains of the receptionists.

Do you have a health insurance card?

Excuse me, have you provided a urine sample?

How many months pregnant are you, signora?

That'll be twenty-seven euros and eighty cents.

Fifteen minutes, half an hour; finally, it's my turn.

I walk alone into the corridor that leads to the consulting rooms.

The nurse who attends to me is male, brusque, he has his radio on — he's speaking to his colleagues as I walk in. They're joking around, laughing. This guy couldn't care less if I'm sick. Life goes on, even if I'm in mortal danger. *Don't play the victim.* But it's true: to a sick person, their condition is the most important thing in the world. They feel like everything should stop in its tracks, including the lives of everyone around them. Their illness fences them off, separates them, confines them to a selfish, frightened place: the place of the primordial 'I', which sees nothing but itself.

Quickly, without saying a word to me, the nurse fastens the strap around my arm. I divert my eyes, so as to not connect the sensation of the needle puncturing my skin with the image of my pierced flesh, the blood being drawn from my body.

I'm not scared, I just don't want to associate those things. I don't want to see it happening.

The nurse, who still hasn't spoken to me, removes the needle from my arm. Accept it: you aren't entitled to anything more than this routine, mechanical procedure. Protocol: we're done, goodbye, next.

The nurse's rushed treatment shows; on my way back to Alessandro — I left him sitting in the waiting room — a pearl of blood appears underneath the cotton ball fixed to my skin with masking tape. It travels slowly down my forearm, all the way to my wrist. It's beautiful. I take a photo of it: a dark-red line that gradually grows lighter, thinner, revealing glimpses of the skin beneath it.

The photo marks the end of the morning's adventures.

Now I just have to wait.

I clean myself up in the bathroom, grab something from the vending machine. A hot tea, full of sugar. A snack, anything will do. My healthy eating habits are over. They have failed.

I go back home and go to bed.

I sleep for a couple of hours.

I wake up, take my temperature.

Nothing new.

The mercury confirms it.

This is really happening.

I grew up in Rozzano, postcode 20089

I grew up in Rozzano, postcode 20089: a small town — although not so small, in reality — on the extreme southern periphery of Milan, constructed in the middle of the countryside, along the banks of the Naviglio Pavese, the canal that flows from Milan to Pavia, and fenced in to the south by the A50 Ring Road.

Buccinasco, Corsico, Assago, Rozzano: places known for producing hip-hop artists, or else recognised from the crime pages of the newspapers. Shootings, deadly brawls, youth gangs, mafia connections.

The population of Rozzano is a little under 43,000. It's a bit like the Bronx of Northern Italy. A place inhabited by working-class people, drug addicts, dealers. Low-lives, criminals, welfare scabs. True? False?

Shame on you: there are plenty of good, honest people in Rozzano.

Careful what you write; don't forget, we still live here.

Rozzano, *Rozzangeles* — can you picture it? It's easy to spot, even from a distance: in 1990 they plonked a Telecom tower right in the middle of town, like an oversized Monopoly token. An enormous structure, 187 metres tall, that looms over everything and disappears at night, transforming into a constellation of lights — some steady, some flashing — that resembles some kind of UFO, and can be seen from tens of kilometres away.

The Tower of Rozzano, where I come from.

Look, the tower: we're almost home.

Rozzano is Milan, but it's not Milan.

The town is composed entirely of big, drab public-housing towers. Streets and streets of apartment blocks, one after the other. Ochre, grey, green, pale yellow: the colours of the buildings I grew up in. Clusters of mass-produced apartments — one, two, or three bedrooms — arranged side by side in military-like formations. The buildings belong to a government body called ALER: the Lombardy Public Housing Commission. They're normally eight storeys, although some are only three or four storeys. Tiny homes stacked like the cells of a beehive. One family living on top of another, forming a single organism, branded with the same street name and number.

Almost all the streets that twist through the public-housing towers of Rozzano are named after plants and flowers — Carnation, Verbena, Rhododendron — presumably according to the same logic that saw the favelas of Rio painted in bright Luna Park tones.

Rents are low, sometimes very low, and are adjusted according to income. When mamma and I were living alone, mamma paid a little over 50,000 lire a month. Even so, plenty of people don't pay their rent, sometimes for years at a time.

There are a lot of southerners in Rozzano, but Rozzano is not the South. If anything, it's a kind of sun-less South. An uprooted and hastily replanted South. A place where all the troubles of Calabria, Sicily, Puglia, Campania are combined and condensed, then shrouded in the cold and fog of the Po Valley. A cool South with no ocean, no family ties, no surviving traditions. The South's impetuous, animal force turned against itself: starved, caged.

Rozzano is a kidnapped, captive South: the South in captivity.

There is always fighting in Rozzano. Sometimes people die.

It's happened before, it'll happen again.

A guy arguing with two acquaintances in a courtyard. Over drugs, they'll claim later. He walks away. Heads home, grabs the pistol he keeps hidden in the wardrobe, returns to the courtyard and shoots. It's ten in the evening. Four people murdered right there in Hawthorn Street.

A pensioner dies of a broken heart.

A little girl, not even three years old, dies after being accidentally hit in the neck.

Her name was Seby — Sebastiana. She was our neighbours' daughter.

Rozzano is crisscrossed by waterways: small streams, more akin to gutters than rivers, narrow shards of wilderness that some locals find unsettling. Repositories of filth and waste along whose banks it's not uncommon to spot frogs, mice, coypu, discarded furniture. Some years ago, a dead body surfaced in one: a homeless man, according to the newspapers. A fifty-eight-year-old Bulgarian citizen. Two days later, another: a young woman, very thin, entangled in leaves and branches. A drug addict who fell into the water and drowned?

Rozzano is old — it existed in Roman times — but the Rozzano I grew up in was mostly constructed in the Sixties and Seventies. Raised from nothing, in the middle of nowhere, among the fields and rice paddies.

My grandparents used to say to me: look there, when we first came here that was all green.

There is still a lot of green in Rozzano, but these days it's invisible, or rather, redundant. The trees and expanses of lawn don't matter to anyone. Nobody sees them. The huge apartment blocks and their appendages are the focal point — the courtyards filled with parked cars, the disused caretakers' quarters, the flowerbeds sprouting their sad tufts of grass. The few exceptions are the small green areas attached to privately owned flats: microscopic kingdoms of wealth and wellbeing, aberrant spaces inhabited by people who pay higher rent and keep to themselves — people much quieter, far less conspicuous, than your typical ALER resident.

A kind of cloistered, protected elite.

As a kid, I imagine these people as happy, proud, arrogant. Their lives must be so different from mine. I'd like to live where they live. Why wasn't I born in Via Guido Rossa, in Valleambrosia, in Cassino Scanasio? Why can't I be like Loris, or Dario, or Valentina?

The beating heart of Rozzano, though, is not found in these quiet anomalies, these oases of privilege. The spirit of Rozzano is crammed, like a family of sardines, into the homes of the people who are doing their best to make ends meet, and also those who aren't — the ones who turn to crime instead. It's in the homes of the women who go to the supermarket in their nightgowns, the kids with fake tans and gel-slicked hair whizzing past on their Vespas, the teenage girls wearing tight tracksuits and a full face of makeup at seven in the morning, with *canzone napoletana* blaring in their headphones. It's in the shouts that fill the courtyard and rise up, up, all the way to the top of the apartment blocks and fill me with anguish.

The swallows don't seem to mind, though — they come every year to make their nests under the eaves.

★

Rozzano was a necessity. Rozzano served a purpose.

Migration pressure.

Dormitory town; dormant, desolate.

Poverty and disadvantage are pumped into Rozzano like wastewater.

People compete over who is worse off.

Your neighbour is a bad influence.

Rozzano families — families almost indistinguishable from one another — comprise a kind of subculture. They speak in a code indecipherable to outsiders. Where they grew up, roles are clearly defined: men are made a certain way — they like Vespas, football, pussy — and women are made a different way. You're either on one side or the other. The slightest hesitation, the slightest glimmer of transgression, is swiftly noticed, and punished. Publicly, in the street, wherever. The code must be pervasive and communal, if the code is to survive.

Rozzano demands certainty; there is no room for nuance.

All the Rozzanesi who have made it big — Michele Alboreto, Alberto Brandi, Arturo Di Naples, Riccardo Morandotti, Antonio Sabato, Mauro Suma — are sports stars or sports journalists. The only exception is Biagio Antonacci, a singer-songwriter, and a childhood friend of my parents. He went to their wedding, and came to the hospital when I was born. He appears in a few photos in their wedding album, a big brown fabric-and-fake-leather-bound book that my mother kept buried at the back of the wardrobe for years, underneath piles of clothes and bedsheets. The spine is falling apart, and there's an enormous gash across the front cover. I threw it at your father, mamma told me once, the day I kicked him out of the house.

★

The town centre of Rozzano runs along Viale Lombardia: a perfectly unremarkable street, lined with banks and hairdressers, but for us the centre of the universe. These days it's filled with Chinese-run businesses — restaurants, nail salons, variety stores — and Middle Eastern kebab shops and butchers. During the day the footpaths are dominated by fast-walking housewives and slow-moving pensioners, but in the early morning and mid-afternoon they're filled with children toting backpacks and lunchboxes to and from school.

Sometimes they're accompanied by their mothers: young women sporting piercings and tattoos, cigarettes smouldering between their fingers, berating their kids without taking their eyes off their smartphones.

Stop being a little shit, you're a real pain this morning.

You see them on the tram, too: girls as young as eighteen or nineteen, already a couple of kids apiece, punishing every peccadillo with pinches and slaps. They alternate heavy-handed discipline with earnest conversations in which they address their children like adults, asking them for advice, opinions, life lessons. They talk to them about money, unforeseen expenses, wonder out loud how they're going to make it to the end of the month. Then the smacking and ear-pulling recommence, punctuated by haphazard, neurotic caresses and words of adoration. The children are sometimes sent to patrol the tram for ticket inspectors, but the rest of the time they're ordered to remain still and silent in their seats.

Hey, shithead, move again and you'll know about it.

Not far from Viale Lombardia is the town square, Piazza Giovanni Foglia, named after a past mayor of Rozzano. A stark, circular space, framed by low structures resembling cement huts.

Home to the civil registry, the real estate registry, the electoral office. For a while there was also a library, but then they moved it to Cascina Grande, in Old Rozzano — Rozzano Vecchio. That's right: *vecchio*, in the masculine. Rozzano is masculine, it ends in *o*.

Hammer and sickle: there are communists in Rozzano, too.

My grandparents use the word communist as a slur: *that's where the communists hang out; I hear so-and-so is a bit of a communist.* The communists meet in circles under the porticoes to talk about politics. Walking past you see the yellowed pages of their daily newspapers, hear their hoarse, bilious commentary, spitting and yelling words that, as a kid, I don't understand but find almost as repulsive as their nicotine-wizened, wine-soaked whiskers. The old men always seem amped up; they nudge each other knowingly whenever I walk past with my mother or my nonna.

Nonna, let's go.

We pick up our pace.

It's not just the communists. For a while, around the mid-Nineties, Rozzano was overrun by members of the right-wing Forza Italia. Female candidates from local chapters and neighbouring towns descended on us in fur coats and stilettos. They campaigned in the town square, or at the Saturday and Tuesday markets, approaching women ushering their kids or grandkids out of the discount supermarkets, their dishevelled ponytails held in place by brightly coloured elastics and hair pins. The candidates are there to proselytise, to plant seeds. They leave behind an assortment of trinkets emblazoned with the Forza Italia symbol: pens, badges, tiny calendars.

Signora, can I give you a flyer?

Do you know who you're going to vote for?

Sorry, I don't have time.

I'm not interested.

Some take advantage of the opportunity: why don't you tell Berlusconi to come and lend us a hand, we're getting shat on down here.

Rozzano is also home to Fiordaliso, a shopping centre that, over the decades, has grown to monstrous proportions. It's been renovated and expanded several times, following the model of American shopping malls. What used to be a single building with a modest selection of supermarkets and shops is now a series of interconnected structures: a cinema multiplex, a sports-supplies warehouse, fast food joints, home centres. Fiordaliso connects us with the rest of the world — it's almost a town of its own, a hamlet of shopping and entertainment that makes Rozzano feel a little less isolated.

And of course we have Humanitas, the avant-garde hospital constructed on the border between Rozzano and Milano 3. People come from all over Italy to be treated at Humanitas. Normal people, but also famous people. The locals don't like it. Nobody admitted to Humanitas ever makes it out alive, they say. You're better off going elsewhere.

You're better off going to Milan.

Rozzano is Fiordaliso, it's Humanitas, it's the Sant'Angelo parish church and Cassino Scanasio castle, it's the overpass and the ring road, the new piazza named in memory of Formula One driver Michele Alboreto, the amateur football pitches, the medical centre on Wisteria Street, where my teeth were drilled without anaesthetic — *please hold him still, signora, this will only take a minute.*

But, above all, Rozzano for me has always been three streets: Hyacinth, Verbena, Dahlia. My mother's house, and the houses of my two sets of grandparents. Three compass points, three refuges — although I wasn't always safe there. My story, the story of my family, is inscribed over Rozzano like a constellation, one map superimposed over another.

Rozzano hates me.

I have hated Rozzano.

Why was I born here? I like to read, write, draw. I'm the teacher's pet in every classroom.

I don't belong here with you illiterate brutes.

And yet, Rozzano is where I was born and raised.

Accept it: you're one of us.

I live in Rozzano, but I try to hide it. I don't want people to know what my home is like. I don't want anyone to see the public-housing tower where I live, with its crumbling plaster facade and its appalling inhabitants leering from the balconies. I don't want them to know I live here.

Whenever someone offers to drive me home from Milan, I ask them to drop me several blocks away. I tell whoever is driving (friend, lover, acquaintance): this is fine, thanks. You can just leave me at the petrol station, or the roundabout. Are you sure? They say: it's no problem, I can drop you at your front door. No, no, there are roadworks outside my place, it's total chaos. Here is great, thanks.

There are roadworks three hundred and sixty-five days a year in my street. Every year, every season. Even in the middle of the night, when it's pitch-black outside. The streets and buildings of Rozzano are my identity card, the physical manifestation of my fear of being discovered and judged as poor — as the son of poor, uneducated, working-class people. The kind of people who never finished high school.

I keep Rozzano a secret because I know that, despite everything, it will always find its way back to me. The place is like a black hole, devouring everything around it: a merciless many-armed deity grasping at its runaway children, reclaiming the ones who have tried, naively, to escape, to make something of themselves. I live in fear of being called home, of being dragged back into its depths. Rozzano is a jealous abyss, and it has marked me, to make it clear to everyone where I belong.

No use trying to hide it.

Where do you think you're going?

You're one of us.

Even today, I'm afraid Rozzano will come for me. That it will suddenly emerge from some forgotten trace — an old document, my facial features, the shabbiness of my clothes — and force me back into captivity among the non-existent hyacinths and wisteria.

Writing about it now, I feel its living presence.

Rozzano is inside me; when I talk about myself I can't avoid talking about Rozzano.

I left, but it's all still here.

I carry its buildings inside my chest, its streets on the soles of my feet. I am the garages, the kiosks, the silent, spooky parks. The outbursts in napoletano and pugliese, the profanities, the explosions of laughter. Even here, in central Milan, the shadow of the Telecom tower still darkens my doorstep.

I've had many addresses over the years, but the only postcode I remember is this one: 20089.

I will always live at 10 Hyacinth Street, at the end of the number 15 tram line.

Terrified of the men that are coming for me.

28 January

28 January.

The test results are ready.

Let's hope it's glandular fever, as the doctor suspects. The Epstein-Barr virus. Kissing disease.

I'm getting more tired every day. The fever isn't passing, it hasn't diminished.

Going out, walking around, is more and more exhausting. Getting to the hospital takes everything I have: walking, staying upright, waiting for the bus. Distances feel threatening — units of measurement against which to gauge my failing strength. I try breaking the journey into a series of smaller, minuscule journeys. Each time, I'm afraid I won't arrive at my destination.

My mother texts me every morning.

So, how's it going? Fever still there?

Yes. Somewhere between thirty-seven and thirty-seven point three degrees. Some evenings it reaches thirty-seven and a half.

Something has jammed in my body. My internal thermostat has adjusted to the wrong level. It won't unjam on its own, that much is clear. Waiting won't help. This situation is not reversible.

But how do you know?

I go to the hospital alone to get my test results, on the morning of 28 January. I take too long at the bus stop — the 94 doesn't stop for me. I sit, rest, wait on the steps of a showroom on Corso Venezia, hoping I have it in me to do what I have to do: board, disembark, put one foot in front of the other, bear the weight of my moving body. I look at the other people waiting: can they tell there's something wrong with me?

Separation. *You're well, I'm not.* I'm sick.

The next bus finally arrives. I collapse onto the seat, rest my head against the window. It's dirty — shiny haloes of grease — but who cares. A few stops, then I get off. My weakness mixes with my anxiety: my legs are too heavy. I cross the street and approach the gate of the Policlinico. Last time, Alessandro was here with me. I could lean on him. Today, I'm alone.

I'm disoriented, but I don't want to walk any more than necessary. I head inside and immediately get lost. I'm looking for the place to get my results. There are too many signs, and none of them is the one I need. I ask a couple of doctors; they're in a hurry. You can tell they're used to hearing the same questions again and again.

I follow their directions and end up in a sort of office next to a big flight of stairs. It looks like a caretaker's cupboard. I exchange my ticket for an envelope.

I need something to lean on.

Now, right now. I need to sit down.

There are no chairs.

I find an abandoned desk and stagger over to it. It's practically falling apart. I rest against it as gently as I can and open the envelope. My heartbeat crushes my breath: I'm scared there's something wrong with my blood, something translated here into numbers and acronyms. They've taken my blood into a laboratory, they've studied it, and now I'm about to find out what's wrong with it. Is it good news or bad? Mild or serious? Today is the day I learn if there's a name for what I have, and whether there's a cure.

I open the envelope and scan everything as quickly as possible. I skip over the details — I'm only interested in the anomalies. Aberrant values, signs that say: *here, here's what's wrong.*

Everything looks fine.

Nothing strange, nothing out of the ordinary.

Are these the mononucleosis values?

I don't understand them.

I re-read the figures, cross-checking them against the reference guides.

EBV VCA-IgG Antibodies

105.00 U/ml

EBV VCA-IgM Antibodies

32 U/ml

They seem to be neither positive not negative. They're in the intermediate range — the 'grey zone', it says here.

I message my doctor on WhatsApp. Keep me updated, he'd said.

He replies.

Send me a photo.

I photograph the pages of the report one by one, first smoothing out the creases with my hand.

I send the photos. Two blue ticks on a green background.

He's seen them.

Now get up, come on.

My doctor is calling me.

He reads the figures aloud as I'm walking back to the bus stop.

He doesn't seem that confident — is he improvising?

Is he trying to convince me of something he knows nothing about?

Bingo, he says. Glandular fever.

Really?

That explains your tiredness and the low-grade fever. You have to get plenty of rest, drink lots of water, be patient. I've had it myself. You can't treat it — eventually, it just goes away on its own.

Mamma and papà

Mamma and papà.

Naked.

In the corridor, between the bathroom and the bedroom.

Clinging to each other.

Are they playing?

Mamma, papà, are you playing?

My mother is holding the metal scissors, the ones from the kitchen. Long, shiny, cold, sharp. She's gripping them tightly in both fists. With the same intensity, my father clasps her hands in his, trying to tear the scissors away from her.

Let me go.

I said let me go.

Mamma is straining so hard she's baring her teeth and gums, squeezing her eyelids shut as if trying to make her eye sockets and eyeballs explode. The tendons in her wrist are popping out; she's trying to squirm away, to free herself from papà, who's squeezing her hands and trapping her. The blades of the scissors point down, towards my father's chest.

A smattering of dark hair in the centre.

Muscle, skin, metal.

Mamma and papà are naked and fighting in front of me. They're right there in the hallway as I come out of the bedroom, where I'd been sleeping until a few minutes ago. There's something in my mouth — a bottle, or maybe a dummy. What are they doing? Once, moving his fingers back and forth in front of my eyes during an EMDR session, my psychotherapist asked me: do you remember how they reacted when you came out of the room? When they saw you, when they noticed you, did they stop? Did they say something to you?

No.

I don't know.

I don't remember.

My earliest memory stops there: there's no before, no after. The first memory I have is of my mother and father fighting, naked, with a pair of scissors.

That's not true. That never happened.

My mother tells me I made it up.

When it comes to trauma, the most important factor, according to my therapist — the same one, my third, chronologically speaking — is what happens immediately after the traumatic event. While the trauma itself is often inevitable, the way in which is it managed can be an opportunity to restore our sense of humanity, our sense of how we're treated by others and how we treat ourselves.

But my memory stops there — crystallised, an image that is more than an image.

A trailer. A preview.

This is the story that precedes mine: the story of my parents. Like me, Tina and Roberto grew up in Rozzano. They were young, my parents. Too young?

My mother is eighteen when I'm born, my father is twenty-one. I arrive by accident. By mistake — let's be honest. They got distracted; it wasn't the right time. They were just two kids living in public housing who liked each other.

At some point, my mother gets pregnant.

I have to tell you something.

What do you want to do?

The moment family members find out about the pregnancy, they intervene. They offer to help raise the baby, to support these young lovebirds suddenly destined to be parents. Everything happens so fast — they're just kids, they don't even have jobs, how are they going to make this work? It must be the hand of God.

We want to help you through this, don't worry.

Abortion? Perish the thought.

The Lord has made it so.

Discussions, tears, joy — despair?

The story of Tina and Roberto, my parents, is the story of a love that quickly soured into hate and spite. A Rozzano love story. The town is a kind of matrix that reproduces itself to scale. Rage and conflict radiate everywhere, in miniature. The microphysics of pain. Confrontation is kneaded into everything. Even in Rozzano's apparently more peaceful pockets, the desire to snarl and thrash is never far away. The strength to fight can always be mustered.

Both my father and my mother come from Rozzano, but their families have almost nothing else in common. They are two distinct tribes, two clans devoted to antithetical idols.

My father Roberto, Robby, comes from a family of office workers. My nonna Nuccia is Sicilian. My nonno Pierliugi, Pier, is from Milan.

My mother, on the other hand, grew up in a generations-old Neapolitan family who came to the North in the early Sixties in search of work. My nonna Lidia is a housewife. My nonno Biagio, known as Sisino, is a factory worker. They're a noisy, melodramatic family. Swearing, teasing. Lunch, dinner, television. Start working young, as early as possible. When it comes to schooling: the bare minimum. My grandparents had no education beyond primary school. Their children — my mother, my aunt and uncle — all dropped out halfway through high school, and they barely made it that far. Later, when their love for one another had dried up, my mother and father would fight, and he would call her names: peasant, idiot, ignorant fucking southerner.

My birth brought these two foreign spheres into contact. Or rather, into friction. They intersect at only one point, and that point is me. The worlds of my father and my mother have very little to say to each other, in reality. They say what little they can, and they go their separate ways.

Then, later: recriminations, insults, threats.

1982: my father and my mother meet almost three years before she gets pregnant. They hang out with the same crowd, in the courtyards facing Viale Lombardia and in the basement beneath my father's building in Dahlia Street. Some of my mother's cousins are also part of the group, along with a few of my father's ex-girlfriends, and Biagio Antonacci, a guy my father plays music in bars with.

There are plenty of drugs around in those days, heroin mostly, but my parents don't partake. They watch the lives of others falling apart around them.

It's the golden age of Rozzano junkies.

The story of my parents is a love story between kids. If I hadn't come along, would it have lasted? I only know bits and pieces of their lives before my arrival: half-finished sentences spoken by accident in the space between one conversation and the next.

Their history has been all but erased, a victim of *damnatio memoriae*.

It never existed, it never was.

I know practically nothing about when they were together. In my mind, they are always already separated: mamma — big space — papà.

I know nothing about their love, their affection towards one another.

Nobody tells me, but sometimes I sense it, dimly, from words let slip by my mother or my nonna. It emerges from the depths of things past like a residue, like a mist.

It's your father's fault. Your father is to blame.

I grow up in the shadow of this partisan verdict; I grow up with the fear of turning out like him.

Unreliable, unspeakable, an absolute piece of shit.

I have no idea what we were like as a young family, but I have pieced together an idea of what my mother and father were like as teenagers. I've visualised them, imagined them, reconstructed them from glimpses stolen from the memories of others.

At twenty, my father Roberto has no desire to work or study. He's restless, unpredictable, a lady-killer. He loves cars and Vespas, he plays the drums. He has long hair to cover his big ears, and he's a huge fan of the singer Renato Zero — he even likes to dress up as him sometimes. My father, who will one day keep a photo of Mussolini in his wallet and take pleasure in heckling homosexuals, was once a harmless little mouse.

When Roberto speaks, people listen. He uses this to his advantage: somehow, he always gets what he wants. He starts high school but soon tires of it; he drops out after a year. They try to make him do a mechanic's apprenticeship, but he gets sick of that, too. *Your father only worked when he wanted something — as soon as he'd bought it, he quit.*

Your father has always been like that, he'll never change. My mother will repeat this to me a thousand times over the years. *And you're just like him* — a verdict, a ruling. You're just like your father.

Just as he and my mother are forming a family, my father enrols in military service. It's likely he sees it as more of a backup plan than a calling. After so many years of truncated employment, he finally settles. He gives up. He has a home to set up, a family to head. A wife and baby to take care of: mamma and me, his little loves, his kingdom. The only people worth trying for.

He becomes a police officer.

What does your papà do?

My father — dramatic pause, my pleasure expanding — is a policeman.

My mother, on the other hand.

Five foot two in bare feet, green eyes, brown hair, although in time she'll dye it blonde, then red, then blonde again. Long skirts, floral blouses, ballet flats or moccasin-style ankle boots. She's named Concetta, after her grandmother, my nonno's mother, but everyone calls her Tina. *La Tina:* the most beautiful girl in any group, the most ardently courted. Plenty of men have tried to woo her, but what can you do? She's chosen my father.

Her mother, my nonna, would like her to go out with Yuri, her neighbour's son.

But why not, Tina? Why don't you like him?

Mamma, stop. I'm with Roberto.

Tina la Bella: beautiful, certainly, but also tough, serious, aloof, the opposite of a flirt.

She trusts no one, or rather, she places her trust in all the wrong people.

My mother quits school early, and until she meets my father she lives a life of almost total seclusion. This is the way her father, my nonno Biagio, wants it. She's not allowed out: my nonno controls her movements, her allowance, as though she were still a ten-year-old girl.

Women belong at home — help your mother with the housework, you can leave here when you get married.

When mamma tells him she likes a certain food, he starts buying it for her compulsively. Stockpiling it. Especially if he finds it on special. He buys so much of it that it starts to make her sick.

Papà, I feel like Nutella. Week after week, the pantry is filled with jars of Nutella.

You wanted it, now you can finish it.

But I can't.

So what, I should just throw it away?

Every so often my mother babysits for family friends, or works selling snacks in the kiosk over summer. Word starts to spread that new job opportunities are opening up — it's the Eighties, computers are becoming more commonplace. Perhaps she could figure something out, find stable work. A real job. She receives several offers.

It comes to nothing — my nonno is against the idea.

It's too far, how would you get home in the evenings?

What, is staying at home not good enough for you anymore?

Tina and Roberto: saying, writing those two names together triggers a short-circuit in my brain. It's a fake restitching, because if I'm perfectly honest there's nothing to restitch. We were never a family. At best we were an attempt, an experiment.

My mother and my father conceive me towards the end of summer, watching Totò and Sophia Loren in *Miseria e nobiltà*. They get married in a hurry, to solve the problem of the unexpected pregnancy, but their parents' attempt to miraculously transform them from 'young couple' into 'happy family' is a spectacular failure. Everything turns out horribly.

I am born on 13 June, 1985. The year of *la grande nevicata*, the snowstorm of the century, although I arrive in spring, at ten past ten on a Thursday morning. Gemini, Leo ascendant. Air fanning fire. 10:10, the time that watches in shop windows are always set to.

I'm a large baby: almost four kilos — my mother never tires of reminding me. I am her trophy. A big son, a never-ending labour.

My mother explains, recants: yes, it's true, you weren't planned, but I always wanted you.

Things turned out the way they turned out, but you were not a mistake.

I'm born on 13 June, but not in Rozzano. I grow up in Rozzano, but I'm born in Milan, in the Niguarda Hospital, and as a child this is one of the few things I'm proud of, along with my mother's beauty and the fact that my father is friends with Biagio Antonacci. Let the record show that I, Jonathan Bazzi, spent the first hours of my life in a place that was not Rozzano.

A frenzied trip to the hospital — my mother is only seven months pregnant, I'm too early. But then I change my mind. First it looked like I'd be born premature, then I don't want to come out at all. I always have to have it my way, even at my own expense.

In the end, I'm born two weeks late. My mother goes to Niguarda for a check-up, and doesn't come home. They keep her there, and she gives birth. I'm born with two birthmarks: one like a slice of watermelon, long and pink, on the sole of my left foot, the other smaller, caffè-latte coloured, on my stomach, right next to my bellybutton. When I'm born I resemble my nonna more than anyone — my father's mother, Agata, or Nuccia. We have the same nose. Everyone on that side of the family has foreign-looking features: my great-grandmother, who was born in Catania, had brown skin, and I've always imagined that she had Moorish ancestors. The nurse even comments on the resemblance as she places me in mamma's arms, immediately after the birth.

He looks like he could be your mother-in-law's baby.

Pregnancy and childbirth wreck my mother's body. Her skin is silvered with stretchmarks in several places — as a child, they look to me like tiger's stripes — and she gets knocked around a lot during the birth.

The nurses and midwife climb onto her belly; one of them accidentally displaces her septum with a stray elbow.

I've seen a photo my father took as they were leaving the hospital: my mother sullen in the sun, long fringe almost covering her eyes. She's wearing a misshapen maternity gown. I'm there, but you can't see me: little baby me, the cause of it all, the reason for all this misery, safely ensconced inside a dark blue pram.

My name is Jonathan, because that's the name my mother chose.

Like the seagull, although she doesn't know that.

In those days there was a show on tv called *Jonathan: Adventure*

Dimension, hosted by Ambrogio Fogar. I'm named after a nature and extreme sports program from the mid-Eighties.

My mother gets to choose my name because I'm a boy. My father would have preferred a girl — if I'd been a girl, he would have chosen the name. He would have called me Desirée; he loves soft, meek women. But I'm a boy, so they call me Jonathan. Tina's choice. The rest of the family would have preferred a more traditional name. An Italian name. Something easy to spell and pronounce.

He was born on 13 June, why don't you name him Antonio? After the patron saint of Padova.

My mother stands her ground: *he's my son, I'll decide*. Her whole life she's been embarrassed of her name — Concetta, an old lady's name, a southerner's name — and she doesn't want me to suffer the same fate.

He's my son; I'm calling him Jonathan.

Written properly, with a *th*, which Americans and English people pronounce by putting their tongues between their teeth.

Practically no one in my family can say my name correctly. They call me whatever they want.

Sgionata.

Gionata.

So would it be Giovanni, in Italian?

The name continues to cause problems even after my birth. The priest at the Sant'Angelo church refuses to baptise me. Jonathan isn't on his calendar, he says. There is no Saint Jonathan. My mother refuses to give in. She's forced to find a new church.

Jonathan Bazzi: my father's surname side by side with the name chosen by my mother. A fusion; a crasis. A failed transplant.

My name is Jonathan, but somewhere in me is Desirée, the

daughter my father would have liked, the little girl he would have doted on. And somewhere in me is Antonio, the obedient grandson, the good little Rozzanese boy who would have grown up to command respect, to rescue the local women from their evil boyfriends. Antonio would have defended himself; he would have been a real man.

Our many avatars, whether by addition or subtraction, determine who we are. All our missing names, the stories that were already being written about us before we came into the world. The expectations of others, their dreams, the tasks they entrusted us with, often tacitly.

My name: eight letters.

This is how I see you; don't betray me.

After living with my grandparents for a few months, Tina, Roberto, and I move into the small one-bedroom apartment in Hyacinth Street, close to the Telecom tower and the number 15 tram terminus. My parents' relationship soon takes a turn for the worse. My mother has moved from one prison to another. My father doesn't let her do anything.

You don't have to work; you'll stay at home, look after the baby.

Don't go out like that, your dress is too low-cut.

Let me see what you're wearing; no, too short, go and change.

No one can touch me; no one can even get close to us. My father is controlling, obsessive, a clean freak. He complains about the things my mother doesn't do, or doesn't know how to do. He starts treating her badly, insulting her, humiliating her: dickhead, piece of shit, half-wit southerner.

My nonna — my father's mother — has explained it to me

dozens of times. Justified her son's behaviour, his infidelity, his disappearances. What did she expect? When he came home from work there were still dirty dishes in the sink.

Your mother was a layabout, she sat around all day doing nothing.

I imagine her as a cavewoman, dishevelled and riddled with lice, dressed in rags.

Recriminations start to fly from both sides.

They contaminate the family, breed feuds and vendettas.

I have only a few fragmented recollections from the brief time we spent together. Not one of them is a happy memory. Have I only remembered the bad times? Were there any good times?

For a while, we're not alone in the house allocated to us by the council. Ambrogio, the big English sheepdog who likes to lift me up by my nappy and carry me around the house, also lives with us — I wonder if he was named after Ambrogio Fogar, too? I don't remember him; my parents tell me about him later, when I'm older. One of the reasons I don't remember Ambrogio is that he doesn't live with us for very long — my parents give him away shortly after I'm born. Ambrogio is the first of many pets that will appear over the course of my life, only to disappear without a trace soon afterwards. It's mainly my mother who buys and gets rid of them. After Ambrogio comes Snow White the cat, then Tabatha the puppy, then Charlie the Yorkshire Terrier, then Athos the Rottweiler (my father's only attempt at keeping a pet, which failed after about two months), then Lulù the Persian cat, then Pongo the Shar Pei. All vanished, evaporated into thin air. My mother keeps buying them, but she can never take care of them for long.

Maybe she only likes them when they're young and helpless.

Maybe she's only capable of caring for creatures that treat her badly.

The few memories I have from the two years we all lived together — my parents and I — are not happy ones.

My father goes out with other women, cheats on my mother. He's always done it, but over time it gets worse. She resists, for a while — *please, Roberto, do it for the kid* — but then she stops. She has a nervous breakdown, slides into a depression. They think she might be epileptic, because of her fits: she faints, trembles, drools, throws herself to the ground. She surrenders to the desperation of a love that has become a farce, a lie, a failure.

Tina is crazy; Tina is sick.

My mother throws tantrums, screams the house down.

Don't leave her alone with the baby.

Fix her, give her drugs, antidepressants.

Don't let her out of the house, keep an eye on her.

Keep her inside.

I learnt from my mother, perhaps even back then, to communicate with my body what could not be dealt with verbally or rationally. The body begins to speak for itself; it overflows, says the unsayable. It reveals what has been denied or ignored. It rebels against the eternal regime of fathers, husbands, grandfathers. Hysterical: the label the patriarchy has traditionally stamped on women who refuse to conform.

My archetypal relationship comprises two enemies. Mamma and papà didn't last, there wasn't enough love between them, but before it all came to an end, the little bit of love that did exist managed to reproduce itself.

It created me.

I am the unexpected result of the briefest of love stories.

The love between them didn't die.

It was just transposed.

I don't believe him

I don't believe him.

I'm worried he's wrong.

And if he's wrong, we're just wasting time. The illness will advance, we'll be giving it free rein. It will trample all over me.

Milan man, 30, dies of leukaemia; doctor suspected glandular fever.

Young man's family seek answers: who is responsible, and could his death have been avoided?

I head home and go back to searching the internet for clues. I scour websites and forums for the values on my blood tests and descriptions of my symptoms. Page after page, tab after tab.

No, I don't have it.

It's not glandular fever.

The doctor is wrong. He's saying it's glandular fever because he's at a loss.

I visit him at the clinic again, to take him the results from my blood test — the ones I sent him via WhatsApp.

The values are, indeed, ambiguous, he says. They could indicate that you're in recovery from mononucleosis, or that you've had it before. Maybe when you were little.

In recovery? But I'm sick *now*, and getting worse.

Let's continue with the vitamins and supplements, he says. Actually, today someone brought in a complimentary sample of herbal tablets: they're made from this powerful Chinese root, it'll really give your immune system a kick. You can take a box, if you like. Let me know how they go.

I head home and go to bed. I curl into a ball. I'll have to get a second opinion.

I send an email to Lorenzo, a guy I met at a yoga studio a few years ago. He's a doctor, a gynaecologist, and he also teaches yoga. I'm a little embarrassed to write to him — we don't know each other well — but the more opinions I can get, the better.

He responds quickly: your symptoms are certainly compatible with glandular fever.

I ask him how he would interpret the values on my blood test. I'd have to check with a colleague, he says.

Then silence. No further reply.

He must have forgotten.

It's no use writing to him again.

I find a new consultant: Eugenia. She used to work on tv, but she quit to become a yoga teacher. She teaches Iyengar — the yoga of alignment. She tells me to take fermented papaya: it's a little expensive, she says, but it does wonders for the immune system. As glandular fever has no specific cure, she thinks the papaya might help.

I'm still teaching. When I'm at work, I pretend everything's fine.

I avoid telling the gym managers I'm unwell: glandular fever is contagious, they'll make me stay at home. I can't stop working; I need the money. Instead of demonstrating the yoga poses, I try to guide the classes with my voice alone. If I feel too tired, I lean against the wall or sit cross-legged on the ground.

I do my best not to attract attention.

I'd rather not leave the house at all, but I have no choice.

At the beginning of every class I'm already wishing for it to be over. My thoughts are always turned to rest. At home I shuffle between the bed and the couch. I hide under the covers with the cats; the moment I fall back to sleep, I start sweating.

I wake up, rise, change, lie back down.

This is my new rhythm.

A sequence of movements with no future.

No plans, no desires.

Then: something changes. The fever is gone. Now the roof of my mouth is itchy, I have a blocked nose, mucus, sore throat.

These new symptoms continue for a week, two weeks.

Was it just a gestating flu? Now it's matured, surely it will just run its course and disappear, like every other flu I've ever had.

It was just a phase, a momentary weakness. These things happen.

My mother calls me: how are you feeling?

The same. I won't be going for a run anytime soon.

No, of course not. Baby steps.

My voice sounds different: my vocal cords and airways are obstructed. At least three times a day I fill the biggest pot I can find with boiling water and inhale the vapour. I add a few drops of tea tree oil, an essential oil extracted from the leaves of the *Melaleuca alternifolia*, a native Australian plant used as a traditional medicine by Aboriginal people. I read about it on the internet — apparently it's great for inflammation.

I inhale the tea tree vapour for two days, three days.

It doesn't help.

I try drinking the oil — just a few drops, the internet says. It's an extreme remedy, not to be taken lightly. The oil has a very strong taste, like air freshener. It stays in my mouth for hours.

Three days, four: nothing changes. The tea tree hasn't cured me.

If it's not glandular fever, then what is it?

Why did I have a fever for weeks on end?

There's nothing I can do but keep typing questions into Google. What if I've got a tumour? Leukaemia? Lymphoma? I grow more and more agitated. Marius tells me to stop — there's no point looking online. But what else can I do?

I read the same websites over and over. I learn about the symptoms, progressions, and cures of an inordinate number of conditions. Day after day I drift into a digital sea of hypotheses and worst-case scenarios. From the available options I always choose the most dramatic, the most fatal. I should be trying to alleviate my panic, but it's easier to feed it, to imagine every horrible thing that could possibly happen to me.

That's it. I've decided: it's a tumour.

I'll have to start chemotherapy soon.

They'll tell me the date of admission, I'll say goodbye to my boyfriend and our cats. I'll kiss them — for the last time? — and head to the hospital, where they'll fill me with tubes and drugs that will make me feel worse than before. I'll be far from home, bedridden, incapable of doing anything for myself.

Will you come to visit me? Will you still love me even as I'm fading away?

When I'm admitted they'll take me — *me*, the one who can't bear to spend more than two nights away from home — to some random hospital. Everything will fall out: my eyebrows, my body hair, the hair on my head.

What will my face look like when nothing is left?

I sleep more and more — I sleep so that I don't have to think, or feel afraid. I can't bring myself to read or write, so I sleep instead. I turn off my body and rest. I start skipping yoga classes; people call me, wondering where I am. Often I don't even answer the phone.

Why didn't you come to work? We were expecting you.

Nothing interests me anymore. I no longer have the strength to stay on top of things, to take responsibility, to remember anything — deadlines, bills — and now that I'm working less I can't pay the rent.

Whatever will be, will be.

My fate is already sealed.

I text my doctor again: I'm thinking of going to the emergency room, I'm almost at my limit.

How's the fever going?

Last night and this morning my temperature was normal, but a little while ago it jumped up to thirty-seven point three.

If it'll make you feel better, you should go.

I do go, but they're no help.

It's not an emergency, they tell me. This is something you should consult your doctor about.

Can't you just put me through as a code white?

The prospect of sitting in the waiting room for hours crushes my spirit. I need bed, couch. I need to be horizontal.

I go home.

An afternoon passes. Two afternoons. Five.

I look for something to watch as I'm falling asleep.

I watch video after video on YouTube about Maurizia Paradiso, the tv personality diagnosed with leukaemia in 2015. I watch the videos she posted during her chemotherapy treatment at San Gerardo di Monza hospital. She's swearing, screaming — nothing is censored. She makes jokes, laughs, yells at people to go fuck themselves — it certainly doesn't look like her world is ending. Life goes on, even in a cancer ward. Plenty of people have gone through the same thing: show me how it's done. I find a bunch of videos by a group of young women who discovered they had cancer and decided to document their day-to-day lives. Women in their twenties and thirties: hairless, puffy-faced, grey-skinned, with black bags under their eyes.

That will happen to me, too. But I can't die yet. Not yet. I'll do chemo, maybe have an operation. One step at a time.

I hold out for a few more days, then I go back to my doctor.

Listen, I'm still feeling really unwell.

Let's take another look at your blood tests.

Huh, that's strange; they haven't done an FBC. Full blood count. That's the first thing we'd normally check, the most important test, really. Red blood cells, white blood cells, platelets. If you've got an infection or a tumour, an FBC will tell us.

They didn't do that?

Maybe it was my mistake. I thought I'd requested it, but I must have got distracted. I'm sorry. Let's send you in for the FBC, and while you're there, we might as well get a few more tests done. When's the last time you were tested for HIV?

A while ago.

That's a lie.

I've never been tested.

At the age of one I have a family

At the age of one I have a family.

By the time I'm three it's gone.

After all the fights, the screaming matches, the panic attacks, my parents finally separate.

My mother is the one who ends it.

It's all Barbie's fault.

Barbie is eighteen years old and studies law at the Catolica. Her university is close to my father's barracks, in Sant'Ambrogio. I'm not really sure how they met, in a café or bar, maybe — *so you study here? what's your name?* — but I do know that their affair is the final nail in the coffin of my parents' marriage.

Gorgeous. Stunning. The only words I hear people use to describe Barbara — sorry, *Barbie* — are gushing, hyperbolic. She's blonde, blue-eyed. Just like a Barbie doll. Barbie is beautiful and rich; she lives with her parents in central Milan. She's going to be a lawyer. Might the myth of Barbie's beauty also contain a hidden admission that my father, in fact, was right to cheat on my mother?

He screwed up, of course, but isn't she beautiful? Like a little doll.

My mother is beautiful, too, but she doesn't have blonde hair and blue eyes.

My mother is beautiful, too, but she's not rich.

Your father has found a new toy to play with. He always does.

Barbie is the first in a long series of 'friends' papà will introduce me to.

Is it alright if I bring a friend?

Ciao, amore — this is just a friend of mine.

Did your father come to pick you up?

Yes, he came with a friend.

Paola, Sara, Gisella, Cosetta. The one we went to the zoo with. The one who came with us to the pool. A new one every time. I meet them once, then I never see them again. Some are nice to me, some less so, but it makes no difference — either way, I never get to know them. They appear and disappear without explanation. Some are friendly, talkative, others are embarrassed: after all, I am the son of the policeman they're dating. *Yeah, I saw him again yesterday, but get this: he brought his kid along with him.*

I meet Barbie several times, though. Soon after my parents' separation, whenever I go out with my father, she's there. He asks me not to say anything to mamma. One evening in winter — just before Christmas — we pick her up outside her house. We park the car, and as we're waiting for her to come out my father makes me get in the boot. He shuts me inside, in the dark. To surprise her, he says.

Don't say a word; I'll let you out.

How long do I have to stay in here, papà?

Papà, what are you doing while I'm hiding here in the dark?

Don't tell mamma about Barbie, don't tell her we went out with her.

Okay, papà — I lower my eyes.

The minute I get home, I tell her everything.

Was she there?

Yes, mamma, she was there.

I tell my mother everything. I know how fragile she is.

Papà took me somewhere I'm not supposed to go.

Papà made me eat junk food.

Papà only took me for two hours.

Papà didn't call.

Papà didn't come.

Are you angry, mamma? It's all his fault. Papà is useless; he doesn't do the things you ask him to do. He doesn't love me. He's a liar. He spends all his money on himself and then tells us he's broke.

It starts when I'm three or four years old: the constant tension between my parents, a pressure that mounts and mounts but almost never explodes. This is the magnetic field I grow up in, drawn first to one pole, then the other. Mamma, papà, and me in the middle. I wind them up like rabid dogs, feeding their resentment for one another, hungry for their attention.

I start lying — I'll do anything to be seen.

My father and Barbie move in together. They live in a kind of extended-stay hotel in Pieve Emanuele, close to Opera, southeast of Milan. Their apartment is little more than a bedroom and kitchenette. Things start to sour between them. He makes her life impossible: my father is insanely jealous. When he goes out he locks her in the bedroom to make sure she doesn't leave the house without him. Poor Barbie is practically buried alive. She's eighteen, the age my mother was when she got pregnant, and, like my mother, she soon sees my father's dark side. Barbie escapes, moves back in with her parents in Milan.

After the separation, my mother remains in the Hyacinth Street apartment; my father is the one who moves out.

I don't want anything from you, just some money for the baby.

I just want you out of this house.

In fact, at first my mother pays back all the child-support money my father sends her: she meets with him outside the post office, cashes the money order, and hands him the wad of lire. Legally, he's done his part: my mother has technically received his child-support payment.

I did it for you, my mother has always told me. I gave him back the money so he wouldn't just disappear.

After my parents separate, I go to live with my grandparents. I live with them for several years, all through primary school.

When it comes to the story of my parents' relationship and the end of their marriage, the version of events I end up digesting is the one fed to me by my mother's family: mamma is innocent, papà is guilty. Mamma good, papà bad. Occasionally, when it suits me, I swap the order around.

Mamma, papà: now our lives intersect only on public holidays, or when the court mandates it. I imagine you together more than I see you.

My parents' love is a hypothesis, a fiction to soothe my loneliness.

Mamma, papà: now the only thing that brings the three of us together is disaster, like when zio Mario, nonna Nuccia's brother, drops me face-first on the floor trying do 'the spin of death', a move that involves grabbing me by the wrists and spinning me around in circles. Zio Mario loses his grip, and I smack my nose against the brown tiles.

Jesus, there's so much blood — a haemorrhage.

Zio Mario and papà take me into the bathroom and hold my face under a stream of cold water. They think my nose is broken, so the three of us — mamma, papà, and I — go to the hospital in central Milan, where the doctor inserts a kind of pincer deep into my nostrils (behind my forehead? into my brain?) and says: everything looks okay; his nose doesn't seem to be fractured. We leave the hospital and have breakfast in a café; it's a special day. A holiday? At that moment, eating pastries in Piazza Ventiquattro Maggio, I let myself hope they'll get back together. Mamma and papà, in love again.

Alas, we go home to separate houses.

Mamma and I together, papà alone.

Nothing changes.

From preschool, I take home two drawings: one for mamma, one for papà.

Miss, why does he get to do two?

I move in with my grandparents when my mother starts working. She cleans offices, mostly, but later also the Mediaset television studios in Cologno Monzese. Her boss is a big fan of Silvio Berlusconi (Fininvest, a company owned by the Berlusconi family, is Mediaset's biggest shareholder). When Berlusconi enters politics in '94, the owner of the company mamma works for throws himself into the campaign. His employees follow suit. Soon everyone is head over heels for Il Cavaliere — *Mamma, why do they call him that?*

My mother works in television; one day she brings home the autograph of Gabibbo, the Channel 5 mascot.

She knows all the tv showgirls. She throws out Cristina D'Avena's menstrual pads.

Mamma is in her early twenties, and alone. She starts exploring all the things she was never allowed to do. Until now, she'd never paid a bill at the post office; she didn't even know what a checking account was. With the men out of the picture, my mother becomes the head of the family. Only now, the family is just the two of us.

Now she has to do everything herself, which means she can't be at home with me.

She wants to give me the world, but all I want is her.

She works as much as possible, and puts all her money away. She's worried it's never enough. She's not used to managing money; she doesn't know how much she needs. Rent, shopping, clothes for me — I'm growing before her eyes. She's scared of running out. She asks her managers for overtime; they oblige, perhaps too generously.

Mamma leaves home at five in the morning and returns at eight or nine in the evening.

All she does is work.

She spends nothing — only the bare minimum.

One day she goes to the bank to get a statement. It's the first time she's been there in god knows how long.

Here you are, signora.

The teller hands her the print-out; she reads it.

Eleven million lire.

I'm sorry, this must be a mistake.

This is your account, signora. This is your money.

Tina calls her mother, my nonna.

Mamma, come and meet me, we're buying new furniture.

They choose a new kitchen table, a console table for the lounge room.

Will you be paying by cheque, signora?

No, no, in cash.

My mother opens her purse and extracts the banknotes: hundreds of thousands of lire, maybe even a few million.

My nonna is stunned: Tina, what are you doing? Where did you get that?

Quiet, mamma, I'll tell you later.

She's offered a job as a hostess at a nightclub. All she has to do is entertain the customers, make them buy drinks, and collect the tops of all the bottles they consume. At the end of the night, she'll be paid according to the number of bottle tops she's collected. But she turns it down. She's not interested. Mamma cleans offices, that's it. She does the same job for years.

Later, she cleans the stairwells in Rozzano's public-housing towers.

Then she works the checkout at a supermarket.

Then she sells Avon products.

Then she works in a school canteen.

My mother is always working. I hardly see her. I sometimes spent time with her on weekends, I'm told. But I don't remember that at all.

Did you use work as an alibi, mamma? As an excuse?

Were you trying to forget about me?

When you looked at me, did you see my father?

Occasionally, isolated memories resurface.

Mamma making pastina one evening. Fiorella Mannoia playing in the background.

Another evening, mamma leaving — she's going out dancing with her new friends. She's going to a place called 'The Rose Garden'. She's wearing a fuchsia bodysuit with gold studs, her red hair is teased — she hasn't started straightening it yet. I imagine my mother slipping into the night, between the garden roses, my mother surrounded by strangers, surrounded by all those people who exist out there, beyond our front door. I stay home and watch tv with zia Tata and her friend Luana. Lorella Cuccarini's theme song starts up as mamma is leaving. (I'm in the habit of announcing to everyone at preschool that I want to marry Lorella Cuccarini, and the teachers make me repeat it every so often, to make them laugh: *who do you want to marry, Jonathan? Lorella Cuccarini!*) I'm sitting on the ground, on the linoleum floor, as mamma pulls on her jacket and walks out the security door papà had installed after the apartment was almost broken into.

Put your socks on, you'll catch a cold.

I'm on the floor playing with my Barbie Knit Magic set, surrounded by tiny balls of colourful wool.

I look up.

Mamma is waving.

Ciao, amore. Be good, don't make zia Tata cross.

Then, one morning, mamma is standing in front of the bathroom mirror. My mother, the most beautiful woman in the world. I'm climbing on top of the washing machine to watch her get ready. She always takes so long. She has a bath, washes her hair, straightens it, puts her makeup on. She wraps a towel around her head like a turban, almonding her eyes slightly. She opens her makeup bag and applies products in a careful sequence: blush brushed onto the cheeks, eyelashes curled, then coated in mascara. Lipstick last. I follow her movements, learning gestures that can never be mine. Mamma retrieves a metal box from the wardrobe in her bedroom: it's light green, and on the lid there's an old-timey drawing of a girl running with a kite. The wind is lifting the kite above her head and blowing the girl's hair back. She's smiling and running through a field strewn with wildflowers. It seems like a fairy tale. *Mamma, what fairy tale is that?* Mamma is busy, she doesn't answer. Inside the most beautiful box in the world are mamma's hairbrushes. I'm not allowed to touch them. Mamma finishes getting ready and puts the box back in the wardrobe, on the top shelf, where I can't reach it.

Mamma is absent. Papà is absent.

Your father has never been around, your father has never given a damn.

This is the official line, the story I hear over and over again, until it's metabolised into truth. And my mother? Between the ages of three and nine, I hardly see her. I have almost no memories of her from that time.

Sometimes, on Saturdays, mamma comes to my grandparents' house for lunch. One day she brings me a box of miniature plastic robots from the supermarket. The colourful robots are lined up neatly inside their box, each one about the size of my finger. It's so nice that you came, mamma, but don't you know that I don't like robots? I like dolls and makeup, even though no one will buy them for me. Even though everyone says they're for girls.

If my father sees me playing with dolls he gets angry.

He says mamma and her family are raising his son to be a fag.

You bought the kid a My Little Pony?

He wants a Playmobil doll's house for Christmas?

Are you insane? He's a boy, get him a toy motorbike, or a Ferrari jumpsuit.

The photos from my third birthday party show me wearing a white shirt and an enormous smile — I've just been given a toy stove that makes its plastic steaks and hamburgers magically change colour. Standing in front of the miniature appliance, I'm a happy little cook bathed in shades of pink — the colour of the stove and the set of plates that came with it.

The colour of shame.

The stove certainly wouldn't have been my father's idea.

When my parents separated, it was decreed that my father would take me one day a week and one weekend a fortnight. My father, however, doesn't honour this arrangement, and almost never comes for me. I spend entire days waiting for him, sitting next to my grandparents' grey plastic telephone.

He said he'd call before he comes to get me.

He hasn't called, nonna. Papà forgot.

Papà always forgets, but still you wait for him. You believe him.

Why don't you go and play? Go watch television.

No, I'm staying here. Next to the phone. Waiting for papà. I have to wait for him.

I feel something pulling and tightening somewhere between my throat and my stomach. I can't watch television, I can't play. Even if I try, I can't. I'm afraid that if I don't wait by the phone, papà will never come.

The grey plastic telephone rings and my heart leaps. It's one of nonna's friends.

It rings again. It's my uncle; he wants to speak to nonno.

So papà isn't coming today?

Nonna, can you give me his number? I'll call him.

It rings, but then the call disconnects.

I redial — same thing.

Is papà hanging up on me?

Today was his day off and he didn't come. He's a patrol officer, in the Porta Venezia fast-response police team. I have his shifts written in pencil on a piece of paper that I keep stuck to the wall near the telephone. Morning shift, afternoon shift, evening shift, night shift, rest. I've learnt them by heart. Morning, afternoon, evening, night, rest. If I know his shifts, then I know when to ask him to come and get me.

I can ask him before he makes other plans.

Yesterday he was sleeping because he'd just finished his night shift. Today was his day off, but he hasn't called.

Papà didn't come; he's never coming again.

When papà does come — about once a month — he takes me out to buy toys and eat hamburgers and French fries. He shows me amazing things I've never seen before. We go to the amusement park on Idroscalo Lake. We go to the Nuovo Arti cinema, where they only show animations. We go to the Natural History Museum (my favourite) in Porta Venezia, the one with all the dioramas.

Papà lets me try things nobody else lets me try.

Mamma and I never do anything fun. She gets angry when she finds out papà has taken me somewhere special, or bought me some expensive toy. She doesn't understand that toys and special things are important. Papà teaches me that. Papà taught me that. Was he the one who instilled the idea — the dangerous, immoral idea, according to my mother — that I deserve the best, that I should desire nice things? Was he the one who showed me how to reach towards the things I want? Papà: my reward, my prize, the person who taught me how big the world is. And that I deserve the world, that I am entitled to it. Even if he sometimes forgets to call, or comes late, or doesn't show up at all.

Papà loves to travel. He tells me he's going to take me to Disneyland, in America. He shows me flyers of all the places we'll go to together: New York, Cuba, Polynesia, Santo Domingo. I ask him when we're going — *papà, when are you taking me?* — and he says: as soon as I have the money, don't worry, as soon as I have the money we'll go. Then he takes his girlfriends instead.

That's not true, you're always exaggerating. We did travel together.

We went to Paris. To Disneyland, in fact. But my mother sets the record straight: he only took you because *he* wanted to go. He didn't do it for you.

The last trip we take together is to Dublin.

I'm thirteen. We're only there for twenty-four hours (twenty-two, to be exact), and in order to get there, my father spends all the money in the junior saver's account my grandparents opened for me. One million lire, saved over the course of six or seven years. Enough for the flights and the hotel.

My mother is furious. She's like a wild animal. Seriously, Roberto, does that seem like a normal thing to do? You've spent all the kid's savings!

But he's wanted to go for so long.

It was the only way.

Sometimes papà takes me to House of Toys, in Rozzano. The ladies who work there know me because I always take forever to decide what I want. They even let me into the storeroom out the back. This is my golden moment: I make it last as long as possible. I wander back and forth, assessing the boxes stacked on the shelves.

I've got that one; I don't like that one; that one's too expensive.

Occasionally I meander back to the front of the shop, where papà is waiting for me: *papà, how much can we spend?*

Before choosing a toy I have to make sure I've looked at absolutely everything. I have to memorise the entire inventory. I'll always be like that, with everything.

I know I can't get a doll, because papà won't let me. If I bring him one he says no, and closes his eyes. The ladies in the shop try to persuade him, but he shakes his head. Or he smiles, goes red, tells me to look for something else.

If I choose an action figure of a character from a film or cartoon, that's okay — even if the characters are women, papà doesn't get angry. So I start collecting female action figures.

Wonder Woman, April O'Neil, Poison Ivy.

Catwoman, She-Ra, Storm from X-Men.

After we've spent the day together, papà always takes me back to my grandparents' house before dinnertime.

Be good, I'll see you next week.

He says that, but it's not true. I never know when he'll be back.

My father is an unkept promise.

If he doesn't come for a while, he tells mamma it's because he didn't have any money. You don't need money to be a father, she screams. She says he needs to teach me that it's possible to spend time together without doing something.

It's possible to be a father without special effects.

But papà doesn't understand, or he doesn't care.

For him, being a father means taking me somewhere exciting. Somewhere extraordinary.

He's more like a big brother, a teenager, a baby, than a father.

I don't know who's right.

But I know I don't want papà to stop coming for me.

I'm freezing to death

I'm freezing to death.

I grab the metal door with both hands.

I pull with what little strength I have left.

I try to break it, rip it from its hinges, rattling the screws.

It doesn't budge.

My knees are buckling beneath me, but I don't loosen my grip.

I want to go home.

I brace my foot against the wooden bench and pull the locker door towards me, violently: I displace it enough to see inside, but it doesn't give.

The locker won't open; the padlock remains intact, inserted safely into the door's neat metal curves.

I'm trembling, sweating. I'm scared of hurting myself.

The lock is stronger than the muscles and tendons in my arm. I'm scared I'll break my hand, or end up smashed against the wall behind me. I can see myself slipping, ricocheting, smacking my head, fracturing a bone. If I want to break this door I need to get angrier, but I'm afraid of the consequences. The changing room is full of people — I'm embarrassed. They'd call security.

I give up.

What's the point? I might be dead in a week. I still don't know why I'm so unwell. I'm stuck here in my yoga clothes and flip-flops. The air conditioning is freezing my skin under these neon lights. I'm in an underground gym in Piazza Diaz, next to the Duomo. I'm shivering. The fever is always worse in the evenings. I've just finished teaching a yoga class, and I can't go home. I can't find my clothes — *what have you done with them?*

I left them, as I always do, in one of the lockers in the changing room, but I can't remember which one. When I arrived I was feeling even worse than usual. All I could think about was finishing the class, getting through the hour. I was thinking about the blood test results I have to pick up tomorrow morning, at the clinic down the street, and I forgot to write down the number of my locker. I couldn't wait to get out of there.

I finish the class five minutes earlier than usual. I extend the final relaxation and stretch out with my students in the darkness, in silence.

I bring my attention to my abdomen, the rise and fall of my diaphragm.

I have to stop myself from falling asleep.

Inhale.

Exhale.

Repeat.

I check the time on my phone.

Nearly ten minutes have passed.

That's it, it's time.

I move my lips, pronounce the usual closing phrases.

Now gently waking up the body.

Moving the fingers.

The toes.

Circling the wrists.

The ankles.

Turning the head slowly to the right.

And to the left.

Now finding a comfortable seat.

Joining the palms of the hands at the heart.

We'll come together with one *Om* to conclude the class.

Finally, it's over.

I don't stick around to see everyone out — I escape to the changing rooms as quickly as possible. I would have changed here, right by the entrance.

I open the first three lockers.

No, those aren't mine.

I try around the corner; I almost never choose the same spot. I always look for somewhere private, away from other people — men's locker-room talk makes me uncomfortable. I do a full round, checking every locker.

My clothes aren't there. They've disappeared. Could I have been robbed?

I have my phone, I always keep it with me. But I left my wallet and house keys in the locker. The last of my paracetamol is also in there — I forgot to buy more before work. I keep buying it, even though it doesn't do anything.

It's late January, and I'm practically naked. How am I going to get home?

I sit down for a moment, surrounded by yogis in various stages of undress.

I need to stop, take a breath. Rest my back.

Wait — what about the lockers with padlocks?

I check them all. I use the torch on my phone to illuminate the narrow gaps on either side of the locked doors.

One, two, three, four.

Nothing.

I try a different area — the secret area, hidden behind the mirror.

There's a locker with a grey rubber combination lock on the door.

I peer inside.

I recognise my belongings.

The yellow light of the phone illuminates my backpack, the leather of my shoes, the knotted fringe of my scarf.

Everything is exactly as I left it.

I head upstairs to reception and talk to the girl working there. I lean against the counter to stop my legs from giving way. I force the corners of my mouth into a smile, try to make my face look normal.

Hi, sorry. I'm the yoga instructor, my class just finished. I think someone must have put their padlock on my locker by mistake.

Oh no, I'm sorry.

She gives me an automatic smile. Eyes wide, high ponytail, eyebrows pushed towards her forehead. It's clear she couldn't care less.

Is there anything you can do?

We can't open clients' lockers, I'm afraid. All lockers have to be emptied by closing time — if they're not, then we can intervene. But not before then, I'm sorry.

What time do you close?

Midnight.

It's nine-forty.

Couldn't you make an announcement or something? Maybe the owner of the padlock is still here.

No, I'm sorry. But you can speak to the manager if you like. She's at the café.

I'm lugging around sixty-six kilos of body that just wants to collapse, to crumple in a heap. I head to the gym's café. They're cleaning up, nearly all the chairs are legs-up on the tabletops. There's only one girl sitting down: orange hair, too much foundation. She's slipped her heels out of her ballet flats and is watching a video on her phone, eating a plate of finely sliced half-raw meat.

Hi, sorry to disturb you …

She gives me the same answer: there's nothing we can do while the gym is still open. No, we can't make an announcement. Sorry.

I drag myself up and down the stairs.

I try asking the guys working out near the entrance. All men, almost all wearing headphones. A couple of them are clearly models — I doubt they speak Italian. I approach them, try to communicate with my hands. I don't like talking to people I don't know. I stutter, although less now than I used to. Starting conversations with strangers still terrifies me. I avoid it as much as possible. The *hi, sorry* comes out easily enough, but then I freeze up. I choose my words carefully, favouring the ones I know I can pronounce. That's why you love singing, a Kundalini teacher once told me. It's your fifth chakra, your throat chakra. You need to liberate it. It's not defective, it's just crowded. Overstimulated.

I manage to get my question out.

No, not mine, sorry.

Then in English: *eh, no, I'm sorry.*

No, I didn't use a padlock.

Are they lying to me?

I sit alone in the changing room. I'm hot, cold, my eyes are burning.

I go back to the girl at reception. She's speaking to a colleague who wasn't there before.

They're laughing about something.

Yeah, right. He'll know better next time. Fuck that guy. Seriously, they're all the same ...

I interrupt them; the smiles disappear from their faces.

Listen, the stuff inside the locker is mine, I can see it. Also, I'm really not feeling well.

We've got bolt cutters. At midnight, if the owner hasn't come back, we can break the lock, but until then we can't help you.

I have to convince her. But how?

My body won't let me do anything. I need to sit down. I want to wrap myself up.

I text Marius; he was on set today, he should have arrived home not long ago. He doesn't work every day, but when he does he finishes late. I hate the thought of making him leave the house again, but I have no choice.

Hey, could you bring me some clothes? I need everything: T-shirt, hoodie, pants, socks, shoes ...

He replies straight away.

He'll be here in ten minutes.

I head back downstairs and try to force the locker door open again with my bare hands. There's no way the padlock will break, it's stronger than I am. I sit staring at it, surrounded by men, young and old, in the changing room. They seem perplexed by my presence.

I haven't eaten dinner; my blood pressure is starting to drop. Low blood sugar. Beneath that the fever, the usual exhaustion. It's late, I'm cold — how many times have I written that now? — and I don't have any paracetamol. I don't even know what's wrong with me. Tomorrow morning I have to pick up my blood test results, and I'm scared. I just want to go home. Is there really not a single person here who can help me?

My forehead is dripping wet; sweat stains are starting to seep through the front of my tank top. The green fabric turns black at my chest and belly, forming dark shapes. My own personal archipelago of shame. I head back to the front desk. The girl with the ponytail is still laughing. It's my pride that sets me off, in spite of everything. It's like I'm possessed. Suddenly, I'm no longer Jonathan. I am Tina.

Listen, will you just open this fucking locker for me?

Excuse me?

I asked you before if you could help me, and you couldn't give two shits — you've just been sitting here, laughing with this bitch the whole time. So open the fucking locker right now or I'll smash it open.

You can't speak to me that way.

Go fuck yourself.

I'm caught halfway between my frustration and my guilt. Every time I lose control it's the same. An ex once told me: you're like a knife disguised as a spoon.

Really? I would have thought the opposite.

I'm escorted away from the front desk. I text Marius again.

He's in the Metro.

He's not far away.

I sit down by the stairs to wait for him. I avoid looking at the receptionist.

A few minutes later I spot him through the glass sliding door.

He's walking fast. He butts out his cigarette before coming inside.

Here, check if I've got everything.

He hands me a gigantic plastic bag filled with clothes.

Wait here, I say. I'll go downstairs and get changed, then we can get something to eat and come back for my stuff at closing time, okay?

I have to force myself to translate my words into actions. I walk back down the stairs and look inside the plastic bag.

There's no jacket.

Nothing warm to cover myself up with. It's freezing outside — these clothes are useless. I head back upstairs. I can't lose it with Marius. I made him rush. He's tired, I can tell.

Well?

There's no jacket.

Shit.

We'll have to wait.

We sit at the entrance and wait for closing time.

At least I'm not alone anymore.

A male staff member approaches us. He's tall, black, wearing a red polo shirt that's a size too small for him. He tells me he'll try asking around. There are only a couple of people left in the sauna and relaxation areas, he says. It's no trouble.

I stay with Marius; it's better if I'm sitting down.

The guy returns. He's holding bolt cutters.

Let's open it, he says. It's almost eleven thirty anyway.

We head downstairs to the changing room and I point at the locker: that one. It takes him two seconds to break the padlock. We open the locker. My things are inside. Nothing is missing, and no one has put anything else in it. So why did someone lock it and then leave?

Did they do it on purpose?

Was a joke? A prank? Some kind of punishment?
I get changed and we head out.
I don't acknowledge anyone as we pass the front desk.
I'm done with this place.

Nonna loves me, but sometimes, at night

Nonna loves me, but sometimes, at night, just before bedtime, she puts a tea towel over her head and hides in the shadows to scare me.

She jumps out from the bedroom doorway and puts on a raspy voice like the voice of Isabel, the girl with the leather mask who lives in the attic in the telenovela we watch on Channel 4.

Miranda! Miranda!

Isabel is the twin sister of Manuela, the main character, who has long blonde hair like Rapunzel. Isabel has to wear a mask because she was disfigured in an accident. *Miranda! Miranda!* That's Isabel calling for her mother, who is also Manuela's governess.

Sometimes, at night, I glimpse a faceless shape in the semi-darkness of nonna and nonno's room — the only light source is the orange halo of the Madonna lamp on nonna's nightstand. For a tiny light, it creates a lot of shadows.

I hesitate in front of the doorway.

Bare feet on cold tiles.

Nonna, is that you?

Miranda! Miranda!

I'm holding a bottle of warm milk, my mouth closed around the rubber teat. I move it aside and ask again: Nonna, is that you?

I'm about to cry.

Nonna, where are you?

She jumps out: she was hiding behind the door, between the wardrobe and the chest of drawers where she keeps the bedsheets I help her fold. She removes the tea towel from her face and laughs.

It's me, dummy.

Between the ages of three and nine I live with my grandparents in another public-housing tower, at 11 Verbena Street. It's eight storeys high, but my grandparents' apartment is on the ground floor — the 'courtyard floor', as nonna calls it. Below us are the basements. I live with nonna Lidia, nonno Biagio, and my mother's younger siblings, zio Franco and zia Alessandra, whom I call Tata.

Everyone speaks dialect at home: nonna is from Aversa, just north of Naples, and nonno is from Mugnano 'e Napule. They've lived in Milan since the Sixties, but they still speak napoletano most of the time. There are words they don't even know how to say in Italian. Nonna never learnt to read properly. She has to read out loud, and extremely slowly, tracing each letter with a finger. Whenever she has to write a letter or sign something it takes her forever; she scatters wobbly, elongated characters across the page, as though she'd penned them without looking.

The kid doesn't speak it, but he understands, no?

I do. I understand everything. There are a handful of phrases that I only know how to say in dialect. But if I accidentally say them in front of papà or his parents, I get in trouble. What are you, a southerner? Speak Italian.

Nonna Lidia doesn't work — she stays at home. Nonno gives her money to do the shopping. She always tells him she's spent more than she actually has; that way she gets to keep a little for herself. Every now and then she might save up enough to buy a new dress at the Saturday market, or some scratchies from the tabaccheria in Oleander Street. I spend a lot of time in the kitchen with nonna Lidia, watching her prepare food. Sometimes I help her mix the dough or shell the peas or crumb the veal cutlets. Nonna mostly cooks Neapolitan recipes: pizza, focaccia, lasagne, pasta e fagioli, pasta con le patate, red peppers blackened on the grill (you can smell them cooking all the way from the courtyard), and tortano napoletano, made with fistfuls of lard, which she keeps in big jars that she calls *boccacci*. On religious holidays she makes pastiera napoletana and struffoli: deep-fried dough balls covered in honey and colourful sugared almonds that break your teeth. When she does the deep-frying, she barricades herself in the kitchen alone. I have to leave, closing all the doors behind me one by one — kitchen, hallway, bedroom — so the smell doesn't escape.

Vatten' allà, che poi puzz' 'e mmerd'!

As an afternoon snack nonna gives me bread with oil and sliced olives, or bread with butter and sugar. I'm wild about butter; I want it on everything. It's an addiction. Everything tastes better with butter. I want it in my pasta, my rice, my minestrone, on my vegetables. I want all my meat cooked with butter, too. First course, second course, side dishes — I want butter on all of them. Bread with butter and jam. Bread with butter and sugar. Bread with butter and Nutella. Bread with butter and Marmite. At Christmas, bread with butter and salmon or bread with butter and parmesan.

Nonno doesn't approve of my butter obsession, so nonna has to sneak it into all my meals. She slips it onto my plate and covers it with food.

Shhh, don't let nonno see.

There's nothing I wouldn't risk for a knob of butter. Even the threat of violence doesn't stop me.

Butter is where it all began.

My nonna is extremely vigilant; she knows about everything that goes on in our apartment building. If she hears someone approaching the entrance, she immediately goes to the spyhole to see who it is — she has to stand on tiptoes, because she's so short. If she sees something unusual, she keeps watching, then detaches herself from the door and makes a face.

Mah, boh, chi 'o ssap'.

Every morning she drinks coffee in the kitchen with her friends. While the moka pot is hissing quietly on the stove, they talk about their neighbours, husbands, children.

Splash of milk?

How many sugars?

Nun 'a pozz' propr' verè.

I heard social services took her kids away.

No, no, the mother is dead …

Eh Vitto', che t'aggia dicer'.

The father's already been arrested three or four times.

Sì, sì, the one on the fourth floor, you know her?

The woman's a pig, *è 'na vajassa*, she throws her rubbish out the window, *da 'ncopp' 'o balcon'*.

People are animals. I've got my bastard husband to thank for us living here.

Me ne vuless' turnà a Napul'.

I'd rather be back in Naples.

Nonna Lidia is constantly doing housework. She vacuums,

then scrubs the floor with a rag dipped in alcohol — she calls it spirits, *'o spirit'*. The smell gets deep inside my skull, it's so strong, but nonna loves it. Spirits are a disinfectant, she says. Spirits kill viruses, and bacteria, and illnesses. They protect us, they keep us safe. Sometimes she does the ironing while we watch Luca Barbareschi in *We All Loved Each Other So Much*, or *The Price is Right!* with Iva Zanicchi. Other times, nonna plays music while she cleans: she puts on cassettes and sings Neapolitan love songs.

Pront' si' tu? Nun attaccà, famm' parlà …

If I'm watching tv on my own, without nonna, I watch cartoons. My favourite shows are the ones about magical Japanese girls. I like to imagine that I, too, have a magic wand or mirror or amulet. Sometimes I make my own: I draw them, colour them in, then cut them out. Now I am Magical Emi, I am Creamy, I am Gigì. I am all the little pastel-haired sorceresses I see on tv. I run around the house casting spells. I have new powers; the enchanted makeup mirror has transformed me into a witch, a warrior princess, a paladin. I come from another planet. I'm on a mission. I defend the weak. On my head I wear a tiara of shining stars, an entire galaxy. I trace bright circles around my body with my magic wand — the circles protect me, and make me invisible. Nobody can hurt me now. I have aliens and goddesses and magic on my side.

The Verbena Street apartment has three bedrooms. My grandparents sleep in the biggest one, and the two smaller ones are for zia Tata and zio Franco. I sleep in Tata's room — the same room mamma used to sleep in.

Connecting the bedrooms is a hallway with a storage cupboard. Sometimes Tata locks me in there, in the dark. As a joke. The storage cupboard is where nonno keeps all his tools: screws, nails, hammers, but also shoe polish and spare shoelaces. At the back of the cupboard is a floral curtain hiding the shelves where nonno keeps a stash of bulk-bought water, oil, and detergent. The door is completely covered by a large mirror. The mirror I remember is not the one that was always there. The old mirror had to be replaced because it broke. I was the one who broke it. I was two. I touched it, and it fell off the door and shattered. I'm not allowed to get too close to the new mirror.

If you break it again, nonna shouts, that's another seven years of bad luck.

Is it always my fault when things go wrong?

Nonno Biagio lives with us, but it's almost as if he doesn't exist.

The only time he pays me any attention is when he's yelling at me.

If he's not working at the factory, he's sitting on the couch, in front of the tv. I often hear him talking to himself.

My spot at the dinner table is right next to his, so he can check how much I eat and drink (too much, not enough) and if I'm using my cutlery wrong, or wasting paper napkins, or wrecking the bread. I like the soft white inside parts, but nonno makes me eat all of it, even the burnt black crust. I force it down like medicine.

Nonna defends me, and so do my aunt and uncle: papà, leave him alone, let him be. But if I do something he doesn't like, nonno looks at me in silence. A look is all it takes. I learn to respond to his expressions, to the tiniest of gestures, like a trained dog.

No one is allowed to speak at the dinner table when nonno is there.

Statt' zitt', quann' se magn' se combatt' c' 'a mort'.

We have to sit in silence and listen to the sounds of nonno

slurping the broth off his spoon, sucking food from his teeth, suppressing burps. It doesn't count if it's only annoying to other people.

Nonno and I don't speak. He doesn't play with me, or take me places. With nonno, I only listen. I listen to him cursing various saints, dead relatives, the Madonna. I listen to the insults he slings at nonna Lidia when they fight and it sounds like he wants to hit her, or at Tata, for things I don't understand. One time he slaps Tata, and she cries with her head against the wall, next to our bedroom window, her arm folded to cover her face. Her hair moving in rhythm with her sobs, her little yellow short-sleeved cardigan. I freeze in the face of other people's pain. Is that where my paralysis began? Is that why I don't know how to console someone who's crying?

Nonno hits me, too, but only once.

I never play outside, I never hang out with the other children in the courtyard — I have no interest in it. But one afternoon, after school, I do something I've never done before: I go out to play with my new classmate, Fabio Serafini. Fabio is blond and blue-eyed, like the angels of his surname. I like him, I want to be his boyfriend. He has invited me to play after school. Fabio is reckless — he's not scared of anything.

Come on, let's climb on the metal pipes in the parking garage.

So I do. I go with Fabio. We jump and swing; Fabio teaches me how to do a somersault and hang from one hand. We're a couple of ninjas, we're special agents. I lose all sense of time. I forget.

Suddenly, nonno is there.

He tears me down from the pipes and slaps me across the face, right there in front of Fabio. It's a hard slap — everything goes black.

I'm not used to being slapped in the face. The worst nonna Lidia will do is yank me by the arm, or the hair.

Nonno wanted me back at five thirty, and now it's five thirty-five.

If there's one detail worth mentioning, it has to be that.

Nonna Lidia isn't there, she must be at a friend's place. She's not there to intervene, to protect me. What happened would happen often if she weren't there to trick nonno, to keep him occupied, to distract him from all the things I do wrong and all the ways I disappoint him.

Bear, ogre, *Mazzabubù*. If people know nonno is home, they stay away.

They don't even dare buzz the intercom.

Nonna's friends say so all the time.

When nonno is home I have to be very careful with my movements. The house — his house — is suddenly full of places I can't go, things I can't do. The spaces available to me shrivel away to nothing; I have to follow precise, pre-approved trajectories.

Get out of that bedroom right now. Go over there and play.

Nonno Biagio walks through the house slowly, watching everything that goes on. He spies on us. He storms into rooms without warning, flinging open the doors to check what we're doing — if we're on the phone, if we've got too many lights on, if we've had the hot water running for too long.

Nonno snarls in dialect. He's telling me to go to my room. The only place where I don't annoy him.

That's just the way he is, nonna tells me. Leave him be.

Nonno Biagio comes home from work at five o'clock every day. He doesn't say a word when he walks in. I wish five o'clock would never come. He comes home and eats an apple. Always a yellow one. He runs it under the kitchen tap to cool it, then he cuts it with a knife and eats it standing up, leaning against the fake-marble dinner table. He shuts himself in the lounge room until dinnertime. He falls asleep there, in the dark, with the tv on.

Head thrown back, mouth ajar. His nose is a shark's fin, a bird's beak.

He snores so loudly.

The light from the tv screen projects shadows across the room, and nonno's stretches out long behind him, against the wall and the radiator.

Nonno is a giant shadow. I wish he would sleep forever.

3 February

3 February.

The day I have to pick up the results of my latest blood test.

The fever is still with me. It hasn't gone away.

I slide the referral form into the transparent blue plastic folder that, until last month, held my university lecture notes.

I text my doctor.

Hi, test results arrive this morning. You at the clinic today?

Yes, heading there now.

What time are you there till?

12.30, but I can wait for you.

Okay, should be fine.

I text him again an hour later.

They haven't given me everything. They've left me in suspense.

I'm sorry, sir, hasn't someone called you?

No, should they have?

The woman at the collection desk stepped away and made a telephone call I couldn't overhear.

I can give you these general test results, she said when she returned. Someone will give you a call about the rest.

She didn't tell me what she meant by 'the rest', nor why I should have been expecting someone — who? — to call me. Every word, every glance and movement had been carefully planned, to protect me. To prevent me from receiving the news alone.

Okay, keep me posted, my doctor says.

I wait for my phone to ring.

I want it to ring now, immediately.

I never want it to ring again.

What if nobody calls?

How long should I wait?

When you're truly afraid, fear anaesthetises even itself.

Everything is numb.

Everyone in our house is young

Everyone in our house is young. When I'm born, nonna Lidia has just turned forty, Tata is ten, and zio Franco is a couple of years older than her.

I'm at home most of the time. I don't have any friends, I don't like being around other kids. If I'm not playing on my own, I'm hanging out with Tata or zio Franco. I watch tv with them — whatever they're watching. *Twin Peaks*, *The Exorcist*, *It*, *The Zio Tibia Picture Show* on Italia 1. Horror scares me, but I still watch it, because being scared isn't always a bad thing.

In the evenings, before dinner, I play board games with my aunt and uncle. I ask them to play every night, without fail. Usually they don't want to, but they always end up giving in.

Ugh, you're such a pain, can't you play by yourself?

I keep bugging them until they agree to a game. We play Guess Who, or Monopoly, or Connect Four. Sometimes I play with Tata's stuff. She collects free perfume samples, and likes weaving colourful scoubidou keychains. Her wardrobe doors are covered in magazine centrefolds of singers and actors. Tata also has a few books from when she went to school, although she confesses (proudly) that she's never even opened them.

Look, they're still covered in plastic.

The possession I covet most is her *Candy Candy* book, which is all about makeup and beauty. It's my favourite. The *Candy Candy* book says if you squeeze a few drops of lemon in your eyes they become more beautiful. I don't know how to read yet, but Tata told me that's what it says. In the picture Candy is smiling, with enormous green eyes that take up half her face.

See, it makes your eyes go like hers. Gaga eyes.

One afternoon, when no one is looking, I try it. I take a half lemon from the fridge (nonno always leaves one wrapped in aluminium foil, next to the eggs) and, raising my eyes to the kitchen light, I squeeze the juice in.

It trickles down my neck and into my hair. I can't see a thing — it burns, horribly.

I run to the bathroom to rinse my eye. I wash away the lemon juice, which feels like it's melting my eyeball all the way into my brain.

I look at myself in the mirror: my eye is half closed, and bloodshot.

Candy is a liar.

Tata and I sleep in a pair of narrow single beds that we have to fold out from the wall every night. In time, I cover every inch of the dark wooden bedframe with stickers: Jessica Rabbit, Jem and the Holograms, The Little Mermaid. Before I go to sleep I place a bottle of milk and a plate of biscuits on the shelf above my bed. I drink milk from a bottle until the age of ten. I always put it on the shelf, because nonna told me never to fall asleep with a bottle in my mouth.

You'll die in your sleep, you'll choke to death.

Tata and I only unfold our beds at night, so that we have room to play during the day. I actually prefer to play in zio Franco's bedroom, though. I like to shut myself in there early in the morning, with my superheroine action figures.

Zio Franco is a labourer; he constructs wood-fired ovens for pizzerias. He's addicted to fighting. He wants to fight everyone he sees. He gets into arguments with people all the time when he's driving; he takes off his glasses and gets out of the car in a huff, waiting for a reason to hit someone, waiting to be provoked. If they're old ladies, he leaves them alone. He gets back into the car, mumbling insults (fucking old bitch), and accelerates violently, smacking me backwards into my seat.

Zio Franco has a girlfriend named Lucia, who can sometimes calm him down. She stops him before his rage gets the better of him. Before he loses control. I adore Lucia — she's never grumpy or mean, and she's obsessed with clothes. I always ask her for advice on my birthday, or at Christmas, when my parents want to get me a new pair of shoes or a new jacket.

Lucia is skinny like a ballerina. She has blonde hair, always with a little bit of black regrowth, and a nose stud. She works in a factory that makes motorbike helmets, and to me she seems like a character from *Melrose Place* or *Beverly Hills, 90210*. She sleeps at our house almost every night, because her house isn't safe. One of her brothers is in and out of San Vittore prison, and nonna says there's something wrong with her other brother, too.

At her house, Lucia has to sleep on a camping cot in the kitchen. But at our house she sleeps in the bed with zio Franco. It's only a single bed, but they don't complain.

I'm not allowed to hang out with them in the evenings; after dinner they shut themselves in zio Franco's room to watch movies in bed, and drink beer and eat chips. They buy special snacks when they know there's something good on tv that night. They keep them on top of the fridge, where I can't reach, and nonna tells me I'm not allowed to eat them.

They're for your zio, leave them alone.

★

Tata is the youngest sibling, so she's the one who always ends up babysitting me.

Like everyone else in my mother's family, Tata hates school. She fails eighth grade. She eventually finishes middle school, then quits and gets a job. Ten years have passed since my mother tried to do the same thing — nonno is more permissive now. He lets Tata work. She finds a job at a company that makes soap for hotels.

Tata is very thin, with curly hair. Her name is Alessandra. Nonna wanted to call her Katiuscia after an actress who used to be in photocomics, but nonno and the rest of the family wouldn't allow it.

Tata dresses more like a boy than a girl — she always wears jeans and sneakers. She doesn't wear makeup or skirts. She likes tracksuits and baggy hoodies, comfortable things. As a child, she hung out with boys more than with other girls. She was always playing out in the courtyard, or climbing trees. She's still friends with a lot of boys. Some of them ride Vespas and (rumour has it) deal drugs — the kind of boys who are likely to end up in jail one day. If Tata and I are out together and we run into one of them, she always stops to stay hi.

Yo, Ale, who's the kid?

My nephew. He always wants to tag along, it's a total pain.

Nah, just kidding, he's keeping me company.

Tata argues with nonno at the dinner table because she never wants to eat anything. Nonno starts yelling at her, saying she's too thin — it's true; her arms are like twigs — and makes her force something down, even if it's something she hates. Tata hates vegetables most of all. She calls them 'plants'.

Mamma, I don't eat this stuff. What have you put in it, plants?

She picks up a visible stalk, or a leaf of something, and eyes it with disgust. Nonno doesn't care — he makes her finish it all. Tata eats everything on her plate without lifting her head, so that she can dry her tears in secret.

During the years I live with my grandparents, Tata has a lot of friends: Lilly, Enza, Imma, Luana. They all live nearby, in public housing. When I'm still too young for school, nonna makes Tata take me out with them, to get me out of the house. Tata usually doesn't want me hanging around, but she has no choice — nonna will get angry, otherwise.

Mamma, what a pain, can't I ever just go out on my own?

Alessa', aggia fa' e mestier'.

Calogera, nicknamed Lilly, is a few years older than Tata and already has two kids. She doesn't get along with her boyfriend; he doesn't work, he just rides around on his Vespa with his friends, doing wheelies.

Imma lives in the old caretaker's quarters of the building behind ours. She has a baby, Kevin, who can't speak properly. Kevin doesn't live with Imma — social security took him away to a place Tata calls the 'community' or 'family house'. They bring him to Rozzano every now and then, to visit Imma. Kevin is always smiling, his mouth is always open. Sometimes he drools, and Imma wipes it up with a handkerchief. Imma is a bit strange herself — she's a lot older than Tata, but she speaks like a little girl, and walks with a limp. When Tata talks to her she speaks more loudly and clearly than usual, and it seems like she's always having to explain things. Imma lives alone because her husband left her. He works at city hall, and at night he sings in piano bars. He does Queen covers. Imma has photos of her husband hanging up everywhere at home, and sometimes she cries when she looks at them. Tata says: don't do that, think about Kevin, think about your son. When's his next visit?

Luana, or Lu, is Tata's best friend.

After middle school, Lu goes to beauty school and starts working at Fiordaliso. She opens a perfumery somewhere — it won't last long, she'll be forced to close it. One day I'll hear that someone saw her in the street, under an overpass; she might have been soliciting.

Lu is the daughter of Giuseppina, one of nonna Lidia's friends. Giuseppina is from Puglia. Lu's brother, Michele, died in a car accident — he crashed into a wall at night. He was nineteen. We visit him once at the cemetery in Rozzano Vecchio. There's a photo of him on the headstone; he's got long hair, like an actor from a magazine, and he's smiling.

Ever since Michele died, Giuseppina dresses in black.

Lu has another brother, Cosimo, who's in and out of jail. I like him; he seems nice. He's handsome. He's not very tall, and he has an earring and tattoos. He always wears brand-name clothes and sneakers. Every time he sees nonna Lidia, he gives her a kiss and a hug.

I raised that boy, nonna says.

Nonna says that about a lot of people. She'd like to be everyone's mother.

When Giuseppina's husband dies, she goes back to Puglia.

What's left for me in Rozzano? she says.

Nonna's friends disappear for one of two reasons: either they die of a horrible illness or they go back to the place they were born.

Enza is another of Tata's friends. She lives with her father, just the two of them, in the building next to ours. Enza is extremely skinny, even more so than Tata, and everyone mistakes her for a boy. She always wears baggy jeans and polo shirts. Morning and night, she's out in the courtyard with her wolfdog. Enza goes out with (and eventually marries) Alfonso Braccia, whose family collects the garbage from all the public-housing towers in Rozzano.

The Braccia family pile the garbage into a little three-wheeled truck that everyone calls 'the bee'. Bags upon bags of garbage. The Braccia family have dark, leathery skin, and they're always grumpy. They yell at each other all day as they go up and down the stairs, lugging garbage from the basement. Enza and Alfonso both have trouble rolling their r's, and they both love Vespas; they're constantly fixing a muffler or changing a tyre. Enza seems like the stronger of the two — she's the boss. Alfonso is too kind, nonna says. It almost seems as if they're together out of obligation, or convenience. They didn't choose each other. They found each other — what else were they meant to do? Rozzano chose for them.

Tata has a boyfriend, too. She hangs out with an older Calabrese boy who drives a bulldozer and lays asphalt. They meet in Rozzano. She's thirteen, he's twenty-six. The day they meet, he's working on the road out the front of her school.

His name is Antonio; Tonino, Totò.

I never call him zio. I will never call him zio, not even after he ends up marrying Tata.

Tata wants to get married as soon as possible, which means as soon as she's old enough. She's desperate to escape Rozzano, and nonno, and all the things she's forced to do here. They persuade her to wait one extra year, but no more: at nineteen, she marries Totò and moves to Milan. To Via Mac Mahon. With all the

Africans, nonna says.

How are you, Alessa'?

Fine. It's different here.

Milan *is* different. I want to go to Milan, too, where everything is bigger, and you're free to do whatever you want. Where you can live by yourself and not be forced to eat plants.

I spend a lot of time with Tata and zio Franco, but I spend a lot more with nonna's friends. We watch South American telenovelas together, and *Good Afternoon* with Patrizia Rossetti. In the evenings, after *Dallas*, we watch *Colpo Grosso*, the show with the laughing, dancing girls who open their bras and show their boobs. They keep their panties on, and have colourful little stars covering their nipples. By the time *Colpo Grosso* comes on I'm half asleep, but I can hear nonna and her friends laughing: *maro', che mmellon' che tten' chest'*.

I spend summer afternoons with them in the courtyard. They wear sundresses, letting mosquitoes feast on their arms and legs. Folding chairs, hand fans, insect repellent, pistachios, and lupini beans. We stay out there for three, four hours at a time, doing absolutely nothing, sitting under the pine trees or among the parked cars, migrating with the slowly drifting patches of shade.

I know nonna Lidia's friends by their surnames, which is to say by their husbands' surnames: Ghizzini, Malerba, Corazza. I never hear them referred to by their first names. Nonna's friends walk me to preschool, they let me sleep over at their homes, they buy me girls' toys when nobody else will.

So what if Jonathan wants to make magic potions with groats and crushed biscuits and mix them up with milk and water and flour and spices? So what if he steals things from the pantry and pretends to be a witch, or a shaman?

He's just a kid! Leave him alone.

They visit while nonna is cleaning the house; come with me, let's bake a cake …

Come on, let's go out and buy some lollies.

I'll bring him back at midday, Lidia.

Say goodbye to nonna, we're leaving …

Doesn't he ever play with the other kids?

No, he's like my little shadow. He's not interested in other kids.

Nonna Lidia has a lot of friends, but in the beginning, when I first go to live with her, she never leaves the house.

She only starts going out after her mother, my great-grandmother Immacolata, dies. Or, I should say, after *one* of her mothers dies. From a young age, nonna Lidia was adopted by an aunt and uncle. When bisnonna Immacolata died, she left all her strength to nonna Lidia. Like a kind of supernatural relay race. Nonna says Immacolata gave her the courage to start leaving the house.

Why couldn't you do it before, nonna?

No one knows, or no one tells me.

What I do know is that, a long time ago, nonna Lidia was depressed. She weighed thirty-eight kilos. The photos of her from that time are kept in a wooden box, high up on a shelf in the storage cupboard. The woman in those photos looks nothing like nonna Lidia. Her face is just a skull covered in thin, dried skin. Her eyes are bulging out of their sockets. She's not smiling in a single photo. Her head is tiny, with a scarf tied under her chin. It looks like she could topple over at any moment.

The woman in those yellowed black-and-white photos in the

storage cupboard reminds me of a bird, a quail. Nonna doesn't look like that anymore: she eats a lot, she has big thighs and a soft belly, and she's always joking around with her friends. If they make her laugh too much, she pretends she's peed her pants.

Me so' pisciat' sotto, mo' m'aggia cambia'.

But sometimes on Sundays, as she's washing the dishes after lunch, nonna cries.

I hear her crying and muttering to herself with her head bowed over the sink. She soaps the plates and the saucepans, then rinses them, crying and saying things I can't understand, because the sound of the water covers the sound of her words.

Whenever she fights with nonno, or whenever something bad happens, she says: one of these days I'll up and leave.

I'll up and leave, and you'll never see me again.

She says it, but she never does it. She's repeated it a thousand times, but she's never left.

She's still there now, with nonno, who since his stroke can barely walk and needs help with everything.

She's still there, even though nonno has lost his mind and flies into a rage if nonna doesn't do things exactly the way he tells her to: if she doesn't serve lunch at exactly the right time, if she doesn't immediately attend to the things he fixates on — forms, bills, telephone calls — to avoid thinking about the fact that he could die at any moment. If he were to die, I could go back and visit her. I could have lunch with her, we could watch tv together again, like when I was little.

But not while he's alive. I never want to see my nonno again.

I've never wanted to see him.

Even though I know he's not evil.

Even though I know he didn't ruin our lives on purpose.

The doctor at the hospital won't look me in the eye

The doctor at the hospital won't look me in the eye.

He's staring at the wall between me and Marius.

We're at San Raffaele university hospital. I actually studied at San Raffaele, for a while. Philosophy. I didn't like it. Too formal, too many rich kids — I felt like I was going to an office job.

I left after a semester, and enrolled in La Statale.

We're in one of the underground rooms between the hospital and the university. Somewhere above us is the huge cupola topped with the statue of Archangel Raphael. At a height of sixty metres, the heavenly messenger dominates the surrounding landscape. The moment the dome and its winged ornament emerge in the distance, you get a sense of the kind of aura this revered hospital (founded in 1969 by Verzé, a priest friend of Berlusconi) emits.

A solemn, enlightened aura. An aura of faith — in God and in medicine.

The design of the hospital complex says it all: the basilica at the centre, with an enormous helix of DNA, tens of metres tall, winding its way up the cupola, culminating in a nimbus of glass and light crowned with the statue of the divine healer. San Raffaele is a cathedral of medicine, built in white stone. It blazes in the sunlight, as if rising up from a valley of the afterlife — one where doctors in white coats have taken the place of saints.

Today, though, there is no sunlight; the sky is grey, the air humid.

It's an early afternoon in early February. Marius and I have just had lunch, and I still have the taste of pasta col sugo in my mouth. I'm back at my almost alma mater, but today my dread has nothing to do with classes and exams.

This morning I wasn't given the full results of my blood test. The woman who attended me gave me as much as she was authorised to. I sat down immediately, right there in the waiting room, to read the report. The first thing I checked was my white blood cell count: if it's leukaemia, you'll know straight away because your leukocyte values will be through the roof. I read that on the internet. They can soar to terrifying levels. I scanned the numbers and symbols on the piece of paper.

All normal.

Once again, medicine has failed me.

I'm getting worse and worse, but my blood tests don't seem to notice. Somehow I'm both sick and well at the same time.

The reason for my constant fever remains a mystery.

A nameless emergency. Without a name, my illness has no dignity.

An hour after my visit to the clinic, I got a phone call.

Bazzi? Can you come to the hospital in Via Olgettina for a moment?

A moment? Are they trying to play this down?

Do I need to be there right away?

No; look, how about we schedule it for after lunch?

A man's voice. More than calm. Soothing.

Is this an act? Is he reading from a script?

I immediately messaged my friends in the WhatsApp group we've had for years.

Guys, the hospital called. They want me to go in. I've definitely got it.

What the fuck are you talking about?

It's fine, it'll just be some routine thing they do.

Alessandro said when he gets tested at the centre for sexually transmitted diseases in Viale Jenner, they always get a doctor to talk him through the results. It has to be a doctor, even if your results are negative.

Alessandro, Simona, Gianfranco, Elena: all united in their denial.

I insisted; I was convinced.

They stopped arguing — a surrender?

Let us know.

Let me know.

When we arrive at the hospital, it takes us forever to find the laboratory office. We get off the shuttle — the little driverless train that runs between the Metro station and the hospital — and wander through a subterranean labyrinth of corridors connecting classrooms, offices, wards. I know these corridors well, I've been here many times, but my perception of this place is skewed; I only know how to orient myself as a student. I know almost nothing about the hospital-related areas of San Raffaele. And anyway, I can barely think straight. I'm incapable of doing anything that requires an attention span of more than a few minutes.

I've been sick for more than three weeks now. The fever hasn't gone away.

I want to know what's wrong with me.

Right now, as soon as possible.

Once we find our destination, I'll have to reconfigure my

relationship with this place. I know these buildings, it's true. But what are they becoming, now, under the weight of what's happening? Perception variables: what difference does it make if I receive the news in a place I know as opposed to one I don't know? My university is about to transform into the place where I discovered what was wrong with my body. What if I bump into someone I know? An ex-classmate, a teacher?

Greta.

Maria.

Luca.

Ciao, Sarah … no, I'm actually here for some test results.

Yeah, I'm doing my degree at La Statale now.

Hi, professor … nothing special, just some blood tests.

I try not to make eye contact with the people we pass in the corridors, to minimise the chance of being recognised. I employ my most well-developed social skill: avoidance, evasion, feigned obliviousness.

We walk until a sign stops us in our tracks: 'laboratory administration office'.

We go in; it's the right place.

The doctor isn't there.

Just wait outside, he'll be back in a minute.

We wait on the shiny black plastic chairs lined up along the corridor. Marius and I are both silent. I re-read the results given to me this morning — the only data I have available. On closer inspection, some of my values are a little off, but nothing looks too unusual. The numbers aren't far from the normal range.

Finally, the doctor arrives. I recognise his voice — he's the one who called me.

Hello. Hello. Did you come on your lunch break? I bet you

didn't have much appetite, knowing you had to come in today.

I'll be right back, excuse me for a moment.

Again?

He walks through one of the other doors that open off the corridor. A few excruciating minutes pass. I've been waiting for this moment for weeks. I've been patient, but now I'm at breaking point — I can't stand any more suspense.

The doctor comes back out in a hurry, holding an envelope.

Come in.

I stand up. I'm going in alone.

I turn around; Marius looks at me.

I thought I'd let him stay there on the plastic chairs, holding our coats.

Did I want him to decide whether or not to follow me?

That makes no sense. Snap out of it — there's still time. I stop in the middle of the corridor and turn to the doctor. Is it alright if he comes, too? He's my boyfriend.

Of course, if it's alright with you.

Without a word Marius stands up, grabs the coats, and walks towards me.

He's usually a slow mover.

Today, though, every movement seems rushed.

People in my family dream a lot

People in my family dream a lot.

Dreams are important in our house. Everyone dreams: Tata dreams, nonna dreams, even zio Franco dreams.

Mamma, I dreamt about zio Peppino.

Alessa', m'agg sunnat' a pat'm.

Mamma, mamma, last night I had a dream about Erminia, the aunt who died of a horrible illness.

The dead speak to my family in dreams. They tell us what we should and should not do. They tell us which lottery numbers to buy, and who's going to get pregnant, and when something bad is about to happen, they cry.

I also dream, but never about dead people. My dreams are terrifying. The same ones, over and over again. Two mute children sitting on a bench next to a streetlamp, exchanging something — lollies? The grand opening of a giant spaceship, at night — a black metal platform illuminated by rays of light. A still, dark lake, and a woman with long straight hair whose face suddenly crumples, wrinkles into a mask of stone or wood. The girls from Non è la Rai having a party, with balloons and confetti falling from the ceiling. A notary's office — something bad has happened.

My dreams wake me up at night. I have them for years.

Always the same ones.

When I'm older, they often return when I have a fever. They still terrify me.

★

Nights at my grandparents' house are never quiet.

I sleepwalk. I don't know I'm doing it, but the next morning someone tells me I got up in the middle of the night, went into their bedroom, and spoke to them in my sleep. Never wake a sleepwalker, my nonna says. It's dangerous, it gives them a shock, they could have a heart attack. People have died from being woken up too suddenly. Nonna tells me about a girl who tried to jump off the balcony in her sleep: they stopped her just in time, as she was lifting up the kitchen shutters.

I get up at one or two in the morning and sleepwalk into zio Franco and Lucia's room. No one really understands what I say during my nocturnal visits. I talk about blind kittens, or cemeteries, or baby birds that fell out of their nest, or Jesus. My eyes are still closed, and I'm always holding my bottle of milk. Mamma doesn't like the bottle — I'm too old to drink milk that way, she says. But while I live here, with nonna, there's nothing mamma can do about it. Maybe nonna wishes I'd never grow up.

I often wet the bed at night. Nonna puts a sheet of clear plastic over the mattress so I don't stain it. I always know when I wet the bed because the sheets feel cold. My pyjama bottoms feel heavy. I wake up shivering.

Every so often, I hear my family talking about me: *Does that seem normal to you? Seven years old and he still pisses himself.* They think I don't listen to them, but I do. I hear everything. *Problem … late developer … send him to a specialist.* I don't say anything. I'm not sure why I wet the bed — I'm asleep, I don't know I'm doing it. They tell me to pay more attention: if you feel like you need to wee, get up and go to the bathroom. But how can I pay attention when I'm asleep?

Nonna Lidia enjoys telling me stories about when she was a little girl in Naples. She tells me about ghosts, and spirits, and werewolves, and the witches they called *janare,* and the little monk fairy, Monaciello. Nonna threatens to summon them all to Rozzano, to Verbena Street, if I don't behave myself. Sometimes she even invokes the devil: finish your pasta or he'll come and take you away, you hear? He's already here, he's waiting for you in the storage cupboard.

The *janare* don't frighten me as much. I'm scared of them, but I also like the sound of them. I love listening to nonna's stories about them — they're like evil fairies, and at night they sneak under the doors of people's houses. But nonna, how do they do that? Tell me again.

They flatten themselves against the ground and make themselves very, very skinny, like a piece of paper, and then they slip away quick smart, like eels. They ride the horses in the stables and braid their tails, and when they get angry they smother children in their sleep.

There are rules at my grandparents' house. Unspoken rules.

Never serve the bread upside down on the table. Never cross your cutlery. Never walk under a ladder. Never open an umbrella indoors. Never break a mirror. Never spill the salt. There are so many things to worry about.

Breaking the rules brings bad luck. Curses.

Statt' ferm' cu 'sti mman'.

Nonna is always leaving little piles of rock salt in the corners of rooms, behind furniture and vases and doors. When I see them I ask her what they're for, and she yells at me to go away and mind my own business. Later, I understand: nonna is trying to protect us from the people who want to hurt us. Rozzano is full of those people. Even some of her friends pose a danger. They're liars, phonies. They give me compliments, nonna says, but in reality they're jealous; they envy her because they don't have any grandchildren of their own, or the ones they have are ugly. Not beautiful like her grandson. Not beautiful like me.

Nonna is obsessed with people's eyes. She warns me about *l'uocchie 'nguoll*, the evil eye, and tells me I have to be careful. She has a ritual whenever we go out together: first she combs my hair into a side part in the hallway mirror, then she puts rosewater and sun cream on my face, then she whispers a prayer and makes the sign of the cross on my forehead. She tells me never to listen to anyone, to trust no one.

The people in Rozzano are animals.

Every so often, nonna goes to a psychic. I wish I knew what the psychic says when she reads nonna's palm, or her Tarot cards, but no one ever tells me. Nonna only talks about it with her friends, or with Tata, and when she does, she lowers her voice so I can't hear. I gather that sometimes she asks the psychic to do a kind of ritual to get rid of the evil eye, because there are people out there who use magic against us.

We've been cursed — that's why we're poor, and why things are always going wrong.

Maybe nonna asked the psychic for a spell to make my parents get back together.

If she did, it hasn't worked. Mamma and papà only speak to each other from a distance, or to argue.

I often go to the shopping centre with nonna and Tata.

Sometimes they steal things. They hide between the shelves or in the dressing rooms and remove the price tags from the stuff they want. Clothes, fake flowers, food — they slip them into their handbags, or up their shirts. Sometimes, instead of stealing, they just switch the prices. It's easy to do, especially with price stickers.

They get a 30,000-lire suit for eight lire, or a twenty-lire perfume for five.

The security guards never notice.

Nonna and Tata are cunning. But I'm afraid something will go wrong, sooner or later.

On Saturday mornings, we almost always go to the market in the park underneath the Telecom tower. I'm bored to death by the long, slow route through the fruit and vegetable and fish stalls. But when we get to the animals, I perk up. The animals make me happy. There are turtles, and birds, and goldfish. Sometimes even puppies, or newborn kittens — won't they die of cold out here, in this cardboard box? I wish I could cuddle them all, take them all home with me, but I can't. Nonno won't allow it.

Say goodbye, you'll see them again next week.

If they're still there.

Nonna tells me I have to be careful at the market because it's full of gypsies, and she says gypsies like to steal children. When we pass a group of Romani women, I freeze. Yellow, white, red, purple — they dress in all the colours of the world. Some wear their hair in braids, others wrap their heads in scarves. Between their lips I glimpse gold teeth (nonna, do they really make those with the jewellery they steal from people's houses?) and on their feet they wear wooden clogs or rubber slippers with terry socks. They strap their babies to their chests with pieces of cloth. They stole all those babies, nonna says. See? The babies are blonde, not dark like them. When their mothers are distracted, the gypsies snatch the babies out of their prams and kidnap them.

Nonna, do the gypsies ask for a ransom?

No, don't be silly, she replies. They sell the babies for their organs, or they keep them and raise them as gypsies. They're beasts, savages. They make the children live in the street and beg for money.

Be careful, or they'll take you, too. They'll slip you under their skirts and steal you away.

The other children from my building play together in the courtyard. I don't want to join them — *I'm not going, I said no* — but nonna and Tata force me. I have no choice. They practically carry me down to the patch of lawn where the boys are playing football. I hate football. I'm scared of fouls, and falls. I'm scared of spraining an ankle or breaking a leg. I don't know how to shoot or pass or tackle. I don't know how to do anything. The boys on my team scream at me. The boys on the other team laugh at me. They call me a moron, a retard. I don't know how to play football, and I don't want to learn. I don't even know how to ride a bike without training wheels: mamma and papà never taught me. I don't spend enough time with either of them for the thought to cross their mind. I won't learn to ride a bike until the age of twelve. I'll never be a confident rider: the smallest obstacle — a bump in the road, a tram track, another cyclist passing too close — will be enough to send me crashing to the ground.

No bikes, no cars, no Vespas.

We don't have the money — you can get your licence when you're older.

I'm destined to always and only be a pedestrian.

When the other kids aren't playing football, they're playing chicken in the basement.

Everyone is afraid of the basements in Rozzano. The basements are where the addicts go to shoot up. The basements are full of rats — sewer rats, my nonna calls them. In my imagination the basements are writhing with snakes, and above them are clouds of bats that get tangled in your hair. The basements are a hiding place for drug dealers and serial killers from *Crime Stoppers* — nonna, I'm scared, change the channel please.

There are basements underneath every public-housing tower in Rozzano. They smell of mildew and garbage and rat poison. There are always two entrances, one on either side of each block of apartments. The basements are like dimly lit, zigzagging corridors with lots of doors. Each family in the building has their own numbered door opening onto the basement. In the middle of the basement is the garbage room, where all the trash from everyone's apartments ends up. The garbage — *la munnezza*, as my grandparents call it — makes its way to the basement via a secret chute that reminds me of the waterslide in *The Goonies*.

Close it, close it, nonna always shouts.

Never leave the basement door open — the rats and cockroaches will get in.

In the game of chicken, you have to run all the way through the basement, from one entrance to the other. If you accept the challenge, you're a hero. If you don't, you're a wuss.

The game of chicken is no joke — there are real dangers in the basement. Once, I find a lemon with a syringe stuck in it. Some junkie must have left it there, nonna says; they disinfect their needles with lemon. It's sitting there on the cement, next to our door. Next to the lemon is a pool of blood.

One afternoon, the kids in the courtyard buzz me on the intercom.

I don't want to go downstairs, but nonna makes me.

We head to the usual spot down by the pine trees. We don't have a ball, so we fashion some makeshift ones out of scrunched-up paper. One of the paper balls rolls down into the basement. Who's going in to get it?

We do *eeny meeny miny moe*.

I'm it.

No, I'm not going in there by myself.

You're it; if you don't go, we'll have to drag you in there.

From the door at the end of the steps I can't see a thing. The lights only illuminate the corridor — the rooms coming off it are completely dark.

There's the ball, it's not far.

It's sitting on the cement, between two unidentified stains. I walk into the black corridor.

I'm not alone.

I can hear breathing, footsteps, fabric brushing against the walls.

I reach for the ball, then turn and sprint as fast as I can towards the exit. There's someone down here. Help, nonna, he's following me! He's coming for me, he's going to kill me! I run to the light, to the steps, and as I'm running I sink my teeth into the scrunched-up paper.

I sink my fear into the little paper ball.

One of my teeth falls out. A bottom tooth — it had been loose for a few days.

Who was there? nonna screams.

Someone, there's someone in the basement, I swear.

I'm never going back in there, nonna, I never want to go in there ever again.

It's good for you to get a fright, that way you'll learn.

Nonna is happy — she hates the basement. She never goes down there, not even by accident.

But, deep down, there's a part of me that likes the basement.

There are many ways to be afraid.

The only place where I'm never afraid is preschool, because preschool for me is Jaco.

The boy I'm in love with.

Jaco is blond; he has a beautiful blond bob. Jaco is the most beautiful boy in our preschool. No, in the world. Jaco is the most beautiful boy in the world. By the age of five he already knows how to read — he's an autodidact. People say his parents are hippies, but I don't know what that means. Jacob reads comic books; he arrives in the morning holding his mother's hand and a copy of *Topolino*.

Jaco is so smart, and I like him so much. Tata likes him, too: what a gorgeous kid, he's too cute. It's true, zia. Jaco is my favourite. And in my final year of preschool, at the age of five, I confess my love to him. I tell my friends to invite Jaco to the mushroom house in the middle of the play room, after lunch.

I want to kiss him.

I give my friends very precise instructions: I'll wait for him here, you ask him if he wants to come. Ask him if he wants to kiss me.

They return a few minutes later, without Jaco.

They're laughing.

No, he doesn't want to come.

Jacopo's not coming.

He doesn't hold it against me, though. He still comes to my birthday party at mamma's house. The last birthday party before the end of preschool. Some of my friends come, too: Ramona, Veronica, Evelyn. At my party, Jaco looks amazing. He's wearing a salmon-pink shirt. His blond hair — not blond, gold — comes down to his cheeks. He's like a prince; Jaco is my little prince.

At my birthday party, there are only girls and Jaco. Those are the only kids I play with. No one bothers me about it yet. But already grown-ups have started commenting on the things I like. Saying they're strange. They get annoyed at me.

At the age of six, I want to dress up as Jessica Rabbit for Carnevale. I'd die for her sequin-covered dress, her purple gloves, her high heels. The cloud of red hair covering half her face. But I can't — you can't dress up as Jessica Rabbit. They make me go as Roger, instead.

I always want the wrong things. Who taught me that?

After you

After you.

We turn the corner and the doctor gestures towards one of the doors that open off the corridor. An office, a consultation room, I'm not sure. We file into the room where everything is about to happen. We sit down in the shape of an isosceles triangle: the distance between me and Marius is the shortest.

The doctor starts speaking.

So — he clears his throat — do you know much about HIV?

His gaze skims mine as lightly as possible; most of the time he rests it slightly to the left of me. I find it annoying. Is he avoiding eye contact? We're sitting right across from each other, but something in him is absent, evasive. He doesn't want to be in this room with me. Maybe he's cross-eyed? I look more closely. No, he's just uncomfortable. Because of me. Or rather, because of what I represent in this room, in this moment.

I give a vague reply: yeah, I've read a bit about it.

It's true — my internet research has encompassed even HIV.

The doctor continues.

So, as you'll know, with today's medications …

I'm biased, but to me he seems like a priest. Thin, greying hair, parted to the side. He must be fifty, sixty? Light-blue eyes, pinkish skin. A few broken capillaries, some blotchy patches. Leather shoes — loafers, probably expensive. His long socks are slipping down his ankles, he needs to pull them up.

The doctor-priest knows.

The virus speaks. She's a real gossip.

I'm meeting this priest-like doctor for the first time and already he knows so much about me. He has already assigned me to a community, a narrative, a case study. HIV confirms two things: you're gay, and you've had sex. Maybe too much sex, and in a promiscuous manner.

Well, okay, HIV isn't only for fags.

But in the public imagination, it is.

And that's what matters.

Go on, doc, say it. I'm ready. I'd rather this than the other thing. Modern medicine has HIV pretty much under control; I know that, I've read about it. Sure, I'll get sick and die one day, like everyone else. But not right away, not now, and that's all that matters. The doctor doesn't seem prepared for my reaction. What was he expecting? Tears? Maybe a grimace? Some show of desperation, at least.

Does he want more?

You can do better than that.

When I tell people — my friends, my doctor — about my reaction to the diagnosis, no one understands how it could be possible. They look at me with bewilderment. But it's true: the moment I learn I've got HIV, I feel happy.

Relieved.

The good-versus-bad binary is naive. In reality, there are fragments of good and bad in everything that happens to us. Our experiences are part of a landscape. Peaks and troughs are relative.

I've been unwell for so long; I can't take it anymore.

I don't know what being HIV-positive means, but I already

am HIV-positive. My body is one step ahead of me.

For a while now I've been seeing things differently. I'm no longer that person who was well, who took his time for granted, wasted it, imagining he had an infinite number of days at his disposal, relying on the tacit cooperation of his body.

Sickness and death are no longer theories to me; I have crossed a line.

Now I have an expiration date. I don't know exactly when it is, of course, but that doesn't make much difference.

I've crossed over to the other side.

I'm sick — that's a fact. This illness affects me exclusively — it has chosen me, it has mingled with my body. Like it or not, the illness and I have made contact. It no longer exists outside, elsewhere, as some anonymous, vague misfortune that only ever afflicts other people.

HIV, fine, but what stage am I in?

How much damage has already been done?

I've never taken an HIV test. Maybe I've had it since I was ten years old, and it's already completely destroyed my immune system. Early intervention is crucial, I've heard.

Is it already too late?

Do I have AIDS?

My initial sense of relief begins to fade.

This morning, when they wouldn't give me the complete results of my blood test, I called Marius from the footpath on Corso Buenos Aires. He was on his way to work. He called his boss and immediately headed back home to meet me.

Hi. So they wouldn't give me the results; I think they're probably positive.

Marius is quiet on the phone, he doesn't say anything.

Mouth open, throat constricted.

No, don't do it. Don't cry, I think. *This is good for me. The alternatives were all scarier than this.*

Come on, it's not that bad. I'll just get treatment. It's not like it used to be.

I play it cool to comfort Marius, but in doing so, I come to the conclusion that staying calm *is* the best approach. With that first phone call, I lay the foundations for an attitude I will soon come to adopt wholeheartedly: yes, I'm sick, but I'm working things out. I have what I have, but it's not the end of the world. It doesn't have to be.

Marius is eight years my junior, and in the time we've been together, I've often helped him do things for the first time. I was the one who taught him how much salt to put in the water for the pasta, how to open a bank account, how to look for an apartment and move house, how to write a resumé when you're looking for work, how to look after the cats. How to buy a plane ticket. Now, I'm teaching him how to accept a positive HIV diagnosis.

The essence of that first call is repeated every time I give someone the news. I reassure them, simultaneously announcing and denying my illness, minimising it. The illness is scarier when it is distant: when it arrives, everything gets easier. The terror and panic reside in the space preceding the encounter, or the collision.

Fear is a privilege reserved for the healthy.

So it's up to me — the patient, the sick friend, the wayward son — to describe what it's like on the other side, to give others a sign of life. To show it's possible to say *I have HIV* without bursting into tears, without spreading fear.

I tell my friends in order to make the news seem more real.

Because it has to be done, not because I want to be comforted. I explain and I reassure, in part to avoid extreme reactions — I don't like seeing people lose control, I don't want to provoke any violent displays of emotion. So I clarify, I quell their incipient despondency, I update views that are stuck in the Eighties. I repeat to others what I've read and learnt about my illness, and in repeating it to others, I attempt to make it real to myself.

Above all, it's me I'm trying to convince.

Before going to San Raffaele, I called my doctor.

Even with him, I felt the need to clarify. All good, I told him, I'm feeling okay. He was upset, although he tried not to show it. He's gay — for him, HIV is personal, not just professional. Has he ever been afraid of contracting it?

Here at the hospital, with the doctor who gives me the diagnosis, I do the same thing: I smile, try to communicate as clearly as possible that I'm okay, that this news is something I can accept. The doctor's tone remains regretful, his gaze averted. How many crises, tears, faces deformed by grief must he have witnessed? A diagnosis like this changes everything — it forces you to completely revise the image you have of yourself, in an instant.

Before: I am healthy, I am thirty years old, I have my whole life ahead of me.

After: I am HIV-positive, I have to get better, I will spend the rest of my life getting better.

I've read the latest statistics on life expectancy for HIV-positive people. My life is not over. The sooner I can adapt, the better. All I have to do is come to terms with the loss of privilege.

You have HIV: in the past, those words were a death sentence.

In the space of one or two years my body would have be completely overpowered, and eventually defeated. It wouldn't have been the virus itself that killed me, but rather the opportunistic infections and HIV-associated cancers. The rapid deterioration of my body would have been unstoppable, irreversible. There were no medications, or the ones that existed didn't work well enough — the disease always progressed to AIDS, always ended in death. There were extremely rare exceptions, of course: case studies, miraculous bodies in which the virus failed to develop. These days, it's not like that — I understand this, my mind knows it. But my understanding is one-dimensional, superficial. A thin veneer that doesn't quite hide the terrifying void beneath it.

I discover a deep, hypnotising chasm inside myself, a dimension thoughts can't penetrate. Now, suddenly, my ego is utterly embodied; my ego is no longer an omnipotent, theoretical abstraction, but a body that knows illness. I am the secrets of my body's blood and cells, their microscopic struggles writ large, enormous enough to change everything. I am vulnerable, infected flesh. I am a vessel of impure blood, forever altered. A bundle of organs and veins and cavities in which a virus — an infamous one — can lurk and multiply without my knowledge.

How am I supposed to live knowing I have this in my body?

How can I agree to spend the rest of my life with this invisible, indestructible parasite?

Like a tiny, unforgettable, omnipresent stain.

The doctor at San Raffaele tells me they've already retested my blood samples to verify the positive result. The diagnosis is definitely correct; there's no escaping it.

In my hand, I'm holding the piece of paper they wouldn't give me this morning.

…e words.

…investigation revealed the presence of specific … sponse to the presence of HIV, according to the criteria … the Centers for Disease Control and Prevention of

I have contracted the human immunodeficiency virus.

The last thing I hear is the doctor's voice: it doesn't seem to be a recent infection.

Snow White in the glass coffin

Snow White in the glass coffin.

Eyes closed, hands resting on her stomach, black hair spilling across the red velvet cushion. Circling the coffin, like a ring of mushrooms, are the heads of the seven dwarves.

The dwarves are grieving the death of their friend.

The illustration adorns the cover of one of my favourite books at nonna Nuccia and nonno Pier's house. Nuccia and Pier are my father's parents. They live in a two-bedroom apartment at 2 Dahlia Street, on the eighth floor (the top floor), overlooking Viale Lombardia. Their apartment is very high up, and nonna gets nervous when I stand on the kitchen balcony to watch the cars and people below.

Don't stick your head out, you'll lose your balance — your head is eight times heavier than your body.

If I try to look down, nonna pulls me back roughly by the arms.

Nonna, if I fall will I die?

Are you kidding? Of course you'll die. A falling body gains velocity.

If my father is there with us he laughs: *shit, we'd be picking you up with a spoon.*

I imagine pink jam smeared across the grass and the cars in the courtyard below.

I like going to nonna Nuccia and nonno Pier's place because they buy me lots of books.

When my other relatives buy me gifts, they always give me toys, or clothes. Tina, what does the kid need? A jacket, a pair of shoes for winter. Not nonna Nuccia and nonno Pier. They buy me books of fairy tales, illustrated atlases, books about animals and the human body. For my birthday they give me books about Greek mythology, and the solar system, and ancient legends, and science. I don't like adventure stories with lots of boy characters in them, but if they give me books like that, I don't say anything. I keep them anyway, even if I don't read them.

I like looking at my books arranged on the shelf, all the different-coloured spines lined up one after the other.

I love stories about princesses and fairies and witches. At my grandparents' place, in the mornings (I'm always the first one up), I leaf through the four big books of illustrated fairy tales that nonno Pier's mother gave to my aunt for her first communion. The books have blue fabric covers, with titles embroidered in gold, and inside they have the most beautiful pictures I've ever seen. An orphan looking at the sun through a perforated leaf. Evil stepsisters spewing toads and snakes (a fairy has punished them for their jealousy). The little mermaid transforming into sea foam. A queen walking through a forest of thorns and crows. The pages brim with splendid gowns and jewel-encrusted tiaras and flying swans and magical spells and ineluctable prophecies.

At the kiosk, nonna and nonno buy me sets of read-along fairy tales. I have the full collection — a row of plastic cases filled with cassettes and little booklets. 'In my heart I have a thousand tales to tell', lilts the theme song at the beginning of each story. I listen to them nonstop: five, six books at a time, one after the other. I sit on the couch in the lounge room, surrounded by cushions and soft toys, and listen to the voices reading me the story of *Hop-o'-My-Thumb*, or *Donkeyskin*, or *Hansel and Gretel*, or *The Little Match Girl*. I sink deep into the tales and the cushions. I lose all sense of time. I even forget about mamma and papà screaming at each other over the phone.

There's always a lot of reading material at nonna Nuccia and nonno Pier's house. Women's magazines, puzzle magazines, travel magazines, the *Corriere della Sera* with all the weekend inserts. I'm allowed to look at all of them, and I'm never told to go and read them in my room by myself.

Nonna doesn't like nonno smoking indoors — she hates the smell of cigarette smoke; if she smells it, she starts shouting — so nonno goes out to the landing and smokes on the stairs. He sits opposite the elevator with his ashtray. Often I follow him, taking with me one of my many books. There on the landing, wreathed in clouds of cigarette smoke, nonno tells me about Pandora and Persephone, and reads me stories about Zeus, the king of the gods.

At my grandparents' place I also have VHS tapes. When I'm not there, nonna records my favourite films and tv shows for me. She writes the title on the white edge of the cassette tape, and next to it she writes my name: *Jonathan Ladyhawke*, *Jonathan Labyrinth*, *Jonathan The Cave of the Golden Rose*. She also tapes *Wonder Woman*, my favourite show. As I watch the recorded episodes, I imitate Diana Prince: I spin around the way she does when she has to transform, and explode into a flash of light and sparks. I run around the lounge room and jump up and down on the couch. Like Wonder Woman, I can bend steel and force open armoured doors. I wear the same blue short shorts with white stars, the same red heeled boots, and sometimes the wetsuit she uses when she has to go in the water to complete a mission.

★

When I'm not reading books or listening to fairy tales, I'm drawing.

Everyone tells me I'm an excellent drawer.

My grandparents give me sketchbooks, coloured pencils, watercolours, paintbrushes. Nonno Pier tells me I should go to the Accademia di Brera when I'm older. Open your hand, let me see. He studies my palm and concludes: *you should be an artist.* I don't really understand what it means to be an artist, but I like the idea of it. No one else ever talks about my future; no one imagines anything for me beyond the here and now.

When I was born, nonno Pier was over the moon.

The first grandchild, a son, a Bazzi.

He even dedicated a poem to me. He wrote it himself. He called it: *For Jonathan.*

Nonna, did nonno really write poems?

Sometimes.

Nonno Pier tried his hand at everything.

You could have a conversation with him on almost any topic. Even mamma says so.

And the things he did for you, when you were little.

I caught whooping cough when I was two years old, and nonno Pier took me to the Alps in a helicopter so that I could breathe good fresh air from the mountain skies.

And did it cure me?

Yes, it cured you.

The pure mountain air saved my life.

★

Nonna Nuccia and nonno Pier's house is the only place where I have a bedroom all to myself. It used to be papà and his sister's room, and now it's mine. Well, it's not just mine — my cousin Luca, who is three years younger than me, also sleeps in it. But there's only one bed, so when I'm there Luca doesn't come. We alternate.

Luca and I are constantly fighting.

I'm jealous, because I know he's nonna Nuccia's favourite. He's her daughter's son, whereas I'm the son of Tina, her son's ex-wife. No one tells me this, but I understand the distinction.

Nonna Nuccia is always in a hurry. She always gets my name wrong when she calls out to me. Roberto! Luca! Pierluigi! She calls out three different names before landing on mine. My father, my cousin, my nonno.

When she gets a dog, she starts calling me 'Fuego' — she calls me by the dog's name.

Roberto! Luca! Fuego! My name is never the first one out of her mouth.

I'm jealous of Luca, but that's not the only reason we fight. With Luca, I have to protect myself.

Because even though Luca is the favourite, he wants to be me.

He copies me, and I can't stand it. He wants to eat the same things I eat, he wants to go everywhere I go. If he's not allowed to, he pretends to have a tantrum — he starts crying and throws himself to the floor. His mouth stretches open and he screams as though someone were torturing him, as though he were being branded with a hot iron, or skinned alive, or else he kicks his legs violently to terrorise nonna and his mother.

You're hurting yourself, Luca, please, you're scaring me.

They fall for it, like idiots. They cave to his demands, buy him whatever he wants. They don't know how to say no to him. There are no limits to my cousin's desires. Just like with papà, nonna?

Until nonna Nuccia and nonno Pier retire, I only stay with them on weekends and public holidays. We don't always stay in Rozzano; sometimes we go to Milan, and get gelato along the canal, and look at the boats bobbing in the water. The boats are fake — you can get on them, but they don't move. They've been turned into bars, or restaurants.

Nonno Pier works at the post office (as a postman? no, just in the office), but in the evenings he also works at the pool, as a swimming instructor. Nonno Pier has many passions. He is curious, he swings from one thing to another. He likes to watch Westerns, and war movies, and history documentaries, and Piero Angela's shows. He likes all black-and-white films, but especially the ones with Charlie Chaplin, Laurel and Hardy, Bud Spencer, and Terence Hill. He listens to a lot of music, mostly Italian singer-songwriters. Giorgio Gaber and Jannacci, songs in Milanese dialect. When he listens to music, nonno Pier closes his eyes and moves his hands around as if he's drawing the notes in the air. He goes to cabaret shows. He's a big fan of A.C. Milan and Ferrari. He watches all the news programs and shows about politics.

Nonno is a Lega Nord supporter. He adores Umberto Bossi, even though nonna hates him. Sometimes they fight about it, huge fights, like the ones nonno Biagio and nonna Lidia have. They argue because nonna speaks badly of Bossi, or for other reasons, like bills and household expenses. They have a notebook where they write down everything they spend, and if one of them has spent more than the other they have to 'settle' their debt at the end of the month. Nonna Nuccia and nonno Pier are married, but they keep their money separate.

When they fight, nonno Pier gets angry and yells, just like nonno Biagio. He tells nonna to shut up, to get back to cooking and knitting. When he really loses it, he yells even louder and says to nonna: watch it, Nuccia, or I'll smash your head open. When he calls her a bitch — *strunsa,* in Milanese — his eyes are wide, his voice gasping and catching in his throat. He says things in dialect that I don't understand. He scares me when he raises his hand as though he's about to punch or slap her.

He grabs her by the shoulders, pushes her: fuck you, Nuccia.

She says: do it, I dare you. I'll report you; I've got the kid as a witness.

I swear, Pierluigi, I'll call the carabinieri.

Nonna, are we going to court?

What will I have to say?

After nonna and nonno have been fighting, nonna's hair is all dishevelled, her bun crumpled and falling down her neck. My hands feel cold. Why does everyone have to do that? Why do they all have to hurt each other?

When we're alone, nonna asks me: who do you love more, nonna or nonno?

Nonna, I say. I always love women more.

I'm a boy, but I prefer to be with women.

It's always been that way. It will never change.

Nonno Pier retires a few years before nonna. She keeps working in Assago, at the head office of a high-end shopping centre, La Rinascente.

Mamma's family says nonna Nuccia has a lover. Who knows how many lovers she's got at that office, they say. Signor Gosimo, who is also her neighbour, is definitely one of them. Nonna's lovers are the reason she's not always home to cook and do housework, like nonna Lidia is. Instead of looking after her husband, she goes to work in an office all day, surrounded by colleagues and managers and money and computers.

Nonna Nuccia is a bad woman. A slut. Why not just say it?

Everyone has always said nonna Nuccia and I look alike, although she has darker skin than I do. She looks a bit like one of the Jeffersons. I don't — I have light skin, like mamma. Easily blemished. Nonna Nuccia is short with a round belly. Like a gnome. *It's quicker to jump over your nonna's head than go around her.* She was born in Sicily, in Catania, but she came to Milan when she was three years old. She doesn't speak Sicilian; she doesn't even have an accent. But she knows how to make arancini. She makes them sometimes, but only on special occasions, because they take so long — she has to make the rice, and the ragù, and then fry them.

Nonna always wears makeup, even when she's at home. She puts on pink lipstick, and draws over her eyebrows with black pencil, and sprays herself with vanilla-scented perfume, and dabs orange powder onto her cheeks. She loves sequins, and wearing dresses with interesting necklines. Whenever she goes to a party or a dinner with her relatives she dresses up in something extravagant: velvet, lace, sparkles, leopard print, sheer fabrics. Nonna Nuccia dresses like a diva, a vamp, and we are her audience. Her sisters give her compliments — *wow, Nuccia, what a look!* — and she says, are you kidding? I got this at the market for 5,000 lire.

Nonna likes reading, too.

She keeps all her books on the shelves above the dresser in her bedroom: *The Women's Encyclopedia*, books about knitting and crocheting, astrology handbooks, Isabel Allende novels, travel guides to places she's visited with nonno. Nonna also loves the opera. I always ask her to tell me stories about the female leads in the operas she sees at the theatre with her sister, zia Gina (zia Gina is extremely rich — she married a businessman who died and left her a bunch of money and houses).

Nonna, do all the women characters die at the end?

Nonno Pier is the only one of my grandparents who was born in Milan. Or rather, close to Milan: in Rho.

Nonno Pier is sick; he has diabetes. Every day he has to measure his blood sugar with a little machine: he pokes a tiny hole in his fingertip and places a drop of blood onto a glass plate. The little machine inspects nonno's blood and tells him if it's good or bad. Depending on the result, nonno is supposed to decide what to eat, although in reality he always ends up eating whatever he wants.

In the evenings, nonno falls asleep with his headphones on, in front of the tv in the kitchen. He sleeps sitting up, his body slipping forward in the chair, his head collapsed to one side. When he wakes up he goes to bed, but then he gets up again at two or three in the morning. He's up until dawn. Nonno never sleeps at night — he watches films, makes minestra, and drinks white wine from the fridge.

Does he get drunk?

Nonna isn't there, so he can do what he wants. Is that why he wakes up so early?

In the middle of the night, nonno Pier creates a parallel universe, a world made just for him. A place where no one else exists. Has he always done this? Papà grew up wanting for nothing, with a father who always provided for his family. But at what cost? Did nonno see his family as a weight around his neck?

Nonno should quit smoking, but he doesn't. He drinks wine and spirits — never water, never simply a glass of water. Water is for invalids. He eats pasta with lard, bread with butter and anchovies, cream buns he buys at the bakery every morning when he goes to get bread. He has heart disease; he's already had one operation, but he doesn't care.

I want to live a short life on my own terms, he says, whenever someone reminds him he should stop smoking, or drinking so much wine, or start eating better. At the rate he's going, he won't last long.

Bazzi men always die young, my zia says. They're unlucky.

Nonno Pier slowly lets himself go. He has another heart attack — they operate on him a second time. A triple or quadruple by-pass, I can't remember now. He spends a week in a clinic outside Milan, recovering. We drive there to visit him. Nonna Nuccia is crying. She's never seen him like this. After the rehab he returns home, but his health doesn't improve. He gets worse and worse. He sleeps constantly, develops a bad cough. He turns into a different person — his form and personality change completely. It's as though he's being weighed down by heavy, invisible layers of sadness.

Nonno Pier becomes a lifeless sack, a bundle of bones.

At a certain point, I learn that nonno used to have a special friend. A girl, much younger than him, from Martina Franca, in Puglia. My grandparents have a lot of photos hanging in the hallway — some of them are of places I recognise, places they've visited on holidays, but others are mysterious. Greek islands, empty beaches, plunging cliffs. I imagine one of the mystery photos is Martina Franca, the town my nonno's friend is from. She wasn't the first, although she might have been the last, because nonno started getting sick after he met her.

Hanging among the photos in the hallway is the certificate awarded to nonno Pier by the Comune di Milano, many years ago. Once, when he was young and fit and could swim like a fish, he saved a woman from drowning. The woman had crashed her car into the canal — nonno dived in and rescued her. My nonno was a hero. He flew me to the Alps when I was ill, and he jumped into the canal to save a total stranger.

If it weren't for nonno Pier, that woman would have died, nonna says.

We would all be dead without him.

He's old now, and sick, but when he was young, nonno was the centre of everything. Everyone says so. He was the motor of our family.

Nonno Pier and nonna Nuccia travel a lot: Greece, Tunisia, Egypt. Nonna always asks me what I want her to bring me back from these faraway places.

Bring me goddesses, nonna. Bring me little statues of female deities.

When she goes to Greece, nonna buys me a miniature statue of Athena. She returns from Egypt with one of Bastet, the cat goddess. Sometimes she gets me surprise gifts: a desert scorpion preserved in a plastic cube, a dagger, a pair of pointy Tunisian slippers, like Aladdin's.

Papà likes to travel, too, but he has to borrow money to do it. He never brings me back anything, because he goes in secret. He doesn't want me to find out, because he knows I'll tell mamma, and she'll get angry.

One time, though, papà returns from a trip with a gift for me.

An amber pendant with a mosquito inside, from Santo Domingo.

It's beautiful — transparent yellow and orange, full of little air bubbles that got trapped in the resin before it hardened. It's like a bead of glass, like a little dream. Papà says the amber is very old. Who knows how long that mosquito has been imprisoned in there? Since prehistoric times? Since the age of the dinosaurs? Like Jurassic Park, papà. It's a wonderful gift — I'm the happiest kid in the world. We'll take the pendant to the bank, papà says. I'll put it in my safety deposit box. It's worth a lot of money, you know. Then when you want it back, we'll go and get it, okay?

Okay, papà.

Months pass. I'm dying to look at my pendant.

Papà, papà, can you go to the bank and get my amber?

Sure thing, I'll get it for you.

I know, I know, I forgot, I'm sorry.

I didn't have time.

Next week, I promise.

I never see the pendant again.

A few years later, I find out papà sold it.

He needed the money.

The best thing about nonna Nuccia and nonno Pier's house is the Epiphany.

I always sleep there on the night of 5 January, and the next morning, when I wake up, there's a stocking hanging from the key in the old wardrobe. An enormous woollen stocking, filled with gifts from La Befana: lollies, and chocolates, and clumps of coal made from sugar. It's not the kind of pre-filled stocking you buy from the supermarket. La Befana has chosen these gifts especially for me — only the best things, the most expensive.

She came into my room at night, silently, and hung the stocking on the wardrobe.

Did she come in through the window?

Does she have a set of house keys?

I unhang the stocking and take it back to bed. I empty the whole thing out onto my pillow: bubble gum, Lion bars, Kinder Buenos, KitKats, Smarties, Galatine milk candies, Goleador liquorice straps. They rain down onto my bed like jewels. I eat hardly any of them; I hoard them, like treasure.

One year, after opening my stocking on the morning of 6 January, I decide to dress up as La Befana. I get one of nonna's floral scarves and tie it around my head. I put on some clogs with a little heel, and wrap myself in one of the colourful dressing-gowns nonna Nuccia keeps in the bathroom. I find nonna's mop and straddle it like a witch's broomstick.

I'm ready! Nonna, look at me!

Nonna, take a polaroid!

There I am, standing side-on in the corridor.

My head turned towards the lens.

I write on the white border of the photo, in all caps:

BEFANA '93.

I caught it from him

I caught it from him.

I must have caught it from Marius.

Two weeks after we met we stopped using condoms, but neither of us got tested. We never spoke about it, never came to any agreement, never clarified anything.

We avoided the topic altogether, out of a mix of embarrassment and romantic naivety.

We had just started dating, and it still didn't seem real to me. I couldn't believe Marius actually liked me. He's gorgeous — couldn't he find anyone better to be with? Maybe I'm just a fallback, something to pass the time while he waits for someone else to come along. I was so happy that I was convinced something terrible must be about to happen to one of us — an accident, an illness, a sudden death. Maybe even to both of us at the same time.

Happiness is an affront, an injury that must be redressed.

What seemed like the beginning of a love story was surely just the preamble to a tragedy.

I was so happy that I decided, more or less consciously, to avoid causing any kind of disruption. Marius had been with more boys than I had — or was it just that he spoke about them more openly? — so I knew I was taking a risk. There was a part of me that considered that, but I chose not to listen. I didn't know — I don't know — if Marius had always practised safe sex, if he'd ever had sex drunk, if he'd always been in control of the situation. I don't know; I've never asked him. I turned a blind eye to all that. I chose to trust (in what?).

I know Marius started chatting with boys online when he was fifteen. He was with quite a few people when he lived in Umbria, then many more after he moved to Milan. All older than him — guys in their thirties and forties. All his friends here in Milan are the same, regardless of gender. They fuck strangers then tell each other about it, laugh about it, brag about it. His friends are all young, like him — early twenties. They re-enact their conquests over drinks, share the details on social media, call each other sluts, whores. Their sex lives are an exhibition. They wield sex as a form of self-expression, as a way of creating a personality for themselves.

One night, at a club, Ginger had sex with three separate men one after the other — all of them guys she'd met that evening, all much older than her. First in the club toilets, then outside in the bushes of Triennale Park. None of them used a condom. Miguel has sex with at least three or four new boys a week. He meets them at bars, or online. He's even taken them back to the bank where he works, after hours. Once, after a night out, Gilda and Rachele took two guys home and fucked them, separately, in the same room.

They talk about their exploits freely on Facebook, blending truth with fiction. They post photos from bed the morning after. Still-lives of lube and dildos. It's not just sex, though. They also share memes about antidepressants, and the mental illnesses they pretend to have, and party drugs (using code names, of course). They get themselves blocked on social media for sharing the details of their Grindr and Tinder hook-ups. They insult all the men they've ever been with, humiliate them by posting screenshots of their chat conversations.

Cynicism and profanity. The more shocking, the better.

They compete with each other to see who can attract the most attention.

I'm uninhibited, but only when it comes to talking about others. I never speak about myself. I've never known how to be open about my sex life. After a while, my friends started calling me 'The Virgin of the Rocks'. But the fact that I don't talk about it doesn't mean I don't do it, or that I've never done it.

Why can't I bring myself to be more flippant about sex? I've had casual sex, I've even sought it out, but I keep it to myself — I've never felt the need to talk about it. Does it irritate me that Marius's friends are capable of something I'm not? If I were more like them — free, uninhibited, extroverted — would I have taken better care of myself? Would I have protected myself more?

I avoided asking Marius about the test, always finding new excuses, until eventually the question just disappeared. By sidestepping the problem, I accidentally ended up setting it aside. I always thought love would keep me safe. I thought love was the best form of protection. I thought nothing bad could possibly come from love. Love is a kind of sorcery, or alchemy: it takes evil and transforms it into good, embracing it, absorbing it, taming it. Ushering it inside the magic circle.

That must be what happened — Marius was HIV-positive and he didn't know it.

Like me, he ignored it.

We're both to blame. Neither of us are to blame.

But it's okay. Some part of me chose to take that risk. Some part of me decided it was worth it, come what may. Perhaps this is the price I have to pay for finding love.

Perhaps this had to happen, so that I could be with him.

When I get the diagnosis, the doctor at San Raffaele asks if I want to book a consultation. The centre for infectious diseases is at a different campus, near Piazzale Loreto. That's good — closer to home. The first thing I have to do, says the doctor, is make an appointment with a specialist and figure out the extent of the damage to my immune system.

Okay.

Great, let's book you in.

The doctor makes the call right in front of me.

He nods: ah, I see.

The waiting period is more than a month.

If you prefer, he says, you can book your initial consultation elsewhere. You might even like to do it privately.

Where? At some random hospital?

Can I think about it for a minute? He makes an appointment for me anyway, in a month's time. He has to. Protocol. HIV-positive people must be monitored, traced. They must start receiving treatment as soon as possible, so they don't spread the virus. They're loose cannons. A danger to society. My new condition has legal implications as well as medical ones.

Marius and I make our way back to the station. Cascina Gobba–Porta Venezia. We head straight home.

As we sit in the Metro, I message my friends in the group chat.

I confirm the diagnosis. Gianfranco, Simona, Silvia, Camilla, Alessandro, Elena, and Stella send me heart emojis. They reply to me one by one, in private.

Stay strong, Pam. We're here for you.

My friends call me Pam. Pamela, like the Richardson novel. But the reference isn't a literary one. When I was in high school I used to sign my drawings with my initials, J.B., and someone drew a parallel with the name of Pamela Anderson's character in Baywatch. C.J./J.B.

I don't know what to say.

This doesn't seem real.

It's okay, everything's going to be fine.

I'm so sorry, is there anything I can do?

I reply to some and not others.

I put it off — *I'll reply later*, I think, then I forget.

How am I meant to live with the idea that I'm no longer whole, pure, a blank page, a blank canvas? How am I meant to go on day after day feeling this thing inside me that shouldn't be there, knowing my body is forever fused with this unknown, this time bomb, that it should have eliminated but couldn't *(I'm sorry, but you'll be living with this illness for the rest of your life)*. How am I meant to live knowing I'm permanently flawed, faulty, broken?

When we get home I fall asleep on the couch with Mashed Potatoes. When I wake up I decide to call my mother. I text her first: can we talk?

She doesn't reply.

Five minutes pass.

She calls.

As the phone is ringing, I take it into my bedroom. I pace back and forth on the carpet: door to window, back to door.

Well?

Nothing, I got my test results back.

And?

I tested positive for HIV.

What do you mean positive?

Yeah, okay, but don't worry. It's not like it used to be (my go-to phrase, my mantra). These days you just take medication and get better.

My mother is quiet, she doesn't say anything. Even without seeing her face, I know it's folding in pain.

Hey, don't do that. It's not so bad these days, they've got it under control. It's like a chronic illness. It's a bit like having diabetes.

A bit like having diabetes — I'm just repeating phrases I've read online. I don't yet know what it's like to have HIV. I'm retrieving the most comforting information my short-term memory has to offer and launching it at my mother, to neutralise her reaction. To restore some sense of normality. The important thing is to stay calm. Me, her, us, everyone. We're not used to sharing our emotions. Or anything else, for that matter.

I don't remember my mother ever cuddling me as a child.

More recently, yes — in the last few years, since I moved out — but not as a child.

Mamma was always too angry, or worried, or absent.

What you give is what you get.

Here we are facing each other, at a distance, with this news hanging between us. This news that still doesn't seem real to me, and that she has interpreted in the worst possible way. I reject her interpretation: I refuse to be a victim. I'm like you, mamma. I've had to learn to be strong, to solve everyone else's problems, even if it means becoming hard, as impenetrable as a stone. The dam has burst, but I'm still here. It's enough for me to know that I'm not going to die right away — that I have time, space to breathe.

My mother tries to speak again, in a voice she can no longer keep from unravelling.

He's my son; I'm calling him Jonathan.

My son is HIV-positive; my son will be sick forever.

Tina, my mother, my little mamma, tries to speak. She blows her nose, lets the handkerchief absorb her tears.

But that means you'll be taking medication for the rest of your life, going in and out of hospital …

Well, better that than the other thing.

I'll never know how much mamma has cried over me — at night? during the day? in the mornings before work? — or who consoled her — my sister? her husband? my zia? — but I can imagine. I have imagined. I'll never really know if or how she has come to terms with my diagnosis. In my family, everything always happens at a distance. We were pioneers of virtual reality. When chat rooms appeared in the late Nineties, I was ready and waiting. Indirect contact is my natural habitat, my essential precondition. I never let anything touch me — not really. Is that why I'm able to bear the things that scare people the most?

You were lucky, someone will say to me, much later. You had Marius.

It's true — in the wake of my diagnosis, my boyfriend remains calm. In appearance, at least.

He doesn't seem to think about it at all.

Marius is good at stowing his problems in places where he no longer has to look at them. He buries them somewhere at the back of his mind and only digs them up when absolutely necessary, although sometimes he runs the risk of leaving them there too long, and by the time they resurface they've grown enormous, or multiplied like potatoes. I'm not like Marius; I'm a slave to my anxiety. I always need to know, to prepare a series of possible solutions, to find a way to fix things. A collision of complexes, in the Jungian sense — that's how a psychoanalyst once put it to me. We compensate by making choices, whether healthy or dysfunctional, and we get stuck returning to the same old wounds.

But then again, didn't I also act like nothing was wrong?

Maybe, when it comes down to it, Marius and I are the same.

After my diagnosis Marius has to get tested, but he doesn't seem too worried about it.

Is there any way of knowing if I was the one who gave it to him?

Will he leave me?

I can't decide if I hope he has it, too, or if I hope he doesn't have it. Vacillating between selfishness and altruism, I find myself face to face with the myth of unconditional love.

Is your partner worried? my doctor writes. He's Marius's doctor too, now — like me, Marius didn't have a doctor before all this.

He doesn't seem to be, but it's unlikely the test will be negative. I mean, never say never, but we've been having unprotected sex for three years.

I'll write him a referral, he says.

You can get an HIV test pretty much anywhere without a referral, but while we're at it, the doctor is requesting some general blood tests.

In the meantime, I have to sort out my initial consultation.

A month is too long to wait. I have to speak to a specialist — the sooner I can start treatment, the better. I want to be free of this fever. It still visits me, especially at night. I tell my friends about the wait time, about the possibility of looking elsewhere. Finding a different hospital. Alessandro writes back: I can try Serena, he says. A friend of his from high school is an infectious-disease specialist at Sacco, one of the best hospitals in Milan for treating HIV. I'll call her now, he says, see if she can help.

Ten minutes later, he messages me on WhatsApp.

He's spoken to her.

They can fit me in.

They make me an appointment for the next day.

Twelve o'clock.

Building 56.

First floor.

Consulting room D.

Fruit

Fruit.

Nancy.

Poof.

Fag.

Primary school sees the debut of a new set of songs that will accompany me for the rest of my school days. A never-ending intermittent chorus chanted by my peers, my classmates, even kids in other year levels. Word gets out. Before long, even the walls are singing at me.

I never want to leave home in the mornings. I don't want to go to school. I eat breakfast at the dining room table in my grandparents' house, watching tv, waiting for the dreaded moment when nonna will tell me it's time to get going. The minutes evaporate too quickly. I glance at the clock constantly. I wish I could stop its hands from moving. I wish I could stay here forever, watching tv in my pyjamas.

I raise a spoonful of milk and cereal to my mouth, my eyes fixed on the clock.

Seven twenty.

Seven forty.

The minute hand moves down the clockface, then climbs back up.

It's time.

I don't want to go.

Johnny, come on, it's late. Time to get dressed, let's go.

Nonna, can't I stay home with you? I don't feel good.

You stayed home yesterday. If you don't go to school today, mamma will get angry, and she'll take it out on me.

At primary school I have two teachers, Miss Mimma and Miss Rosalia. Miss Rosalia teaches us religion, and helps my classmate Nina, who has trouble understanding things. At school I never hang out with the other boys. They're always playing football, or trading cards with photos of football players on them, or talking about the football match on tv last night. At recess I play with the girls. If it's cold we stay in the classroom, and if it's not we crawl underneath the big hydrangea bush out in the garden and talk. Huddled in a circle, we hold secret meetings. Often, though, the girls want to talk about things I'm not allowed to hear, because I'm a boy. When that happens, I have to leave. I'm exiled from the bush. Other times we dance in a circle to songs by Ambra. *T'appartengo. Margheritando il cuore. L'ascensore.* The girls who go to dance classes are always in charge of the choreography. The rest of us copy them.

Sometimes I play Power Rangers with two of my classmates, Massimo and Loris. They're the only boys in my class who hang out with me. When we play Power Rangers I'm always Kimberley, the pink ranger, whose weapon is a bow and arrow. Massimo is blue, or sometimes yellow. Loris always wants to be green or black — he only plays boys.

Loris is my favourite classmate. He has curly hair and long eyelashes. Like a fawn. Loris loves anything to do with science: inventions, experiments, books about animals and insects. He has a watch that tells you the temperature and is also a compass. He's always bringing special things to school: litmus paper, Magic Eye pictures, a box filled with sliding metal pins that makes an impression of your hand or your face. I get along with Loris, but his best friend, Dario, is also in our class, so Loris usually prefers to hang out with him.

Loris and Dario even see each other outside of school — they're not just classmates, they're friends.

When the bell rings for recess, my stomach turns. I pretend to busy myself under my desk, to buy some time. I organise my lunchbox, rearrange my pencil case, open and close my books. At recess I am no longer protected by the teachers, by the order of the classroom. Outside, there are no rules. We're free. And I have to tell the other boys that I don't play football, that I don't want to play football.

Massimo and Loris don't always stay inside with me. The other boys invite them outside to play football. I always hope they'll say no. I hope they'll choose me. If I'm left alone — if all my classmates, boys and girls alike, are off playing elsewhere — then I go and make coffee for the teachers. I fill the moka pot with water in the bathroom and bring it back so they can heat it on their portable electric stove. I talk to them as they drink their coffee. Or rather, I listen. They sit down with teachers from the other classes and talk about the syllabus, about the topics they've been teaching that day. At a certain point, the teachers always ask me to leave. I'm not allowed to hear everything. After all, it's recess for them, too.

Eventually, I start spending recess with Mario.

Bushy black hair, enormous glasses — he looks like my cousin Luca, but darker.

Mario is one of the boys who like to make fun of me. He hurt his foot and couldn't play football for a while. We get to talking. We accompany each other in our boredom.

When it's just the two of us, Mario doesn't make fun of me. He's a year older, and knows a bunch of things I don't. He enjoys enlightening me. He tells me about the body, about boys' things. He says if I rub myself down there — *have you really never done it?* — something happens, and it feels nice.

Try it, he says. You have to try it.

One afternoon, when I'm home alone, I do. I feel something I've never felt before.

A wave; a tremor?

It doesn't last long.

How many seconds?

I like it a lot — it becomes an obsession.

I form a habit of rubbing myself against the stuffed toys at my grandparents' house, the ones that are almost as big as me.

I do it more and more often, as often as I can. I wait until I'm home alone, then I lie on top of the long-haired white gorilla or the bear with the bow tie that nonna bought at the supermarket with her reward points. Afterwards, I clean them with toilet paper, and dry them with the hairdryer, so I won't get caught.

From third grade on, the bullying is continuous. They call me *ricchio'*, a Neapolitan slur, the long *o* dragging on forever, becoming a sing-song call like the cries of the old men at the market who want to sell nonna their vegetables. Leo — Leonardo, another classmate of mine — always makes the same gesture when he mocks me, touching his right earlobe two or three times.

Frì frì, femminiell', ricchio'.

He does it in front of the others, and it catches on.

He laughs; everyone laughs.

Leo lives close to school, with his mother and his sister. His father is in jail, since I don't know when. Leo is disruptive in class: Miss Mimma has to send him outside almost every day. He doesn't give her a chance to explain anything, she can't do her job when he's in the room. After he's been sent outside, Leo opens the door again and again: can I come in? Can I come back to class? He does it out of spite. He opens the door, sticks his head in, and makes faces. We all burst into laughter — Leo likes being the centre of attention.

Leonardo, enough with the nonsense or I'll send you to the headmistress.

Miss Mimma is constantly being interrupted.

One day she loses her patience. She starts screaming at him, her face turning red, then she runs after him and smacks him.

Leo throws himself to the ground, and she stands over him.

So now you're crying, huh? You think you can just do whatever you want?

Miss Mimma is screaming at him, the veins in her neck are popping out. Her face is completely red, her curly hair shaking like a tuft of cotton wool. Leo is on the floor, covering his face with his arms. Miss Mimma's kicks send him sliding on his back against the wall, underneath the window above the stairs that lead to the entrance. We all rush to the half-open door, to get a better look. It doesn't last long. Miss Mimma stops hitting Leo and comes back into the classroom. She picks up where she left off, explaining set theory and intersections, without saying a word about what just happened.

The next day Leo's mother comes to school to speak with the teachers and the headmistress.

I don't know what they say, but Leo stays at home for a few weeks.

When he comes back, he's exactly the same.

Nothing has changed.

Whenever I clash with my male classmates, they tell me they'll be waiting for me after school.

We're going to kick your fucking head in.

I spend the whole day dreading it. I can't concentrate on anything except my fear. I can't fight — I don't know how to punch or kick someone. But there's no way around it. I can't stay inside the school grounds forever. I hope someone, nonna or zia Tata, is there on time to pick me up.

I hope they're not late.

Mamma always tells me off — she says I should stand up for myself, not let them walk all over me. I should be more like her. Once, when a man tried to rob her at an ATM, she chased after him and threw him to the ground. She kept him there until security arrived.

Mamma is strong; she knows how to fight back. I don't. At the first sign of conflict I start to feel weak; my legs go soft, my hands have trouble holding on to things. How am I supposed to punch someone in this state? With these limp hands? I wish I could just disappear, or that someone would come and rescue me. I want to be teleported somewhere safe, some place where I never have to defend myself.

As we kids leave the school grounds, on our way through the courtyard that lies between the entrance and the front gate, we're alone. Our teachers are no longer there — they're still inside. Our parents are not yet there — they're waiting for us outside the gates. It's the perfect opportunity. That's where they punch me, slap me, shove me, pull me to the ground by my backpack (it's always so heavy, I lose my balance immediately). When it happens, no one stands up for me. The other kids see it all, but they don't help me. I can feel the blood rising to my face, my cheeks burning.

I don't know how to fight, and in Rozzano knowing how to fight is important. More important than having money, because no one has money anyway. If you know how to fight, you can at least earn respect.

You can protect yourself.

You can feel safe.

At school, my mother is a parent representative. The days when she comes to school for meetings are extremely exciting for me. I tell everyone in my class.

You have to see her. Come and see my mother, look, she's arriving now.

There she is, she's about to come up the stairs.

I've been imagining this moment for days.

I run down to the entrance.

Come! Come and see!

Your mother is so young …

She's so pretty!

Miss, miss, is that Jonathan's mamma?

Miss, she's beautiful.

How old is she?

It's true, my mother is beautiful. She has long red hair with a fringe, and green eyes. All the other mothers are fat or ugly or badly dressed: mine is the youngest, and dresses like the women on tv. Men stare at her on the street, and compliment her as they drive past. If they say something she doesn't like, mamma gives them the finger, or yells: go fuck yourself.

When mamma comes to school, I'm happy. Is that what it means to love someone — to reflect their light?

The transitive property.

To be worth something thanks to their beauty.

Sometimes the teachers take us out on excursions.

We go to see performances at the theatre, or visit the municipal library in the town square. When we go to the library, there's almost always a man there who tells us stories. We sit on colourful cushions on the ground, surrounded by gauzy curtains. The library becomes a magical lair, a secret haven just for us.

The library is my favourite place.

The only nice thing about Rozzano.

Before we head back to school, whoever wants to can sign up for a library card.

It's free — really?

I sign up, and occasionally I ask nonna or zia Tata to take me to the library to borrow books. They can't say no, because it doesn't cost anything. They always take me, even though they're not the slightest bit interested in books themselves.

When I go to the library, it takes me forever to choose what to take home with me. Just like with papà at the House of Toys. There are certain books that I borrow over and over again, even though I've already read them. Like the illustrated one about the life of Joan of Arc. I want another look at the armour, the battles, the talking angels, the trial, the stake. I want to be Joan of Arc, I want to know everything about her. I do the same with the series of books with the pink spines, the ones full of stories about girl heroes: apprentice witches, girl detectives, cavegirls, alien girls camouflaging as humans. The one about the girl who, after an accident, discovers that her brain has been transplanted into the body of a chimpanzee.

Nonna and zia Tata take me to the library and leave me there while they go and run errands. I prefer being alone. If they stay they get bored, and tell me to hurry up.

There's only one problem: to borrow books I have to speak to the attendants at the front desk. I never want to. Or rather, I can't. I'm physically incapable of speaking to people I don't know. Fear seizes my body. I start sweating, I feel like I'm going to wet myself.

I was born with a flaw, a fault, a defect. I must have been born with it, because I don't recall a moment in which words came out of me differently. I've been like this since I can remember. A stutterer. My parents noticed early on, when I was around three. They immediately took me to the paediatrician — doctor Barzani, a very serious man with a long beard and small, round glasses.

It's just a phase; as he gets older he'll grow out of it.

He was wrong. I didn't grow out of it.

While I was little, it seemed normal. A lot of kids stutter at that age. And besides, it was endearing. The stammering, the bumbling. I had too much to say; I was in a hurry.

Slow down, they told me. Think before you speak. One word at a time.

But thinking has nothing to do with it. Unless you stutter, you can't understand what it's like.

I'm like a jammed machine; the sounds catch in my throat

and won't come out. They refuse to form themselves into letters, words, sentences. The consonants at the beginning of a word are the worst. My tongue gets stuck; I want to tense my lips. For fear of making strange sounds, like the stutterers everyone makes fun of in the movies, I keep quiet. I play dumb. Or I leave long pauses between one word and the next. People get impatient with me; they don't have time to waste. They finish my sentences for me. They put words in my mouth that are not the ones I was trying to say.

This is why I refuse to go to the corner shop to buy myself a snack. This is why I never answer the telephone at home, letting it ring and ring until it stops. I hate the telephone: if you don't speak, you're not there, you don't exist. On the phone, your body can't help you. Your gestures and expressions can't fill the gaps left by your voice.

At the library, once I've chosen the books I want, I wait for nonna or zia Tata to come back so they can borrow them for me.

I get them to talk to the librarian for me, or the lady at the front desk.

Seriously, Jonathan, when are you going to grow up?

You're eight years old, it's time you learnt to do things on your own.

Every so often the library organises special workshops.

The problem is, you have to go with your parents.

One time I ask nonna Lidia to take me to a puppet workshop. The puppets act out stories, then everyone gets to make their favourite character. It's embarrassing because nonna isn't my mother, and also because she can't read well and only speaks napoletano. The parents who take their kids to the library are not the kind of parents who live in public housing. They work in offices and read newspapers; they have a different way of speaking.

I don't want to look bad in front of them.

I'm afraid they'll mock me, laugh at me and also at nonna, but I have no one else to take me. If I want to go, it has to be with nonna Lidia.

I give in.

I ask her to take me. Nothing bad happens.

In fact, we have fun.

Nonna is affable, she makes friends with everyone. We make puppets out of sponges and glue and pieces of cloth. Nonna helps me make the hair out of wool, and the eyes out of buttons. She's good at sewing — she even helps the other kids with their puppets.

I like the library. I'm safe there.

The library is nothing like school.

In third grade I finally make a friend.

One day, as we're sitting in the canteen eating lunch, Cinzia, one of my classmates, passes me a folded note. I open it and read: *Who do you want to go out with?*

There are two boxes: Cinzia or Marika.

I tick Marika.

With that, we're boyfriend and girlfriend.

Marika and I become inseparable. Every day I ask the teacher if I can stand next to her when we line up, so we can hold hands. The other boys tease Marika because she's hairy: she has a dark moustache, and hair on her legs. Not just a little bit of hair, a lot. And it's long, longer than mine. You can see it poking through her stockings.

You look like a fucking monkey.

Jonathan, your girlfriend is a sasquatch.

Marika doesn't take it quietly. She hits back at the boys, sometimes physically. She's not afraid. She's stronger than I am. When I'm with her, I feel a little braver.

Marika is beautiful; I like her, but I don't want to kiss her. We've never kissed, and we never will. We're only eight or nine — still too young for these things, right?

At what age are we no longer too young?

Marika and I see each other after school, too, in the afternoons. She comes to my house, or I go to hers — she lives close by. We give each other gifts on Valentine's Day. Baci Perugina chocolates, handmade bracelets, little silver necklaces with heart-shaped pendants that split in half: one for you, one for me. We even start going to karate classes together, although I soon quit. Marika continues for years, becoming a brown belt, then a black belt.

We remain boyfriend and girlfriend until the end of primary school.

On the last day of school I'm overwhelmed by an unexpected sadness. I burst into tears; I can't stop crying. I'm going to miss everyone; I don't want to leave my classmates and teachers, the people I've spent every day with for the past five years. Even the boys who made fun of me are nice sometimes. I'm sad, and the sadness spills out through my eyes.

Miss Rosalia is stunned. Who would have thought, she says. You, of all people.

I don't understand — I think about it constantly, for days. Why did she say that?

Should I be happy that it's all over?

On exam day I wear the Buffalo tower shoes I made papà buy me. They have a huge, smooth platform heel, taller than the footpath. The first time my mother sees me wearing them, she thinks they're rollerblades.

Oh madonna, Roberto's bought him rollerblades ...

I wobble around in them — I have to hold on to my father's arm to stay upright. I resemble some kind of grinning scarecrow, completely enamoured of my new accessories. They're different, unique, special. No one has shoes like these yet — these are Spice Girls shoes.

No, mamma, they're not rollerblades! These are the shoes that are fashionable now.

They cost almost 200,000 lire. Mamma is furious when she finds out.

We could have bought him three pairs of shoes with that money! What kind of ridiculous fucking shoes are they anyway? Where is he supposed to wear them?

Mamma thinks I won't use them; she thinks they're a waste of money. But I wear them everywhere, even when the older kids laugh at me, and call me a poof, and try to spit on me. They always come in groups: three, four, six, seven of them. I've lived up to their expectations, and I'm certainly not hiding it. As with butter, so with my shoes: I refuse to give up the things I love, regardless of the consequences.

I walk around in my platform heels with my hair twisted into little spikes like Luca Tommassini, the dancer from Buena Domenica, except I have to use hair ties because my hair is too thick — Sicilian hair, like nonna Nuccia — and no amount of gel and hair spray will do the trick. The hairdresser on Viale Lombardia tried once, but gave up after an hour because his fingers were cramping. He advised me to use hair ties, so I did. I bought a packet of those little colourful ones from the stationary aisle of the supermarket. Every morning, before school, I cover my whole head in tiny spikes. I look like one of the daughters from *The Cosby Show*.

Then there's the hair dye: yellow, blue, green, blond with pink tips. At twelve I get my belly button pierced, like zio Franco's girlfriend, at a shop in Porta Ticinese — it's cheaper if they use the earlobe piercing gun. I wear blue tartan pants (they're for gays, the kids at school tell me. Why? I ask. Look in the mirror, they say) and cropped shirts that expose my midriff, like a dancing girl in a discotheque.

I attract the attention of the boys in Rozzano. I avoid them where possible — cross the street, take detours. But sometimes I'm too slow. If they see me and start insulting me I look straight ahead and walk a little faster, hoping they'll leave it at verbal abuse.

They almost always do.

In any case, it's best to be prepared. When I went to the safari zoo with papà I stole a pocket knife with a handle in the shape of a deer's antler.

I slipped it into my backpack as we were leaving, without telling anyone.

The pocket knife is like She-Ra's sword.

My own secret weapon.

Marika and I don't see each other after primary school.

We're placed in different classes.

A few weeks later, word spreads that Marika is going out with an older boy, Pietro, who got kept back two years in a row.

Apparently they have sex — he took her virginity. Did you cry, Marika? Did it hurt? I like Pietro, too. I get it. He's handsome. A proper boyfriend. He'll kiss her, touch her, do all the things I never intended to do.

The kids at school start calling Marika a slut. They make up songs to tease her. They say when she started middle school she'd never done anything with anyone, and now she does everything with Pietro. Someone secretly hangs posters around the school: *Marika is a whore.* I feel bad for her — everyone is against her — but deep down I'm also a little pleased. They're avenging me. They're making her pay.

Sometimes Marika and I cross paths in the corridor.

She looks at me for a moment, from the corner of her eye, as she's being shoved or ridiculed. She's different. She's no longer the Marika from last year.

Is she growing more beautiful from a distance?

We don't talk anymore — we won't talk again.

We act as though we never knew each other.

She was the only friend I had.

He's scared of needles

He's scared of needles.

He hasn't had a blood test in years.

Before my appointment with the infectious-disease specialist at Sacco, I accompany Marius to get his HIV test. We sit together in the clinic waiting room. I feel more confident in this place, now. The sense of anguish and dread is gone. My diagnosis has liberated me. It was the uncertainty I couldn't bear. Now that I know what's wrong with me, I have a strict process to follow, one that provides specific answers to a problem that has been identified, named, circumscribed.

In the clinic on Via Spallanzani, I tease Marius about his fear of injections (*what if I pass out?* You won't pass out, and if you do, at least there's no shortage of doctors here) and people-watch in the waiting room. Old men, pregnant women, busy staff. It feels like I'm watching them from a great height. Look at you all, sitting here in the dark, getting tests, giving blood, terrified you might have something. Well, I already know what I have. I know everything there is to know. And yet, here I am. I'm back. My diagnosis wasn't the end of me.

I have returned to the site of my fear to take care of things, to get everything in order for my new life. The eternal student in me has leapt into action. I need to know everything about this virus; the more I know, the better I can heal. There are dozens of pamphlets on the coffee table in the centre of the waiting room. Some offer information about HIV, others on places in Milan that offer free testing, or organisations that help people living with the illness — specialist centres, support groups, psychological helplines. I take one of each, placing them carefully in my backpack as if they were lecture notes or textbooks.

Marius gives his blood sample — *It didn't hurt that much*; I told you so — and we head home. On our way back we pass through Piazza Oberdan, the place where we met.

19 April, 2013.

Almost three years ago.

At about five on a Friday afternoon, under a sky that threatened rain, I went out to meet a guy I'd found on Gayromeo. I really liked his photos, even if he did give off a bit of a stray-dog vibe. He looked like he could be an addict, a rent-boy, a frequenter of fetish bars. His profile picture was a photo of him squatting in briefs and combat boots. Nose ring, acid eyes. He looked like he'd just walked out of a Berlin goth bar. I'd shown his photos to my friends. Simona looked at my computer screen and said: he's disturbing, he looks like an old baby, like a baby that got old.

Needless to say, I didn't have high expectations.

I thought it was unlikely we'd have anything in common.

We'd arranged to meet in front of the gelateria in Porta Venezia, which is no longer there. He arrived half an hour late. Tall, thin (*I thought you'd be shorter*), the skin on his cheeks and nose red, slightly cracked. He was wearing a red plaid shirt — or was it fuchsia? — and black jeans cut off halfway down the calf. He looked like a gutter punk, or one of those kids who skateboard to school and sneak beers into their backpacks at the supermarket.

Hi, sorry, the tram was late.

What do you want to do?

Boh, don't know.

Is there anywhere you want to go?

Nope, you?

Park?

We entered the Porta Venezia Gardens from the side overlooking the Bastioni. We walked aimlessly for a while, then sat down on a park bench. One of two benches next to the café that, in the summertime, becomes a madhouse of screaming children fed by a thirty-metre-long queue, the sight of which is sure to cure you of hunger, thirst, and the will to live. Facing the café, with your back to the planetarium, ours is the first bench on the right. We still go back there, every now and then. It's a pinned destination, forever geolocated in our minds.

He had an Umbrian accent, although he was born in Romania — he came to Italy when he was six years old. I've always liked Umbria. For its mystics: Saint Francis of Assisi, Filippo Timi. We sat down on the bench in the Porta Venezia gardens and started talking. To my surprise, he spoke about his family: his childhood, his mother, his brother and the trouble they used to get into as kids — breaking things, drinking bubble-bath liquid, crashing around the house, fighting and racing each other. I spoke about university, yoga, my cats. He laughed, but he also listened, with his downward-slanting eyes that seemed a little sad, although in the light they are blue, and blue eyes can never be completely sad. As we spoke and listened to one another, I understood that he had none of the defensiveness boys in this city often seemed to have. He wasn't afraid.

All of a sudden, it started to rain. We got up and made our way back to Corso Buenos Aires — the drops falling from the sky were becoming intrusive. It was almost seven, and I was hungry. I proposed an aperitivo at a place nearby, but he had a prior engagement. Or rather: he told me he had a prior engagement. Months later he confessed that, actually, he hadn't brought his wallet with him. Most likely he'd already spent the money his parents used to send him at the beginning of the month.

We went back to our respective homes.

The next day he called: he wanted to meet my cats.

You know, they're actually the reason I replied when you wrote to me in the chat, he'll tell me later. I wanted to see them in real life.

The day after that, Sunday, he came to my house, to the apartment I shared with my housemate Steve. We sat on the floor, in my attic bedroom with the terribly low ceiling, surrounded by piles of clothes and university books. Nothing had happened between us yet.

The first moment of contact: bodies in exploration.

Me lying on the ground, him resting his head on my abdomen. I had to tense my muscles to maintain the position.

I didn't say anything — I bore the discomfort in silence, as lovers always do, at least in the beginning. But my body betrayed me: my muscles started to spasm from the exertion.

Sorry, can you move your head for a second, I'm having like a prelude to a tremor.

A what?

He might have laughed, I don't remember.

I turned, and with a pencil I found on the desk behind us I wrote, on the wall, in small letters, the words PRELUDE TO A TREMOR.

I wrote them right next to one of the wooden beams crisscrossing the walls, between the clumps and hollows of cracked plaster.

I haven't lived in that apartment for years, but I know the people who ended up renting that bedroom.

They said the words are gone; there's nothing written in pencil on the wall of the attic room of the top-floor apartment at 1 Via Lulli.

Someone must have erased it, someone who didn't realise those words were the title of a love story.

She flies through the windshield at five in the morning

She flies through the windshield at five in the morning.

She bursts through it and onto the road.

Prone, exposed, motionless.

It's winter; the sky is still dark.

Get her up, there are cars coming.

Johnny, mamma has had an accident.

She was in the white van with Tino; they were on their way to work, off to clean offices at dawn.

Mamma smashes the glass into a thousand pieces, and as she flies out of the cabin she wraps her fringed shawl around her — an impulse, a reflex — to cover her face. She lands a few metres from the wheels of a truck that didn't see them coming. A little further and things would have ended differently.

Johnny, mamma is very sick.

Johnny, mamma can't make it home today.

As she hurtles out of her seat my mother protects her face with the black lace shawl, to avoid shattering the windshield with her bare skin, to avoid grazing her face on the asphalt.

She's lucky — no broken bones.

Only scrapes, cuts, abrasions.

Cheekbones, knees, hands.

She stays in bed for weeks, covered in bandages. Mamma has turned into a mummy. She managed to protect her face, but not completely. When eventually she gets a new job and starts working as a cashier at the supermarket, customers will remind her constantly.

Signorina, I think your mascara is running.

Excuse me, ma'am, you've got some pencil under your eye.

If she's sick of repeating the same reply, my mother simply thanks them and leaves it at that. If she's in the mood, she says: no, signora, thank you, but it's not makeup, it's a scar.

Some are taken aback, others make a joke of it.

My mother is left with two dark marks under her left eye, where a bit of asphalt got stuck under her skin. They will never go away; she'll have them forever. She talked to a surgeon about removing them with a laser, but it would have been too expensive. She'll get used to them, eventually. Mamma is barely thirty years old. First, pregnancy tattooed the skin of her breasts and hips with stretch marks, and now this. She can almost hide the scars with foundation and concealer, but not completely. What goes through your mind when you look in the mirror, mamma?

At least she's not alone anymore. She has a new boyfriend.

His name is Tino. He's one of the managers at the cleaning company.

Tino is Sicilian, from the province of Messina, and he only came to Milan a few years ago. Tina and Tino. Tino's name is actually Tindaro, in honour of the sanctuary of the Black Madonna. When mamma and Tino get together, she starts working less. I'm allowed to move back in with her, into the apartment on Hyacinth Street.

Tino comes to live with us, too. He brings his brother Salvatore along. Tino and Salvatore had been living together before they moved in with us. Tino can't be expected to leave his own brother in the lurch, just because he's got a girlfriend. Mamma understands, of course she does.

I sleep in the lounge room, on a fold-down bed, and Salvatore sleeps on the sofa bed.

We make do; we always make do.

When I'm with mamma and Tino we always do the things they like to do. Or rather, the things *Tino* likes to do. Mamma's tastes slowly metamorphose into those of her new companion. When we go out, we visit furniture stores and antique markets. On Sunday mornings we go to Melegnano to have brunch in the piazza — why there, of all places? — and in the afternoons we go to Pavia to window shop, even though everything is closed. Long, rambling days of pure boredom.

In the car we listen to the music they like. At Blockbuster they choose which films to rent.

Mamma sees me as a kind of appendage, an extension of herself. Since she's decided to follow Tino around, adopting his interests as her own — his handmaid, his little geisha — I've been forced to do the same. I am a parallel structure, a dependent variable, easily manoeuvred.

As I grow older, though, I become less docile.

Adolescence starts to rear its head.

Killjoy, arsehole, piece of shit.

One day, in the car with mamma and Tino, just as we're pulling into the courtyard at Hyacinth Street, I insult him. He's just scolded me for something — nothing serious, Tino isn't the kind to get upset. I lock eyes with him in the rear-view mirror. Fuck you, I say. You're not even my father.

We'll deal with this at home — my mother's voice.

Take the keys, go upstairs.

In her head, she's already decided.

As Tino is parking the car, I head through the front entrance and up the stairs.

My mother follows closely behind.

When we get to our apartment, mamma opens the hallway cupboard and takes out her nonna's walking stick. Bisnonna Immacolata's wooden cane. I'm not seven years old anymore — mamma must have decided her hands are no longer enough. She needs the help of the cane. I have to pay for ruining her plans, for talking back to the man whose presence means she no longer has to work twelve hours a day. Whose presence allows her to buy shoes and dresses in nice boutiques, to be even more beautiful than before, to visit tourist resorts, to hang giant prints of famous paintings on the walls in expensive frames made of real wood, to swap out the old couch and bed for brand-name ones, complete with matching sheets and quilt cover.

Mamma wants to beat me to death.

She wants to break bisnonna Immacolata's cane over my head.

She chases me around the house, screaming.

I barricade myself in the lounge room.

I close the door and lean all my weight against it.

Tino has just repainted it white — for years it was faded and yellow. Tino has made the whole house more beautiful. He provides us with everything we need, and this is how you treat him? Well, I made you, you little bastard, and I'll destroy you.

I learn something new that day: I'm stronger than her. I manage to keep the door closed, even as she throws her entire body against it. I'm capable of defending myself, even from my own mother. She's always so angry. Sometimes I'm afraid she'll lose her mind and grab the biggest knife we have from the kitchen: the one she uses to slice the raw steak, with the red plastic handle. Now that I'm causing trouble, I think my mother wants to get rid of me.

Mother murders son; partner complicit.

Mamma wants to have a family again. With Tino. Everyone says he's an idiot, a moron. But she's stubborn, she tries anyway. At least, until she discovers that Tino is still seeing his ex-wife. The ex-wife is also Sicilian — a childhood friend? She lives in Rozzano as well, but not in public housing.

Mamma investigates. She follows Tino. She's like a detective. In times of stress she is lethal, unerring. She trusts no one. One afternoon she shows up at Tino's ex-wife's house. She finds them together and slaps them. She slaps Tino and his ex-wife right there in the stairwell, on the landing of their apartment in Via Roma.

You son of a bitch! After I let your brother live with us in my home. In *my* home, you hear?

Tina, we were just talking — I didn't tell you because I knew you'd get like this.

True; false. What's one more betrayal, mamma? It doesn't change anything.

She starts to feel bad.

She always does this: first she flies into a rage, then she crumbles in a heap.

Like an invertebrate Amazon.

Mamma slips into her second depression. The first was caused by my father, the second by Tino. Always men. Always the men in my mother's life.

She stays in bed all day, starts taking medication. Packets of tablets, little brown medicine bottles — psychopharmaceuticals, tonics. Mamma and I stay at nonna Lidia's for a while. Tino comes to visit every now and again, and he and mamma talk alone in zio Franco's room. Tino promises to take mamma on a holiday. We'll go to Ostuni, he says. To the mountains. To Trentino, to the Valtur Village Resort. We can take the kid, too. We'll take Jonathan.

An all-inclusive holiday resort, the kind rich people go to. Let's start over, let's reset to zero.

Nonna Lidia cries and prays in front of the little Madonna with the glowing halo.

An image from my memory: mamma huddled in bed, talking to me in the voice of a little girl. I'm scared. Mamma has regressed, she's turned back into a baby. She says things that make no sense, she doesn't recognise me anymore. Is she possessed? Has she gone mad? Will they take her away to an asylum?

My other family members try to hide her from me.

Tino arrives, turns out the light, and sends me out of the room.

He's come back to us. My mother can't be alone.

Negative

Negative.

Marius comes home, and his test result is negative.

Marius doesn't have HIV.

Only I have it.

I waited for him at our apartment on Via Kramer while he went out to get the results. I tried to distract myself as best I could — computer, music, food. Nothing worked.

I waited for him to return, lacking the courage to message him on WhatsApp, delaying the moment of revelation. Our entire understanding of the situation we're in hinges on these test results. They could even decide the course of our future together.

I have HIV. We have HIV.

When the intercom buzzes, the sound grabs me by the throat.

Marius comes through the door with the piece of paper in his hand. One measly piece of paper that holds the key to everything. No manila folder, no cover, nothing to reflect its significance, the value it holds for me, for him. It's common for couples to break up after a diagnosis of HIV. If I've infected him, the same thing might happen to us.

You've ruined my life.

You were older.

It was your responsibility.

After the diagnosis, everything is different — the relationship that existed before is no more. The survival instinct accelerates the formation of rifts, feeds crises, exposes blemishes, lifts veils, tears down walls. In the end, all that's left is the truth.

But none of that will happen to us, right? At least, not yet.

When Marius walks in and tells me the results are negative, his expression is incredulous. I'm stunned. Even he was convinced he must have been the one to infect me. But his blood has been interrogated, and it tells a different story.

It's better this way, I think. He won't have to go through what I'm going through.

I won't have to see him get ill, his body won't deteriorate. His eyes, his skin, the shape of his body will remain just as it is. I won't have to watch him grow weak and fall apart. This problem is mine, not his. Only mine.

An asymmetry is established. We are no longer a single entity, the codependent fusion of beings we were in the early days. We moved in together a week after we met, and were inseparable from that moment on. We shared everything: shoes, underwear, food, saliva. Now we learn that we are in a 'serodiscordant relationship' — that's the technical term for it. One of us has contracted the virus, the other hasn't. Our status isn't new; we've always been serodiscordant, we just didn't know it. I didn't know. And I should have known. I *could* have known, if I'd got tested. But I didn't. Not ever. Not when I was nineteen or twenty and meeting strangers from chat rooms for sex. Not when I was twenty-two and living with my first boyfriend. Not at twenty-eight, newly single and back on the dating apps.

I've always been too scared.

I chose sickness over fear. I chose sickness over the *fear* of sickness.

Idiot. Coward. Reckless. Masochist. Criminal. What would you call me?

The landscape has changed, now. If Marius didn't transmit the virus to me, if I already had it when we met, then who gave it to me? In three years we've made love dozens, hundreds of times, without protection. In bed, on the floor, on the balcony, on the couch, in the shower. In Via Lulli, Via Tito Vignoli, Via Venini, Via Varanini, Via Kramer, Via Tucidide. I've never cheated on him, so if he's negative that means I can't have caught it recently. I must have had it when we met. So who gave it to me?

Does it matter? Do I need to know?

Everyone asks me about it, they can't help themselves. Do you have any idea who it could have been? Have you retraced your steps, racked your brain? Do you know how long you've had it? They're trying to protect themselves, trying to understand where I went wrong so they can avoid making the same mistake.

But I have no idea.

I thought my defences were enough.

In my efforts to avoid some other, greater contamination, I defended the parts of myself that I didn't want to see destroyed.

One Sunday my mother invites me — invites us — to lunch. She does it on purpose, to force me to leave the house, even though she knows how reluctant I am to go outside.

Mamma, sorry, but can't you come to us?

No, you come to me, it's not far.

It's an hour and a half on the tram.

Marius and I take the number 15, passing through Piazzale Abbiategrasso and Viale Missaglia.

Sitting at the table in my mother's house, after some small

talk about the weather and what tv shows we're watching, she tells us she has something to say. She must have been planning this moment for days; I know what she's like. Her true nature is cold-blooded, clear-headed. She's not in shock anymore — she's back in her spiked armour. To protect herself, my mother attacks.

It's 2016, she says. Surely you don't just catch HIV by accident these days. You have to go out looking for it. It's not the kind of disease that just comes along and you think, *poor thing, he was so unlucky*. I thought I'd raised you to have a good head on your shoulders, and now …

So it's my fault.

She's not entirely wrong.

Go on, just say it.

I don't blame myself.

I don't know how I caught it. There's no point in knowing, but I attempt to find out anyway. It's another way for me to feel like I'm dealing with things, another way of keeping myself busy. I try getting in touch with the only two people I've knowingly had unprotected sex with, aside from Marius. They're both named Marco. I dated one of them, my ex — my only other long-term relationship — on and off for several years. I thought I was in love with him, for a while.

Neither of the two Marcos has it.

They both ask me if I want to talk about it, if there's anything they can do for me. They're kind, they seem genuinely worried. I have no reason to think they're lying. So if not them, then who?

When did it happen?

Was it the guy who lived in the building behind me in Viale Monza, four or five years ago? I'd never topped before, and, as we were having sex, he'd asked me to try it with him. I didn't have a condom, but I pulled out straight away — I didn't want to risk it. Could that have been enough?

Is a moment all it takes?

Or maybe it was that guy, only recently arrived in Italy, who came to my apartment one afternoon — three, four years ago? — unbeknownst to my housemate at the time, and afterwards told me we could meet up again if I paid for his train ticket; he lived in Brescia but didn't have a lira to his name. We used a condom, I'm sure of it. But I took him in my mouth without one. Could that have been it?

A blowjob?

Low risk doesn't mean no risk.

There's an AIDS organisation in Milan where you can request support from a volunteer after your diagnosis. I call them, and make a booking. I go to their headquarters in the Ticinese district one morning. My support person is a woman: dark skin, distinctive features, voice frayed by cigarettes. She might be wearing a wig.

She's brusque, sometimes she provokes me. *She's trying to get a reaction.*

Have you told your mother? Really, so soon? You know, sometimes we unload our problems onto others to make ourselves feel better.

When I tell her I don't know how or when I was infected, she seems perplexed. I know it couldn't have been oral sex, I say. She stops me.

What do you know about HIV and oral sex?

That the risk is low.

But low doesn't mean non-existent, she says.

She looks me in the eye, her face serious. Low doesn't mean zero. Low doesn't mean absence of risk.

Improbable, but not impossible. If your sexual partner has contracted the virus and doesn't know it, if they're not in treatment and have a very high viral load, even oral sex can be enough.

I promise myself I'll think more about it, maybe write a list of names, but not yet. Right now all I want to know is how to get rid of this fever that seems to want to stay forever, this exhausting fever that won't let me do anything at all.

It'll be at least a month before I can start treatment.

At least a month.

The infectious-disease specialist tells me this at my initial consultation, at Sacco.

Alessandro is with me again. He's a Pisces — he's attracted to suffering.

The doctor is young, around my age. Tall, thin, olive-skinned, with black hair and uneven tufts of beard. He looks like a Spanish musketeer.

I'm glad he's my doctor.

The evening before the consultation I looked him up on Facebook. In his profile photo he's leaping over a bush at what was once my university. Jumping the hedge is a graduation-day tradition at La Statale.

Scanning his wall, I found photos of him at soccer matches with his friends. A typical heterosexual man in his natural habitat.

I feel inclined to trust him. When we talk about homosexuality, about sex between boys, he doesn't seem embarrassed or uncomfortable. He smiles. He doesn't seem to have a problem with what I represent. *Therapeutic alliance,* they call it: an important prerequisite for successful treatment. I can tell he's an early-career doctor, but he's good at his job. He provides me with kindness and detailed explanations, two things that are neither required nor expected of him. He's never in a rush; he lets me take up all the time I need. He explains to me how the virus behaves, drawing pictures and diagrams to help me understand the evolution of the disease, and the meaning of the values on my test results. I like this way of expressing interest in one another: not through physical affection or jokes, but through conversation, through thoughtfully placed words.

He gives me his contact details: email, telephone number. I can write or call whenever I want, he says. When I do send him an email — calling him is out of the question; I still hate expressing myself verbally without the help of my face and body — he replies straight away. Sometimes within a few minutes. Is his diligence just a performance to impress his supervisors, to secure his future at the hospital? Possibly. All the same, his punctual, reassuring replies make me feel safe. This man, roughly the same age as me, knows how to heal me and promises to do it. We'll do it together, him and me. This is what he's saying when he conjugates his verbs in the first-person plural.

The first time we meet, he's very clear about my treatment goals. First and foremost, CD4 cell recovery. The virus attacks the immune system, targeting this subgroup of white blood cells in particular. It uses them to reproduce itself, destroying them in the process. The main objectives of my treatment are two-fold: on the one hand, to suppress the viral load until it is undetectable; on the other, to restore and preserve immunologic function. To meet these objectives, CD4 cell counts are essential — the count tells us how well the treatment is working. Are the numbers going up, or are they staying the same?

A healthy person with an uncompromised immune system has somewhere between 500 and 1200 CD4 cells per millilitre of blood. If your count drops below a certain level, it means you have AIDS.

If you reach that point, it might be too late.

My doctor carefully explains the process that needs to be followed if I'm to get better. There are a number of different tests we have to do before we start treatment. We need to paint a detailed portrait of the situation inside my body. The antiretroviral resistance test is the most important — it's possible to be infected with a version of the virus that is insensitive to one or more of the active ingredients in the antiretroviral medications.

These tests take time.

At least a month, maybe more.

You have to be patient, my doctor says. You have to rest.

Take paracetamol if your temperature gets too high.

In that first consultation, my doctor asks a lot of questions.

He asks me if I drink (a little, two or three beers a week), if I smoke (no, I quit years ago), if I take recreational drugs (just the occasional toke, and I once tried poppers), if I have a family history of cancer (mamma's sister, zia Tata, had breast cancer, but they caught it in time — she didn't even have to go through chemo).

He notes down my answers, filling in the fields on a thick dossier with long pages that fold in on themselves, like a magazine centrefold. Then he examines me. He does this on our first meeting and every subsequent one. He follows the exact same procedure every time.

He asks me to lie down on the examination table. He listens to my heart through a stethoscope, then uses his fingers to press underneath my ribs until he finds my internal organs. I sit up, and he asks me to breathe deeply in and out of my mouth while he places a cold metal disc on my back to listen to the sounds inside my rib cage. He feels the lymph nodes in my neck and armpits to see if they're swollen — infection? lymphoma? He asks me to open my mouth, and explores it with a little pen-shaped torch that he takes from his shirt pocket, inspecting my throat, the roof of my mouth, my tongue — lesions? ulcers? mycosis?

Okay, we're done, he says as he's washing his hands.

I sit back down on the chair next to his desk.

Waiting to be told when we'll see each other again.

Rozzano is full of weirdos

Rozzano is full of weirdos.

But the weirdos in Rozzano aren't bad people.

There's Gurgone, the beanpole, tall and thin with a bald patch in the centre of his head. A monk without a robe, but wearing a kind of uniform nonetheless: a short-sleeved shirt when it's warm, a beige raincoat in winter. He walks around Rozzano all day, bouncing on his long legs. Mamma says I walk like Gurgone — I bend my knees too much, I need to tense my legs more.

Hey, walk properly, you look like Gurgone.

Sometimes Gurgone is calm, sometimes less so — occasionally he hits himself on the head as if trying to remember something. His family has money, according to my parents. His father is a doctor, or an engineer.

Why do they live in Rozzano, then?

There's the short blonde woman who talks to herself, voice like a duck, eyes wide. A half-smile that never leaves her lips. Tata tells me she was raped when she was young, and that's why she went crazy. *The poor thing, they destroyed her — she's been traumatised.* The boys in Rozzano make fun of her when she walks past, mimic her. She ignores them completely. She's too busy speaking with someone we can't see to even notice them.

There's the panda-eyed woman on the number 15 tram, thick circles of black eyeshadow spreading from her eyebrows to her cheekbones. She looks like a voodoo doll, a rogue puppet.

Then there are the residents of the sanatorium on Viale Liguria. Some stand at the gate in their dressing-gowns, others are curled up on the ground or singing a kind of nursery rhyme. I see them when I walk past on my way to my grandparents' house. Their faces are so white, as if they've been covered in chalk or flour.

The weirdos in Rozzano aren't dangerous.

I'm far more scared of our neighbours on Hyacinth Street.

I'm far more scared of Carmelo, the neighbour who's always smoking out on the balcony, shirtless.

Carmelo is from Naples, like my grandparents.

He was in jail for a long time, and in jail he got a bunch of tattoos, each one uglier than the last. Mermaids, naked women, monsters, crucifixes, quotes full of spelling errors. The tattoos, mamma explains, were done by Carmelo's cellmates. They cover every inch of his swollen, asymmetrical body, from his pregnant-woman's belly to his bare chest, which is cleaved by an enormous diagonal scar. His face looks like a scar, too. His eyes are two slits; he looks like a boxer after a week-long fight. Carmelo is convinced he's the mob boss of our building. At 10 Hyacinth Street, whatever Carmelo says becomes unwritten law. The front door to our building, for example, has to be kept open day and night. If someone closes it, Carmelo smashes the glass. Every time the people from ALER come to fix it, he smashes it again. The next morning we find the front steps covered in shards.

Carmelo's wife, Rosy, is short and fat. In the evenings he drives her out to the ring road to turn tricks. She wears makeup — like a clown, mamma says — and a miniskirt, with only a bra on top.

Who would pick *her* up?

Someone must.

Carmelo drives her out to the ring road and waits in the car while she goes with the clients. Does he stay there all night?

Carmelo is Rosy's pimp. He's there to make sure everything runs smoothly, that nothing bad happens. But only while she's working. At home, Carmelo and Rosy fight constantly, and when they fight, he beats her up. We can hear her screaming and crying; mamma tells me he shoves her head in the oven.

Carmelo and Rosy have a son, Vincenzo, who might not actually be Carmelo's son.

When Vincenzo grows up, he and Carmelo fight a lot, too.

Vincenzo tells mamma: Tina, I have to get out of here. If I don't leave, I'll end up killing him.

Carmelo is an alcoholic. When he's drinking, he barricades himself in his apartment and turns the music up as high as it goes. High, higher — how many speakers does he have in there? Does he have a whole sound system, like at the cinema? He plays Neapolitan music: Nino D'Angelo, Mario Merola. It's impossible to get anything done when Carmelo is putting on one of his 'shows', as the other residents of the building call it. The windows of our apartment tremble. We turn on the tv to drown out the noise, shut ourselves in our rooms, hoping the doors will dull the blaring music.

It goes on like this for years, but nobody says anything.

If someone calls the carabinieri, Carmelo pretends to calm down for a while, but then the music resumes as loudly as before.

He gets worse as he gets older.

Eventually, Carmelo gets sick. Cancer. He has episodes: he cuts himself with a knife and drips blood all over the stairs. If the carabinieri try to take him away, he threatens to lock himself inside and turn on the gas.

I'll blow myself up.

I'll blow up this whole fucking building.

I'll show you, you pieces of shit.

Carmelo really did send a man to try to break into our apartment that night, when I was a baby and mamma and I were home alone. Papà was right. At the time, my father had just joined the police force. He'd tried to intervene. He'd wanted to dismantle Carmelo's racket.

Did he give up? Did he decide it was best to just act like nothing was wrong?

He did it for us — he gave up on Carmelo to protect us.

Or did he just stop caring, after he moved out?

When I move back in with mamma, my father never comes to pick me up at our apartment. Not once. He won't even come near the building. He parks his car in a neighbouring courtyard.

Is that dickhead still not dead?

That's what he calls Carmelo — *that dickhead.*

I do it for you, he says. I don't want him to see me and then target you.

But papà, I have to walk past his door every day. I live here. And every time I walk past his door alone, I'm scared he'll come out and shoot me. I'm scared he'll use the guns he keeps in the basement — the pistols, the shotguns, the assault rifles — and fill my guts with bullets. I'm scared he'll leave me to die on the stairs, lying on the broken tiles nobody can be bothered fixing, with the dead mosquitoes stuck all over the walls, next to the supermarket trolley someone brought home and abandoned in the stairwell by the wall of mailboxes. That's why I run. On my way home I sprint up the stairs two at a time. Sometimes even three at a time, leaping like a spring, never stopping until I reach the top, never looking behind me. That's why I don't take the elevator, because in the elevator you're trapped. If Carmelo surprises me in there, there's no way for me to escape.

When it's hot Carmelo spends all day out on the balcony, shirtless, checking who comes and goes. I never wave, I never say a word to him. Mamma does, and so does nonna Lidia — they laugh and make jokes, like old buddies. I act as if he's invisible. It's my small act of resistance. It could get me into trouble: my silence is an affront, a challenge.

Will he make me pay for it?

His illness gets the better of him before he has the chance.

Carmelo's death is a liberation for Rosy. She gets her life back together, starts living respectably again. She starts looking after herself, dressing better, fixing up the house — she receives a small pension, and uses it to raise her grandson, Vincenzo's kid. But then we hear Rosy has started drinking. She's an addict. First drink, then the harder stuff.

She loses her mind.

One day Rosy disappears. She dies.

Carmelo's house is left empty.

Asia is Rosy's friend. She lives in our building too, but higher up, on the sixth or seventh floor, where I never go. She's also a prostitute — *yes, but I told you not to use that word.* Asia has no teeth and a red, swollen face. She's always walking around half naked, in a tiny Lycra miniskirt and crop top, as though it were always summer. She's a drinker, mamma says. She's always been a drinker. But she's kind: whenever she sees me she gives me compliments.

What a handsome young boy you've turned into.

Does she want to be my girlfriend?

On the ground floor, next door to Carmelo, lives Tommy, a kid who had his hand blown off by a New Year's Eve firecracker. The firecracker was defective — it exploded in his hand here on Hyacinth Street, just behind our house, on the lawn separating our building from the parish sports field.

He may be missing a hand, but you should see what he can do, mamma says.

Tommy is a mechanic, and he can repair pretty much anything. When I get home from school I almost always see him lying underneath a car, changing parts, fixing things. His arm ends at the wrist but he uses it anyway, as best he can. He has two children, a boy and a girl. They're more or less my age. At some point, his wife abandons them: we stop seeing her around.

Eventually, word gets out that she ran away with Vincenzo, Carmelo's son.

The apartment underneath ours is inhabited by Signora Battaglia, a child-sized widow with a dog named Birillo. After Signora Battaglia is found dead in her home, Alfredo moves in.

Alfredo was recently released from jail. He's nuts. He fights with everyone. With his girlfriend, who is older than him — she looks like she could be his mother. With his neighbours. With the men who come to visit him occasionally, his *connections*, whom he sells stuff to. When he gets mad, Alfredo shouts, growls, slams doors, kicks things. He seems to have money, but he never goes to work. Is he on holiday? Unbuttoned white shirt, luxury cars, cigars. He's constantly bragging about how much money he has.

He treats the other residents of the building like scum.

This place is crawling with fucking welfare bums, he yells.

Why does he live in public housing, then?

It's a cover — he actually owns three or four apartments, he's even got a villa somewhere.

Alfredo is sick, too. Not surprising considering how much he drinks, how much cocaine he snorts. He's sick for years. Why isn't he dead yet? I'm forced to keep crossing paths with him, saying hello. I hate him. I'm scared of him. I can't sing when Alfredo is home; I can't play music as loudly as I want. Mamma doesn't let me.

I don't want to get into an argument with the guy downstairs, she says.

I don't want anything to do with him.

Carmelo and Alfredo do whatever they want; we can't.

We're not allowed to do anything.

Donata and Pino live in the apartment above us.

Husband and wife, both in their fifties. No children. They take holidays in May, when it's cheaper, and in the summer they sunbake on the balcony. Their home is a place of strict routines that must be respected. Donata's life is only as big as Pino allows it to be. He decides everything, from the clothes she buys to the shows she watches on tv. No, Pino doesn't want to, Pino's not interested, Pino doesn't like it. The hierarchy is clear. Donata is like her husband's servant, she has to ask his permission before doing anything. When Pino is at work Donata comes downstairs to chat, but when he's home she doesn't move an inch. We don't see or hear from her.

Donata is also a gossip. She pretends to be mamma's friend,

but then she goes around spreading rumours about us. She tells everyone my mother was with a bunch of different men after my father moved out, but it's not true. My mother has only been with Tino.

Oh, and Rocco.

But he was in love with her; mamma didn't even like him.

Anyway, Rocco died not long after they met. In a motorbike accident. I was home with mamma when they called to tell her. We were in the kitchen. The telephone rang, mamma answered. I heard her wailing.

Mamma, why are you crying?

I thought that, but I didn't say it.

Marina, mamma's friend with the yellow hair and the thick fringe, whom she's no longer in touch with because people are pigs and friendship is a sham, took the cigarette out of her mouth and said: take the kid into the other room.

I'll leave the envelope at the front desk for you

I'll leave the envelope at the front desk for you.

Inside you'll find the specimen containers for your urine samples.

Fill them up, then come back and see me.

Along with the specimen containers, I collect a thick stack of referrals for my pre-treatment tests. A few days later I return to the hospital, and the nurses suck an alarming amount of blood out of my veins — I never thought I'd see so much of my own blood in one place like that, collected into tubes, extracted from where it should be. Twelve vials in all. I count them, one by one, as they're filled and placed on the little metal tray. I visualise my body being drained, an internal lattice of dried veins. When the needle has taken what it needs, I get up from the recliner.

Antiseptic, cotton wool. I roll my sleeve back down.

Surely I'm going to faint the moment I stand up.

But no — I feel nothing. No sudden drop in blood pressure, not even a vague sense of dizziness. How much blood can we do without?

Time for a big breakfast, says the nurse, as I gather up my coat and backpack.

I walk out of the room and head to the hospital café. I'm glad my mother isn't with me — she would have forced me to eat every last one of the reheated pastries in the glass cabinet next to the cash register. Before I got sick, I was vegan. Not anymore. Over the past few days I've started eating eggs and milk again. Being vegan makes no sense when my survival depends on drugs that are almost certainly tested on animals.

My ideals are dead — all that's left is grim reality.

Everything is going to be different from now on.

Marius accompanies me to my second appointment at Sacco.

The doctor explains why it's not so strange that I haven't transmitted the virus to Marius. There have been plenty of cases like ours. It's more likely in heterosexual couples, but it happens with homosexual couples, too. Transmission depends on a number of different factors. The viral load of the HIV-positive person, but also their partner's propensity for infection. Some people are simply less susceptible than others. The biological predisposition for HIV decreases, he tells us, the further you get from the equator.

Marius was born in Romania — he's light-skinned, his hair is almost blond. Suddenly, everything seems allegorical, predestined. I'm with Marius because that's the way it was meant to be. He was naturally protected, one of the chosen ones. White, Danubian, Orthodox Christian, immortal. At least, that's what I tell myself. I buy into the narrative that HIV is less a disease than a symbol. Not an illness, but a metaphor.

In a candid moment, I confess to my doctor that I haven't had much to do with hospitals until now. I've never had surgery — no broken bones, no emergency appendectomy.

He smiles.

I guess it's something you'll have to get used to.

I don't dislike hospitals. I find them fascinating. Hospitals are places of terrible anguish and fear, but they're also places where lives are renewed. Sites of sickness, but also of healing. Bursting with people preparing to go back out into the world. And newborns, preparing to see it for the first time. In my adolescence, I associated hospitals with birth. Late-night trips with family members, the long wait during labour, the sense of being united, together as a family.

I'm not bothered by the constant hospital visits. Marius is, though. He hates hospitals. He doesn't understand how I can feel anything but hostility towards them.

He only comes with me a couple of times.

I go to most of my check-ups alone.

After my initial consultation, I turn back to the internet for reassurance. I need to know everything in advance — I want to be the model patient. I read every bit of advice I can find, every personal account. I search for information on the life expectancy of HIV-positive people, on common side effects of treatment. I'll be starting antiretroviral therapy soon, and it's something I'll have to continue for a long time. For the rest of my life. It's possible to live with HIV these days, that's true. But will I stay the same as I am now? Will the virus, or the drugs, or both, alter the way I look? Will I lose or gain weight? Will my face change?

Online, everything is layered: answers create new questions, new and old information are mingled indiscriminately. Both HIV and the drugs that treat it will leave their marks on my body. They might affect my metabolism, causing *metabolic syndrome*, or even *lipodystrophy* — an irregular distribution of body fat that hollows the cheeks and balloons the hips and belly. Lipodystrophy can also produce a buffalo hump: an accumulation of adipose tissue at the nape of the neck.

Will I turn into a skeleton with an overgrown abdomen, and breasts?

Alive, but grotesque?

Are these the conditions I'll have to accept if I want to live?

Will I have to get cosmetic surgery — cheek fillers, like the guys on tv, or liposuction, to suck out the fat that's migrated from my face and limbs to parts of my body where it doesn't belong?

No, it's not like that anymore (I read somewhere). The potent cocktails of drugs they used to prescribe, decades ago, have been replaced with gentler medications. They no longer rely on lethal substances like AZT. Lipodystrophy is an obsolete side effect. HIV-positive people are no longer easy to spot, like they used to be. It's difficult to determine what's true and what's a legacy of the Eighties and Nineties. If in doubt, say the anonymous users of the forums, ask your doctor. Forget about the stuff you read on the internet.

They're right. I should take their advice.

But I can't — the impulse is stronger than I am.

It doesn't help that I have nothing else to do. I've stopped working, I've stopped reading, I've stopped writing, I've stopped meditating, I've stopped taking photos, I've stopped going on Facebook. I only leave the house when I absolutely have to. I'm drawn back online again and again, inevitably.

People no longer die from HIV, but they're still susceptible to a range of cardiovascular problems and run a higher risk of developing cancers and other pathologies associated with premature ageing. On the other hand, they're also much more closely monitored than most — how many people have blood tests and check-ups three or four times a year? So these secondary illnesses are usually detected early.

I won't die immediately, then, but will I get cancer in a few years?

Will my heart fail?

I'm thirty years old now. What's my life expectancy? Thirty-five? Forty? Surely I'll make it to sixty-five, or seventy. Plenty of people do. Then again, many don't. I would have liked to live into my nineties, become a centenarian. I've never been one of those people who say *please, for the love of god, don't let me get that old*. Now, though, I have to make peace with a revised estimation. With the idea of barely tasting old age.

I find myself obsessively calculating the number of years I can expect to live, mentally traversing the distance that separates me from death. When you find out you have HIV, your mind inevitably turns to death. Even today, when everyone is constantly reminding you how much medicine has progressed, how all you have to do is get treatment and you can live a normal life. Death is no longer imminent, but it lingers all the same, a dark presence that must be continually exorcised. The rituals of medicine are what keep it at bay — tests, check-ups, drug therapies.

Death is the reason I have to go through all this.

Death is always there, just around the corner, ready and waiting.

The day I'm hit by a girl

The day I'm hit by a girl, I'm on my way home from school.

I'm in seventh grade at Bernardino Luini Middle School, in central Rozzano.

I've got a sinking feeling in my stomach — it often happens at this time of day.

I wonder what mamma has made for lunch.

The girl is waiting for me in front of the Sant'Angelo church. She's older than me, but not by much — a couple of years, maybe. I recognise her. I've crossed paths with her a few times around Rozzano. She's a girl, but she looks like a boy: short black hair, freckles, always wearing a tracksuit, like zia Tata. She has a mole next to her mouth, and long, narrow eyes, like a samurai, except she's not Japanese. She lives in public housing, but in one of the single-story buildings near the café on Viale Lombardia, where the drug dealers hang out. She's a friend of Patrizia, one of my classmates.

Last week Patrizia and I went door to door, selling WWF stamps to the inhabitants of the public-housing towers near school.

Would you like to buy one, signora? It's to save the Italian wolves.

Patrizia is nice to me, but she's prickly — she gets irritated easily. The other day we fought, and I called her a slut. At my grandparents' house we swear all the time, sometimes as a joke.

According to zia Tata's friends, I would stand on the balcony as a toddler and shout insults at passers-by. You used to call me a whore, they tell me. You used to call me a slut. One of my primary-school teachers, Miss Lucia, once had to call an emergency meeting with mamma, because nonna Lidia had promised to rip out Miss Rosalia's pubic hair — *ce scipp' tutt' e pili 'ra fess'* — when she found out she'd written a note for my parents in my school diary. The next day I went to school and told everyone. Within half a day, even kids in the other classes knew. Mamma had to take a day off work to sort it out.

The child's grandmother has said something unacceptable, signora.

Mamma was so angry with nonna Lidia.

Don't you realise how shitty you made us look, mamma?

Patrizia's friend was waiting for me in front of the church. She knows which way I walk home from school. Who told her? She must have stalked me. Suddenly, she's standing right in front of me, beneath the statue of the angel with the outstretched arms.

Who are you calling a slut, huh? Who?

Everything happens so quickly. Her leg, her football player's leg, used to kicking balls into the back of nets. Her faded jeans, her socks, her white sneakers suddenly coming towards me. Her foot meeting my belly, my poor little belly, delivering a hard blow between my navel and my lungs. My soft abdomen, unprotected by muscles. The impact, my diaphragm contracting, my breath catching. The humiliation rising to my face, the burning humiliation — you're disgusting, you're pathetic.

Even girls are beating you up now.

I get up and start running. I run and I don't stop, hoping she's not following me.

I turn my head to look behind me. She's not there. She's not coming. Is she really going to leave it at that — a single kick in the stomach? I run all the way home. I run through the park behind the parish where I go to catechism class. I run past the church where in a few months' time I'll complete the Sacrament of Confirmation. I run and run, past the peeling walls of the public-housing towers, underneath the people sitting on their balconies (I hope none of them saw what happened), through the basements of Rozzano, beneath the house of the guy I'll catch crabs from in a few years' time. I run even faster than I run in P.E., all the way to my building and upstairs to our apartment. But I don't tell anyone what happened. It wouldn't do any good.

You're twelve years old now, you should be able to deal with your own problems.

But I'm not. All I know how to do is play with my toys and read books and watch tv. All I know how to be is the little fag I am. Dressing in bright colours, even though I shouldn't. Singing in my room for hours, my voice so high — it will never break, not completely — that the neighbours mistake me for my mother: *feeling good this morning, huh, Tina?* Dedicating songs to people who aren't there, who have never been there. To the boys I like, or to my father, who occasionally remembers I exist and still makes promises he'll never keep.

When I sing it might seem like I'm in my bedroom with the door closed, but actually I'm on stage. The people I'm singing for are out there in the stalls, among the audience. *This one goes out to you.* I shout, I shout the words I've never been able to say in real life. Now that I'm famous, now that I have the lyrics of the greatest songwriters in Italian history on my side, I finally have a way to express myself.

I'm sorry you didn't see my worth earlier.

I would have happily shared my success with you.

But now it's too late. I'm untouchable. You'll have to make do with my little dedications.

Papà, this one's for you. There you are, the lights are on you — I arranged it with the stage director before the show. This one goes out to you, papà.

Don't cry: there's no point.

What happened is in the past now.

Let's just enjoy this moment.

I'm the smartest kid at middle school, but that's not enough to protect me.

I do so well at school because I memorise everything, for fear of stuttering. I need to have my words prepared in advance, like poetry recited by heart. They need to come out without my having to think about them.

I do everything I can to minimise the pauses, the moments of silence.

I have to seem normal.

When I have to do presentations and oral exams, the question isn't whether I'll be prepared but whether I'll be able to speak. In the morning, on my way to school, I look for signs to tell me how the day will go. Buildings, posters, street signs — these become my oracles. If I see thirty red things between here and the school gate, everything will go well. Twenty-seven, and things won't go as expected.

Only eighteen? It'll be a disaster.

The worst thing is reading aloud. Literature is the class I dread the most. We take turns reading one or two paragraphs from a book. The literature teacher calls on us in order, according to where we're sitting. When it's almost my turn, I try to save myself by asking to go to the bathroom. Sometimes I really do have to go: the fear gives me stomach cramps, awful stabbing pains in my intestines.

I count down. Three names to go.

Now two.

I try to pinpoint the perfect moment to raise my hand. Too soon, and I'll have to be out of the room for half an hour; too late, and it won't be believable. When I return to the classroom, the teacher calls on me anyway. He asks me to make up for my missed turn. I have to try. Maybe this time it'll be okay.

It's not okay, and everyone notices.

I sound like a robot, stopping and starting, pausing in the middle of sentences, getting stuck and falling silent. I read without intonation. If my pauses are too long, or too frequent, my classmates start whispering among themselves. I'm terrified of hearing what they're saying.

Is he retarded or what?

Do you think he does it on purpose?

The teacher intervenes. Do you read at home? You need to practise.

I do read at home — it's practically all I do. But when I'm alone, even if I'm reading aloud, I never stutter. For a stutterer, reading aloud in public is the worst, because you don't get to choose which words to say. You have to read what's written in front of you. There's no escape route.

Literature class is the nail in the coffin. I'm a lost cause.

Even introducing myself is a stumbling block: when someone asks me my name, the *j* — a hard, uncomfortable letter — easily gets stuck between my teeth.

Like at the Pian dei Boschi camping ground, in Pietra Ligure, where nonna Nuccia and nonno Pier take me every summer. They force me to join the other kids and play with Betta (short for Elisabetta), the woman who looks like Lara Croft and runs the Kids Club. Every afternoon Betta organises soccer matches and treasure hunts. She makes us sit in a circle and introduce ourselves. Everyone has to tell the group their name before we can start playing. When it's my turn, the perfect flow — Micky, Samuele, Sara, Nicoletta — is interrupted. All eyes are trained on me. Waiting.

Well? Go ahead.

My mouth is open, but no sound is coming out. The other children burst into laughter.

Don't you know your own name?

Did you forget it?

There are countless scenes like this in my childhood, scenes I've removed, edited out of my memory. You're not here, you don't exist. You can't even speak.

I stutter in middle school, but there's so much going on in the classroom that sometimes it goes unnoticed. Some of my classmates come from families assisted by social workers. Like Valentino, who has a support teacher, even though he's far from stupid. Valentino has trouble paying attention — he throws our pencil cases out the window, threatens to hit the music teacher, asks the maths teacher to show us her boobs.

Miss, whip out a tit for me.

I didn't find out until a few years later: *of course, didn't you know? He was sexually abused, poor kid. Raped by an uncle. Really messed him up.*

Then there's Katia: both her parents are drug addicts, and her older brother is in jail. You wouldn't know it to look at her — she's always happy. She's tall and skinny, and wears rolled-up socks in her bralettes to make her breasts look bigger. At school we make fun of her because she always wears the same clothes, and because she has a dark birthmark at the back of her neck. She's dirty, the kids say. She doesn't wash. We tease her relentlessly.

We only stop when she starts crying.

I'm the smartest kid in my class, but it doesn't stop Davide Sommariva from unleashing his fits of rage on me. When nobody's watching — when we're walking to the gym, or hidden from sight behind a pillar, or in some isolated corner of the corridor — he slaps me on the back of the head and pinches my arms. He doesn't do it half-heartedly. He hits me with all the force he can muster. He tries to rip my skin to shreds. He turns red in the face, his cheeks go blotchy. He bites his bottom lip, and his eyes roll back in his head.

He enjoys it — he seems excited by it.

Smacks, knuckle punches.

Shut the fuck up, poof.

Is that when I started wanting men to hurt me?

I don't tell anyone what happens with Davide. I could tell the teachers, but that would mean admitting weakness. I'm not a girl. I should be able to defend myself, but I don't even try. Despite Davide's ambushes, I have a reputation to uphold at Bernardino Luini Middle School. The teachers are kind to me; my grades are always good. And then there's the English teacher.

Bianca Villani Moore.

She was born in Salerno, but she married an American, from Boston — a fact she reminds everyone of constantly.

I'm infatuated with her. Ms Villani dresses impeccably, and wears a special perfume I've never smelled before — it smells like flowers and spices, and fills the entire classroom even after she's left. She's always wearing incredible shoes: purple heels, or mustard flats. I never see shoes like that in Rozzano. I wonder where she buys them. My classmates say I'm in love with her, but it's not true. I know I like boys. But I do get excited when it's time for English class. That much is undeniable. Even the night before, when I'm preparing my schoolbag, I get butterflies.

Ms Villani teaches us about American traditions: the Fourth of July, Thanksgiving. She makes us craft pumpkins out of playdough for Halloween, and watch karaoke videos of Disney songs. Our class is an absolute train wreck. No one knows any English, and no one seems capable of learning. Ms Villani tries to teach us as if we were babies, with nursery rhymes and colouring books and cartoons. Some of my classmates have a hard enough time with Italian — they normally speak dialect at home. In class they just fight and run amok, laughing and throwing things at each other.

On the worst days, Ms Villani makes us do a kind of meditation — that's what she calls it. She draws the blinds and has us put our heads on our desks. Then she tells us to imagine we're at the seaside, listening to the sound of the waves beneath a blue sky. Maybe it's the only way she can get through the hour?

At school meetings, Ms Villani complains to our parents. It's impossible to teach your children, she says. We're constantly shouting over them, we're exhausted.

Mamma comes home indignant: who does that woman think she is?

She thinks she is who she is, mamma: my muse. The first real teacher I've ever had. Before Simone Weil, Edith Stein, Elsa Morante, Hannah Arendt, Cristina Campo, Roberta De Monticelli, and Laura Boella, there was Bianca Villani Moore, my middle-school English teacher.

Ms Villani doesn't live in Rozzano. She lives in Milano 3, the wealthy town where my father also lives, although my father isn't actually rich. He just pretends to be. *Your father is always biting off more than he can chew.* At the end of seventh grade, Ms Villani is the one who suggests to my parents that I change schools.

We move too slowly here, she says. We're too far behind in the curriculum. Considering the circumstances in the classroom, it's impossible to move any faster. Jonathan is capable of much more than we can offer him. It would be better for him to spend his final year of middle school with children who are at his level. Otherwise he runs the risk of starting high school at a disadvantage, without having covered the basics, and that would be a pity.

Send him to Milano 3; the middle school there is excellent.

Johnny, what do you want to do?

Okay. We'll do it.

Finally, I'm out of Rozzano. I enrol at the middle school in Milano 3.

With children who are at my level.

Ten minutes by bus.

Surrounded by rich kids.

HIV is a hoax

HIV is a hoax, I read.

The biggest conspiracy of the twentieth century.

As I wait to start antiretroviral therapy, I stumble across the online world of AIDS denialism and alternative medicine. People who think the human immunodeficiency virus doesn't exist. People who think it can be cured with probiotics, antioxidants, and strong doses of vitamin C. Supplements and aloe vera and juice cleanses. Diets based on radicchio and raw onion.

I learn that there are HIV-positive people out there who choose not to get better, and not because they want to die. They refuse treatment, or pretend to take their medication, because they believe HIV and AIDS were invented by Big Pharma.

I've never been interested in conspiracy theories or anti-establishment fantasies, but some of these pseudo-experts — the more appealing and esoteric among them — pique my curiosity. I try writing to a homeopathic doctor who aligns herself with such views.

Good morning, I've just learnt I have HIV. What would you recommend I do?

I recommend you educate yourself. Read books, watch videos on YouTube. Overcome your ignorance. Otherwise they'll end up killing you, the way they've killed so many before you. People don't die of AIDS — the drugs, the ostracisation, the fear kill them. Not some virus no one has ever seen.

She suggests I attend one of her seminars.

Tickets are a hundred euros, paid in advance.

Meanwhile, she prescribes fasting, and bathing my genitals in cold water.

The illness is caused by negative thinking, she says. She has invented a method to cure it using words. HIV is only a useful label if you're selling medications. The true cause of the sickness is psychological: non-love.

She really says and writes these things. She professes them freely.

I've decided. I'm going, I want to go.

I don't actually believe HIV can be cured by words and cold baths, but I'm a little intrigued by this idea that the body is completely under our control, that it's possible to solve biological problems with magical formulas. The body as story, as imagination.

Am I playing with fire?

I look up how to get to Peschiera Borromeo, where her seminars are held. I arrange everything. I don't tell Marius. I'm ready to learn the hidden meaning behind my illness, to understand the connection between me and my sickness, to decode the message it is here to tell me.

A day passes. Two days pass.

I check my bank account. I'm not working anymore. Maybe it's best if I spend what little money I have left on groceries. I change my mind. I'm not going.

I'll never know what that homeopathic doctor would have said to me, had we met in person.

I'm sure it would have been entertaining, if not helpful.

Our emotional lives and our physical health are linked — that much seems self-evident. But even if it's true that physical ailments originate in the spirit or the mind, it doesn't make sense to think you can work your way back up the causal chain and change the original emotional state that gave rise to your illness. Once the dysfunction has manifested in the body, it becomes a problem for medicine. It calls for chemotherapy, scalpels, antiretrovirals. The rest is just a gamble: entertainment for people who have nothing to lose, or who aren't sick enough to understand the risk involved.

I give up on alternative medicine and go back to researching the evolution of my illness. When I first discovered I had HIV, I was relieved. *At least it's not cancer.* Now, though, I learn that HIV infection normally causes symptoms early on — during the period of seroconversion — and again much later, when the immune system begins to collapse. I can't possibly be in the early stages of infection, because I must have contracted the virus before I met Marius.

So does that mean I'm reaching the end?

Am I beyond cure?

Basiglio Comprehensive Institute

Basiglio Comprehensive Institute, Milano 3 campus. Good morning.

Good morning. I'm Jonathan Bazzi's mother, he's a student of yours …

Your name, please?

Concetta De Rosa.

Sorry, could you repeat that?

My mother hates giving her full name.

De Rosa. Concetta De Rosa.

Thanks. How can I help?

I'd like to know if my son is at school.

Now?

Yes, I'd like to know if he arrived at school this morning.

Class?

Eight B.

I'll check and get back to you.

Thank you.

My mother hears footsteps retreating, then returning.

Signora, are you there?

Yes, I'm here.

No, he didn't turn up today.

I see.

You weren't aware?

For a moment, my mother's ears stop working.

Signora?

Yes …

Signora, is everything alright? Has something happened?

I'm not sure. His father says he left for school as usual, but then a colleague of mine here in Rozzano called to say she'd seen him walking down by the canal, in the middle of the highway.

Your son doesn't have a mobile phone?

He does, but he's not answering.

I've been in Africa

I've been in Africa. I've been in Haiti. I've been in New York, in California, all over the United States. *Rare cancer observed in 41 gay patients; immunodeficiency correlated to homosexuality.* I've been in Brazil. I've travelled to Europe. I've been ape, hunter, stranger, unwitting partner, betrayed woman, porn star, aspiring singer, dancer, drug addict, escort, hairdresser, executive, athlete, unfortunate patient, unfaithful husband, employee, homeless person, child of criminals, activist, priest, drag queen, transgender girl, professor, housewife, doctor, labourer, poet, photographer, breastfeeding mother, scapegoat, avenger, adolescent, rape survivor.

The virus has been in all these bodies. It has passed through them, used them, consumed them. These people are dead; their bodies no longer exist. But the virus has endured. It is immortal. The virus transcends, adapts. It was passed on — and on and on — until it arrived here.

Part of me made this epic journey through space and time before becoming me. Before I became what I am now.

I belong to an invisible community.

Of victims and survivors, of ghosts and living relics.

The test results are in.

It's HIV-1.

The virus I have is type 1, the most widespread type in the west.

The most aggressive, the most contagious.

Type 2 is mostly present in Africa.

The tests say my virus exhibits no resistance to any antiretroviral drugs. That's good news: it means we can choose the best treatment. The latest one, the one with the fewest side effects.

My CD4 cell count isn't too alarming: 497.

Slightly below the lower limit of normal.

My viral load — the numbers of copies of the virus present in my body — is ridiculously low: 1221 copies per millilitre (I've read on the internet that a viral load of 10,000 is still considered low). Although the infection isn't recent, the virus hasn't reproduced much. My body has been fighting back — confirmation that I'm special, that I can still set myself apart.

The results are encouraging.

Maybe too encouraging, I think.

Optimism is often just ignorance of danger. We must be brave enough to recognise negative omens even when they're in disguise, when they're attempting to mislead us, to make us drop our guard. So you think you dodged a bullet? Poor fool — surely you're not that easily deceived.

If my values are this low, then why did I develop symptoms? Symptoms appear — symptoms *should* appear — when the immune system begins to fail, but not before. The virus can inhabit a body silently for a number of years.

What if my fever has a different cause?

What if it wasn't HIV that made me sick after all?

My suspicions ferment into conviction. You're wrong: the virus is a red herring diverting doctors away from the real origins of my fever.

The true cause is still hidden.

I walk through the icy fields

I walk through the icy fields, surrounded by thick fog.

Skirting the irrigation channel, I pass two gigantic black crows.

It's freezing, but I can't feel the cold. I hate this feeling: sweaty, but unable to disrobe.

I've got no money; I've already spent the pocket money nonna Lidia gave me last week. I've got a packet of crackers in my backpack, and a peach juice box. If I have them now, I won't be able to buy anything else if I get hungry later. I decide to save them.

I'm somewhere in the countryside separating Milano 3 from Rozzano. I hope no one sees me.

Is it true that if a farmer catches you on their property they can shoot you?

I walk from Milano 3 to Rozzano, then I turn around and walk back. I spend the rest of the morning sitting on a park bench, surrounded by foreign nannies and rich Milano 3 babies. Infants born in this place that looks like one of the scale models in the architecture studios mamma and Tino clean.

I sit for two, three hours.

I didn't go to school this morning.

It's not the first time I've skipped school this year. Today we had an oral exam for history class. I'm sick of looking like an idiot. I don't know how to speak in front of people. I can't make sense of the teacher's corrections. I don't want to be made fun of anymore.

Enrolling in middle school in Milano 3 was a bad idea.

I took my English teacher's advice, but she's not here with me.

On top of everything else, I don't even get to see her anymore.

Everyone in my class has known each other for at least two years.

They're all beautiful, intelligent, fierce. Aspiring doctors and lawyers. The girls with their blonde highlights and Louis Vuitton bags, the boys like miniature versions of their fathers, tiny entrepreneurs. In the afternoons they play tennis or go to the stables to ride their horses, while I take the bus home and watch Maria De Filippi as nonna Lidia reheats pasta for lunch.

I have nothing in common with them. They recognise that immediately.

I have no money. I stutter. I don't know how to kiss a girl. Early on, I almost manage to deceive them. I start going out with a girl in my class: Flo, Floriana. For a brief moment, we're the 'it' couple.

Look at them, aren't they cute?

We're together for a week before Floriana dumps me.

I was expecting this — it was only a matter of time. She'd been the one to ask me out, but I knew it wouldn't last. Floriana is very beautiful. I said yes, but all we did was hold hands. A whole week of dating and not a single kiss.

Does that seem normal to you?

In the changing rooms after P.E., the boys in my class wanted to know: so, did you get some?

At the very least, they thought we must have made out. Maybe more.

They expected things from my body that it couldn't deliver, that it would never be able to deliver.

When we break up, Floriana cuts off all her hair. It used to be long and brown: high pony, low pony, side pony, braids. She cuts it super short, and doesn't talk to me for the rest of the year. She doesn't talk *to* me, but she talks *about* me to our classmates. She tells the other girls I was scared to touch her, that I wouldn't even brush against her accidentally. They get angry; the news disturbs them. They draw a circle of gossip and derision around me. There's no coming back from it.

The spell works: my role is assigned.

In Rozzano, everyone was an individual. School was chaos, there was no special sense of belonging. Here in Milano 3, things are different. They are the class, they are the standard, and I am the uninvited guest. They know I can't be assimilated, they can tell just by looking at me that I'm different, second-rate. At Bernardino Luini I was just another poor kid among poor kids, but at least I was smart. Here I'm stupid, worthless.

What does your mother do for work?

I lie. She's a cook, I say. A chef.

I don't tell them she works in a supermarket.

So you're from Rozzano? Where in Rozzano?

Another lie: Cassino, Valleambrosia, Via Guido Rossa.

I don't tell them I live in public housing.

Here, I'm transparent. Milano 3 has given me the gift of invisibility, a superpower none of my superheroines possess. At best I'm a caricature, a punching bag, a pressure valve. I'm entertaining, in my own way: every point of difference is a portal to ridicule.

Don't be so dramatic, there must be someone you connect with.

The only kids I get along with in my class are Giacomo, the little brother of a famous sports journalist (Giacomo is also from Rozzano, but he doesn't live in public housing) and Ettore, whose parents live a few doors down from my father. But those two allies are not enough to balance the scales in my favour. In any case, neither Giacomo nor Ettore would risk his reputation for me. When it comes down to it, it's clear which side they're on.

Then there's Laura, the daughter of a colleague of my mother's boyfriend.

Laura invites me to her house sometimes, but in class she doesn't stick up for me either.

It's just a joke. Don't get offended.

I ask my mother to come and ask my teachers if I can be exempted from reading aloud in class. The least she can do is support me on this. I have to insist, but in the end she gives in.

Who's your nicest teacher?

My Italian teacher.

A substitute, recently graduated, obsessed with Leopardi.

Mamma goes to the school and talks to her. The meeting goes well: all good, Johnny. They won't make you read anymore. Happy?

I'm still scared, though. I'm scared my teachers will forget, that they'll get confused and call on me anyway. As it turns out, I'm a Cassandra, a little Pythia. My prophecy is fulfilled. The religion teacher is the one to betray me.

She hasn't forgotten about my mother's request. She does it on purpose.

Tall and large, enormous, and always enveloped in something

— a poncho or a shawl. She thinks she knows better than me. She thinks I just have to unblock myself. She's convinced my refusal to read is just a childish hang-up that can be fixed with a bit of unsanctioned exposure therapy.

It happens one day while we're reading photocopies from a book about the history of the monotheistic religions (Christianity, Judaism, Islam). The teacher doesn't follow a predictable pattern when deciding who to call on next.

I hear her voice.

Bazzi.

I haven't misheard.

She's called me.

We had a secret agreement: I don't read, ever. And she has violated it. There's nothing I can say. My classmates don't know, mustn't know, about our arrangement. I obey. I perform. Or rather, I try to perform. I try, but nothing comes out. Have my vocal cords stopped working? My silence is met first by surprise — *what's wrong with him?* — then euphoria. The words I can't say crash through the orange tiled floor beneath me and drag me down with them. The class bursts into laughter, one giant cackling mouth. My moment of consecration: I am the fool, the pariah, the leper.

It doesn't take long for me to adapt to this new version of myself, to accept it, to integrate it. I don't have the strength to fight. I don't have the strength to be the person I should be, to become again what I was before: different but smart, bullied but special. Unique. I surrender to mediocrity. My grades plummet. (*What was your graduating GPA in middle school? It's a secret*). I don't know how to be part of a group. Either I'm on top or I'm worthless.

Eighth grade is all about waiting for middle school to be over.

★

Despite it all, I am fond of Milano 3. It strikes me as a kind of English shire, a haven, a cave of wonders. I've been coming here for years, because of my father. Milano 3 is Berlusconi's artificial village, all burgundy apartments and lawns and tree-lined streets, an over-designed suburb artificially wedged between the farms and rice fields of rural Lombardy.

My father lives here. He's like you.

My father lives in Via Verdi, in an apartment building called Willow House. In Milano 3 everything is named after plants: willow, elm, birch. Not flowers, like in Rozzano. Here they name things after big, majestic trees. Meaningful plants.

Rozzano. Milano 3. The family schism launches me from public-housing tower to luxury apartment, although here, too, the buildings are all clones of one another, following the blueprints of Berlusconi's construction project. The synthetic coldness of Milano 3 is, for me, at once a dream and concrete proof of my failure. There is an air of elitism here, of exclusivity. Families that look like they've stepped out of a tv commercial, with their enormous cars and their designer clothes. Celebrities and soccer stars enclosed in their villas. Occasionally, though, anomalies emerge — the coke head, the ruined showgirl from the Eighties — to restore a sense of familiarity.

After all, Rozzano is just down the road.

I'm intoxicated by these amaranth houses with their empty stairwells, their wall-to-wall carpets, their silent, smooth elevators unspoiled by profanities and graffiti. Rozzano fades into the background during these brief, sporadic journeys into the world of the rich — a world of freezer meals and keeping up appearances. Milano 3 is real paintings (not prints) hanging in the stairwells. Pleasant fragrances. Safe, immaculate basements. Cleaning ladies from the Philippines. The lake with the beautiful but ferocious swans I scatter stale bread for — *watch your hands, they'll bite you.* The mini shopping centre with the supermarket that sells things you can't buy in Rozzano. The colonies of Hermès mothers waiting at school gates. The purebred dogs. The subscription magazines peeking out of letterboxes, unstolen.

I'm enchanted by Milano 3, and at the same time I'm crushed by it. By the tantalising possibilities it both offers and withholds. By the image, the mirage, of a different way of living in the world. A lighter, more spacious way.

I don't live in Milano 3; my father does.

I'm just a visitor. I'm allowed to borrow the lifestyle, but only under very specific circumstances. I need a reason to be here. And now I have one: despite everything, I'm enrolled in the middle school in Piazza Leonardo da Vinci.

I love Milano 3, but it's an unrequited love. I love it even though my father's sister (she lives in the same street as him) says the people here go without food so they can spend their money on fancy things to elicit the envy of their neighbours. So they can buy the latest handbag, or drive a car that won't embarrass them in the underground garage. Even if all that is true, the fact remains that the people in Milano 3 are different. I've got no chance of fitting in, of slipping under the radar.

I didn't know that before, and now it's too late to go back.

Different stock, different pedigree.

It's not true that we're all born equal.

★

When we first decided I would change schools, the plan was for me to stay at my father's house during the week. *It's easier that way — you're already there.*

But the plan fails miserably.

I live with my father for no more than a month before he takes me back to Rozzano.

This is impossible, you haven't brought him up properly.

You see, Jonathan? This is how your father solves his problems.

Papà says I'm undisciplined, unmanageable. He's obsessed with cleanliness, and I don't cooperate. Shoes have to be removed before you walk in the front door — papà makes everyone do it, even the people who protest. He vacuums after every meal, even if no food has fallen on the floor. When he mops, he has to check the tiles against the light to make sure they're clean. After he cleans the bathroom, he tries to stop me using it for the rest of the day (I have to brush my teeth over the bath, because if I use the basin I might dirty the mirror). When I'm in the shower, he checks to make sure I shampoo twice. He comes in and gives me instructions: lather, massage, rinse. And again: lather, massage, rinse.

Any violation of the hygiene rules, however small, sends him into a rage.

There's a specific way to do things, and that's his way.

The only option is to accept it and move on.

My father has a lot of expensive things in his apartment, which just means he has big debts. The banks are always chasing him for money — they call him, but he doesn't answer. He never answers calls from unknown numbers. When things get really bad, nonna Nuccia intervenes. She pays off his debts, taking on more of her own in the process. Nonna always forgives him, always defends him. He's her Robby, her baby.

Nuccia is the one who ruined your father, it's her fault he turned out the way he did.

Big televisions, a Dolby surround-sound system, new phones, computers, gaming consoles. My father also has a large collection of curios, mostly souvenirs from his travels. Shells, corals, starfish, carved wooden statues. Each object has its own place on the shelf or the bookcase. His possessions are like theatre props — if I want to look at them, I have to put them back exactly where I found them, and it's better if I don't touch them at all.

Papà remarried after he and mamma split up. His new wife is Antonella, a policewoman from Verona. Stick-thin and a bundle of nerves. She grew up in the country with eccentric parents who would cut her hair in her sleep if she did something naughty. Antonella hates me — she hates me and she hates my mother, because we represent the past. One time she tells me off for sitting at the table the way I still do today: with my legs tucked underneath my bottom, or folded like a little Buddha.

Nice. Are you a monkey? Does your mother let you sit at the table like that?

Mamma calls papà: tell that anorexic bitch to keep her mouth shut, or I'll come and shut it for her. Does she think I give a fuck if she's a cop?

People say papà married Antonella for her money.

They say they broke up because she wanted to have a baby and he didn't.

To err is human, says papà, but to persist …

One time over dinner, after too much wine, papà confessed to me: I can't help it, after a while I just get bored.

Once his marriage with Antonella is over, papà gets together with Leila, a French girl with Algerian heritage. Leila is overweight (papà says she looks like Maria Grazia Cucinotta, or Mietta, or Monica Bellucci) and has a kind of perennial cold. Her nose is always red and blocked, and she's always carrying a fistful of balled-up tissues. When she cries, it's hard to tell if she's sad or if it's just sinusitis. And as time goes on, Leila cries more and more frequently.

In the beginning, my father treats all his women like queens. Then, slowly, he destroys them.

Barely a year into their relationship, he's already cheating on her. They break up and get back together. Leila lives with my father for a bit, then rents her own place in Milan, closer to work. But things don't work out between them. She goes back to Lyon.

I'll never see her again.

I thought I loved her.

Papà doesn't marry Leila, but he does marry Michelle, a single mother fresh off the plane from Brazil.

They meet at the Latin American festival in Assago.

His third marriage.

My father marries Michelle and becomes the stepfather of Pedro, Michelle's son. Once they're married they fly Pedro to Italy, to Milano 3, from Brazil, where he was living with his grandparents.

Four or five years pass. Pedro calls my father papi, papà.

He doesn't give a shit about you anymore, he's too busy pretending to be that bastard's daddy.

My father showers Pedro in gifts, buys him everything he wants. Then suddenly it's over.

My father and Michelle break up. Michelle and Pedro go back to Brazil.

Is the game over now, papà?

My father is obsessed with sex. He says so himself: *I've got a sickness. He's in charge* (and he points between his legs). When we're out in the street, in a shop, anywhere, he comments on every woman he sees. From fourteen to sixty. He'd fuck them all.

Anything with a pulse, my mother says.

The wolf may lose his teeth but never his nature, she adds.

My father harasses women in the street, even when his wife or girlfriend is standing right next to him.

She looks like she needs a good spanking.

This one here's a screamer.

It's not the size, sweetheart, it's what you do with it.

Or if he's driving, and a woman is trying to cross the road: I'd rather have that under me than under my car.

Nonna Nuccia finds it all very entertaining. Roberto, cut it out, she says, giggling.

Papà is always talking about sex, bragging about all the women he's been with. All the men in his family are the same. When they get together over Christmas dinner, or Easter lunch, they egg each other on. Giancarlo, nonna Nuccia's boyfriend (nonno Pier died suddenly of a heart attack one afternoon, at home, after a nice lunch), says he put the Baby Jesus inside her last night. Zio Mario describes the positions he and zia Anna, nonna's sister, tried recently. Papà tells everyone about the time he did it with two nurses from San Raffaele.

While the women cook lunch, the men get together and watch porn on their phones. I'm eleven, then twelve, then thirteen. It doesn't seem like I'm paying attention, but I hear everything.

Whenever the conversation turns to women, I just hope they won't ask me to contribute. I hope they won't ask me to appraise some actress's tits, or rate the hotness of some neighbour.

Uff, that one there. I'd like to lick her all over.

Papà tells zio Mario he has a great tape to lend him — a friend of his runs a videotheque in Milan.

One morning, at his apartment, I find the stash of tapes in a cardboard box in the storage cupboard. At least a dozen VHS cassettes, hidden high up on the top shelf. Just above the collection of horror paperbacks papà buys me from the kiosk. Papà is outside washing his new car — the Puma, or the Tiger. Papà loves cars named after animals. I take advantage of my window of opportunity.

I masturbate in the lounge room, in front of the expensive tv.

My first porno.

All the actresses are trans.

Two days after receiving my diagnosis

Two days after receiving my diagnosis, I get a call. My father has leukaemia.

Bazzi men are unlucky; they always die young.

The illness I was convinced I had, the one I obsessively searched for traces of in the results of my blood tests, in my white blood cell counts, on every medical website I could find. He has it. My father actually has it. He'd been feeling unwell for a few days, a persistent tiredness — like mine? — followed by a sharp pain in his side. The spleen.

They took him to the emergency room, and a blood test quickly revealed the cause. The monstrous number of white blood cells explained everything.

Cancer of the blood.

Neoplastic proliferation.

They don't yet know if it's chronic or acute leukaemia.

They don't yet know if there's anything they can do to stop it.

When I receive the news, it's been nearly a year since I saw or heard from my father. Over time, our relationship revealed itself for what it really was: an accident, a flimsy, ill-fitting arrangement. I'm not a kid anymore. I'm no longer that suggestable, hypnotisable child who would sit at home, paralysed, waiting for him to call when he said he would, never anticipating the inevitable let-down. Now, on the rare occasions when we see each other, neither of us has much to say. I can't stand his unfunny jokes, his unbridled hedonism, his inability to focus on what's important. I imagine he sees me as a kind of obstacle that re-emerges every so often, presumably thanks to the interventions of my nonna, his mother.

When nonna calls to tell me about his diagnosis, I still haven't told her about mine. I will, but first I need to get my head around the situation.

My father has blood cancer. I have HIV.

Cancer is a crazed proliferation of cells. HIV is cell death. Cancer is internal revolt, the body wanting too much, growing, expanding. HIV is an attack, an invasion, a capitulation. Mirror images (a miracle? a cruel joke?) formed by two parallel bodies, two physically and emotionally distant organisms that, somehow, are still capable of conspiring to make a mockery of the laws of logic and probability. The laws of biography and chronology. Our two bodies bridging the chasms and trenches of the mind to remind us that there are forces beyond our understanding, and that these forces are connected, communicating, colluding behind our backs.

You can ignore them.

You can force yourself to forget, for years.

Roll a stone over them, psychically sever the bonds that connect us. But we are embedded in ancient matrices. The belonging we deny in the mind is affirmed in the body.

We spend our lives skating on a thin sheet of convictions, on a brittle layer of ideas that have been carefully separated and controlled, their edges smoothed and soothing. We draw hasty conclusions: my father had no paternal instincts, my father has never been a real father, my father is not my father. And all the while, the incandescent roots of our shared nature glow beneath us: father and son in synchrony, like characters in a terrible screenplay.

I tell my mother about my father's diagnosis and she says: write to him, reach out.

I should — *he's still your father* — but I can't bring myself to.

I am cold, arrogant. I feel guilty, but only because I don't feel what I know I should feel. I resent being forced to make contact with him again.

My father is dying. I thought he was already dead? Where did we bury you, papà?

I know I should exhume you, try to re-enact the pain everyone expects from me now. Now that you're really dying.

I can't recall how old I was when I stopped missing you.

I report the news to my doctor: in my medical record, under family history, we'll need to make an amendment.

What do you want to be when you grow up?

What do you want to be when you grow up?

I don't know, you?

I'm still deciding.

I need to choose a high school. Time is slipping away — pre-enrolment has already opened. I spend hours browsing the guide they gave us, which lists every high school in Milan. Who are you? What do you want to be? I can go wherever I want. Liceo classico, liceo linguistico. Gastronomy and hospitality school. Technical college. At home, nobody understands the difference anyway.

No one in my family has studied past middle school. If I decided to quit school and find a job, they wouldn't mind.

In the end I copy Giacomo and Ettore, my classmates at Milano 3, and decide to follow them to Liceo Scientifico Italo Calvino, in Rozzano. Even though I hate mathematics. I hate anything that can only be done one way. Right or wrong — follow the rules.

I considered music school (opera singer? no, songwriter) but I was terrified of the idea of ending up in a class full of strangers. Again.

I don't want to be alone anymore.

At home, everything is changing. Everything has changed.

★

Towards the end of my final year at middle school, my mother meets Alex. They work together. He's the delicatessen supervisor at the supermarket where she works as a cashier. He's recently separated and has a three-year-old son, Omar. His colleagues say he has a horrible temperament and is impossible to work with. He argues with everyone about everything — it's best to say nothing, to let things go. Quiff, leather boots and jacket, solarium two or three times a week. James Dean, Bon Jovi, George Michael, Miguel Bosé. Alex is cool, a Latin Lover. He could have any woman he wanted. And he's chosen my mother, Concetta De Rosa. The woman who trusts no one, who always keeps her distance, who uses the formal register with all her colleagues. The one who heads straight home after work, and has no problem putting you in your place if you cross the line.

Alex and mamma start dating. *Are you jealous?* No, I like him. Early on, I often go out with the two of them. Park, bowling alley, excursions to the mountains. I'm a central part of their courtship. Evenings, weekends, holidays. Alex seduces me, too. He buys me gifts, takes me to the cinema, drives me around in his petrol-green Alfa Romeo, plays basketball with me — I don't like basketball, but I still enjoy the attention. I hold his hand when we walk down the street together.

Zia Tata jokes about it with mamma: who's the girlfriend, you or Jonathan?

I know, mamma replies. He adores him.

Mamma has broken up with Tino (for Alex?), but Tino refuses to give up. He keeps calling, begging her to take him back.

Tina, please. Don't those five years mean anything to you?

One night he takes a gamble: he turns up at our house.

He stands out the front of 10 Hyacinth Street and buzzes the intercom. He doesn't know we're not alone — he doesn't know Alex is with us.

Mamma picks up the intercom phone.

I'm not coming down. I have nothing to say to you. Please go away.

He buzzes again.

Alex springs into action. He opens the door and flies down the stairs (quite literally — he barely touches the steps), sending the metal balustrade quivering.

We hear a shout, then another.

I start trembling, the way I always do when something bad is happening.

Alex returns, his chest enormous, swollen. He's puffing, as if he's just finished an intense work-out.

That arsehole won't be breaking your balls again anytime soon.

What did you do to him?

Headbutted him, broke his nose.

Tino is a loser, he doesn't know how to fight.

Is that why you left him, mamma?

Alex loses control easily. The incident with Tino is the first time I see it happen, but it won't be the last.

When he gets angry Alex punches the wall, breaks down doors, bashes his fists against the table. One time, when he and mamma are fighting, he breaks the bones in his hand against the white bathroom tiles. Another time he breaks the glass in one of the doors and has to get stitches. He also beats Pongo, the Shar Pei mamma and Tino bought together. I have to look away when poor Pongo is being kicked, yelping in pain at the random thrashings that have replaced Tino's careful treatment of his dermatitis and respiratory problems.

He's a delicate dog, the veterinarian used to say.

Sweet, good. A big couch potato.

Like Tino?

It's best if we give him away before something happens. Mamma always finds a way to fix things — stress is her great motivator. One rainy afternoon, Pongo disappears without much explanation.

We took him to a place.

Did they just abandon him somewhere?

Pongo disappears. Lulù, the white Persian cat we'd had for years, disappears.

Our house is Alex's house now.

Alex fights over his son with his ex-wife, Deborah, a Jehovah's Witness who lives near Pavia in one of those tiny villages with no amenities, completely isolated from the rest of the world. They argue for hours on the phone over money, over child support, over when Alex can or cannot, must or must not go and pick up his son. When things escalate, Alex calls her every name under the sun. He sits in the kitchen holding the banana-shaped phone to his ear. Sometimes mamma and I are right there in the same room, listening.

Bitch! Cow! Have you forgotten how I used to pound you like a fucking farmyard animal? Have you forgotten the time you almost lost the baby because I fucked you so hard?

He screams into the receiver, flings it across the room, storms out and slams the door.

He also walks out during his fights with mamma.

He leaves and stays out all day, or all evening. Why?

What would happen if he stayed?

It's not always like that, though. Alex isn't always a ball of rage. Sometimes he's as weak as a kitten. He faints a lot. He has an extremely low pain threshold, he says. He can't even handle getting a tattoo. He's tried more than once, but as soon as the tattooist touches his skin with the needle, he passes out. Is cocaine the reason he's like this? Neurological damage, acquired brain injury? He's off cocaine now, though. It was a phase, just a phase.

Detox made me go mad, he says.

And what are you now?

As the months pass, Alex and I don't get along the way we did at the beginning. Now that he's won us over — won *me* over — there's no more need for flattery, gifts, drives in the car. The moment he moves in with us, everything changes. Alex expands, takes up space. He fills Tino's cupboard with all his stuff. The energy he put into impressing us is diverted into occupying our home, taking possession of its rooms, its rhythms, its rituals.

Nonna Lidia hates Alex, but she can't tell mamma that. She knows how her daughter would react. So she tells me, instead. Of all the men she could have, nonna says to me in secret, your mother always winds up choosing the worst one possible.

Scart' frusc' e ppiglie primmer'.

Ha scartat', ha scartat' e fernut' rint' 'o scart'.

Mamma searches high and low for Mr Right (I imagine her as a character in a fairy tale, walking in the woods at night, lantern in hand, looking for tiny miniature men hiding in bushes and weeds and burrows) but she always ends up with the same man. Bad mannered, easily provoked. A man who replaces the sadness inside her with a little bit of fear.

Fear for your life?

Because this isn't just a story, mamma. We actually have to live with this person.

I've just started high school when mamma calls me into her bedroom. She's been acting strange for a few days. She doesn't feel well. Half-reclined in bed, her back supported by a pile of cushions, dressing-gown wrapped around her.

Johnny, I have to tell you something.

What?

I'm pregnant.

Mamma made the same mistake she made thirteen years ago. She messed up her contraceptive. Two unplanned babies.

Despite everything, at least I've had mamma to myself until now. Over the last few months, we've even started creating new rituals together. We've been taking walks around Rozzano, and buying gelato at Ottocento, the café next to the Fellini cinema. Two chocolate affogatos — mother and son have the same taste. All that is over now.

If my mother has another child, I'll be worth nothing.

No more chocolate affogatos. Do you have any idea how demanding a newborn baby is? Please, mamma, don't do this to me.

Nothing will change, I'll still love you just as much as before, she promises.

I can already see it in my mind's eye: my mother pushing the pram, glowing, majestic, maternal. Everyone stopping her in the street to congratulate her.

I don't want you to have a baby. Please, mamma, you have to get an abortion.

How many weeks? Is there still time?

Alex said: it's your decision.

The woman decides.

And she's decided to keep it.

I can already feel you, my love. You'll be the one to give me strength.

Again, mamma decides to keep the baby. Just as she did thirteen years ago. With me, the son now burning with resentment over all the things she never lets me do, over the money we never have. Why did you have me? You should only have children when you're ready, I'll tell her — an implacable judge expounding a universal law. You should only have children if you're capable of raising them.

After all my sacrifices, this is the thanks I get.

After everything I've done for you.

Have I ever asked you for anything?

A new leaf, my mother thinks. A fresh start. This time, everything will be better.

A real family, with a mother and a father.

When she tells me she wants to keep the baby, I start crying. I turn to the window, looking out over the little parish soccer pitch and the number 15 tram terminus, and let out a wailing sob.

I can't stop crying.

My cheeks wet with tears.

I never should have trusted him.

We're ready

We're ready.

I'm finally starting treatment.

One tablet a day.

It won't have an immediate effect, the doctor said. It could take a few weeks.

More waiting.

In fact, the fever disappears after a few days. But then I fall ill again. For a while, immediately after my diagnosis, I felt like I was getting better. Now I'm back on high alert.

Yes, I have HIV. That's what the test results say. But HIV isn't what's making me unwell. I have something else; I know it, I can feel it. HIV isn't what caused the fever. Maybe I don't have HIV at all; maybe I've never had it, and the test results are wrong. Maybe they're lying. *False positive.* It happens. The doctors told me they verified my diagnosis with a second test, the western blot, but all I've seen is a result written on a piece of paper.

That's the only evidence I have.

Why should I trust it?

I'm physically weak, but that's not all. My memories are blurry. I forget things.

I can't remember song lyrics.

Walking home after going to the supermarket to buy cat food, I sing a Björk song to distract myself from the exhaustion. I can't remember how the chorus ends. I used to know the whole song by heart. I haven't forgotten it completely — just a couple of words. Five words, just five. Is that normal? I try with some other songs from my adolescence: Carmen Consoli, Cristina Donà, PJ Harvey, Alanis Morrissette, Madonna, more Björk. *Ah, so you listen to lesbian music* — the words of a guy I met when I was nineteen. I still remember most of the lyrics, but every now and then blanks appear. Or uncertainty. I'm not sure if that's how the verse actually ends. I haven't listened to these songs in so long. Maybe it's normal.

No, it's not normal. I'm losing my memory. HIV also attacks the brain, I've read. Or is that AIDS? Is the virus linked to dementia? Maybe fever was just the first alarm bell. Now the sickness is spreading, showing me what it's capable of.

Except it's not the virus. The virus has nothing to do with it. I'm fading away, but no one seems to notice. I'm shrinking, I have no appetite, I have to force myself to eat. Then, without even realising it, I start gaining weight. I grow fat, like a cow put out to pasture. I don't move anymore. The couch sags under the weight of my body, lying motionless for twelve hours a day. It's been months since I practised yoga. Last time I tried I had to stop after three sun salutations. My legs started to give way, the force of gravity pulling me to the ground, the irresistible call of the earth. Each movement felt like it might end in collapse.

I feel hollowed out by the thought that everything is about to end.

This is it. I'm going to fall over and never get up again.

I wait for a sign.

And it comes.

I head out to do some grocery shopping, and as I'm turning the corner onto Viale Piave something happens to my right leg.

It feels heavier. My hip is making an odd movement. My foot is meeting the earth strangely.

Am I limping?

My senses are amplified, fixated on my right leg and foot. I have to be prepared. It must be something neurological. If the blood tests didn't pick it up, it must be because the problem is in my brain. That's why I'm forgetting song lyrics. That's why my legs are failing me.

After two days, the sensations shift from my right leg to my right wrist and hand. Then my whole arm, all the way to the shoulder. I notice it when I'm holding something, when I lift my fork at the table, when I go to pick up the sugar bowl.

It feels like my arm is losing strength, becoming a dead weight.

Maybe I have multiple sclerosis, like Pavarotti's widow?

An imaginary illness, the unlicensed homeopathic doctor would say. The complaint of childish, capricious women. The body's way of seeking attention.

I go back online to look up my symptoms. I have to decide whether I'm ready to self-diagnose or whether I should wait. I imagine how it will feel to receive an official diagnosis, to begin to live with it. Maybe I'll end up in a wheelchair, in a tracksuit and slippers with a tartan blanket over my knees — which is at least better than being dead.

I keep searching. I have to prepare myself for what's coming.

Finally I find it. My worst-case scenario.

I stumble upon testimonials from people with ALS: amyotrophic lateral sclerosis. I read about how they discovered they had motor neurone disease, a devastating and incurable illness that progressively paralyses you within the space of a few years. I read the accounts of surviving family members: children recounting the suffering of their mothers or fathers, wives reliving the moment they noticed something wasn't right with their husbands.

My father passed away last year.

My mother fought until the very end.

I lost my brother. For the last three years of his life we barely left his bedside.

It always starts in the limbs — in an arm or a leg or a hand — and spreads from there.

This is it.

I have ALS. The disease that took Piergiorgio Welby and Stephen Hawking and Luca Coscioni. The neurodegenerative disorder that affects an unusual number of football players — some say it's caused by excessive physical exertion, others by supplements or doping. Could it have been all the yoga? My obsessive asana practice, pursued with all the dedication of a gymnast or a competitive athlete? Two, three hours a day, jumping forwards and backwards. *Sirsasana*, headstand: excessive pressure on the central nervous system. Did yoga betray me?

The disease generally manifests later in life — at sixty, seventy — but there are exceptions. And I find them. The internet is my accomplice. I read about people in their twenties and thirties afflicted with young-onset ALS. Interviews, fundraisers, public displays of solidarity.

How long do I have to live?

Two, maybe three years.

Some people last five or six.

I'll spend the last days of my life unable to move, prostrate, confined to my bed, although I'll still be able to read and write.

These days they have sophisticated machines that allow you to communicate through eye movements — would they be covered by insurance? If they're too expensive, I'll crowdfund. I check the prices online. I research the disability pension, and home-care options. I imagine hearing my voice through the speech synthesiser, which will repeat the words I compose using eye-tracking technology, one letter at a time. I watch videos of people with the disease; I read their stories. I listen to their appeals for institutions to do more, to better help them and the people who care for them. I do all this in secret, clearing my browsing history at the end of each day. Marius mustn't find out what awaits us — that he's destined to wipe my drooling mouth and weepy eyes, that he'll need a suction machine to remove the saliva and mucus from my mouth so I don't suffocate.

Should we move to Rozzano?

We'll have to. We'll never manage here, on our own.

They'll set up a special bed for me at my mother's place, with all my equipment. In the lounge room, maybe, which is the biggest room in the apartment. Everyone will take turns looking after me: mamma, Marius, my sister, my nonna. At some point I'll need twenty-four-hour care.

Marius might stay here in Milan. There's not enough room at my mother's apartment. Or maybe he'll rent a room in a share-house, to save money. Then, a thought like a flash of pain: what will happen to Blueberry and Mashed Potatoes? My mother has two little dogs, Sissi and Raya. I won't be able to take the cats with me. Will they live with Marius, in the Milan share-house? Will I only get to see them in photos, or on FaceTime calls?

In the end-phase of the disease (I have to think ahead, I have to consider everything), I'll need a ventilator to help me breathe.

Many people refuse the ventilator; they'd rather just die. They're tired of the humiliation, the pain, the disturbance, the constant invasion of their bodies. I've decided I won't refuse the ventilator. As long as I can still read. And write. Not novels, of course. But poetry, short stories. Even if it's just a few sentences a day. I'm not a prolific writer, anyway. I tend to work sporadically, in fits and starts. As for reading, I can listen to audiobooks. Sure, I won't be able to move, but I've always lived more in my mind than out in the world. I feel like if anyone can bear paralysis, I can.

I won't suffer as badly as some.

I carry out tests to keep tabs on the disease's progress. Most people don't discover they have ALS until they can no longer button up their shirts, or tie their shoelaces, or turn a key in a lock. I start repeating these revelatory movements every day, constantly. Little diagnostic rituals. These actions will reveal the truth to me. They will confirm my doubts. Although, if I'm honest, my doubts have already hardened into facts, into grim reality. I stand in front of the mirror in our bedroom, or in the bathroom, and perform the Mingazzini test to check for muscle paresis.

Eyes closed, feet planted firmly on the ground. I hold my arms out in front of me.

Thirty seconds later, I open my eyes.

Is my right arm lower than my left?

Not yet.

I'm still in the early stages of the disease.

I try with my palms facing up, then down. I try every possible variation, to see if anything changes. More tests, more exercises. I'm never satisfied. Some I find on the internet, others I just make up. I tap the fingers of my right hand together to check my coordination.

Thumb and index finger, thumb and middle finger, thumb and ring finger, thumb and little finger.

One night Marius and I go to the Chinese restaurant in the street next to ours, and the whole time all I can think about is whether or not I'll be able to use the chopsticks. The chopsticks will be my litmus test: if I can't use them properly, it must mean something is really wrong. It must mean the disease has started spreading through my nervous system.

I pick up the chopsticks and try lifting a piece of tofu.

I can do it, but the strange feeling in my hand, wrist, and arm is still there.

I have to lean my elbow on the table to bear the weight of my arm. I'm afraid I'll collapse, fall in a heap, paralysed.

I don't say anything to Marius. I just tell him I'm tired, always tired. He acts like nothing's wrong — he almost never worries about what lies ahead. He takes things as they come, follows the most linear path. He avoids complications and conspiracies.

You've got HIV; you get treatment; you get better.

End of story.

Problem solved.

Simple. Direct. Obtuse? Ruthless?

This is why he can't see what's happening to me. This is why he's still with me, despite the fact that I'm a disgusting blob. I shower once every three days, at best. I never change out of my pyjamas. My muscles are covered in fat. If it were up to him, we'd still be doing things the way we did before. We'd still be taking turns washing the dishes — one of us at lunchtime, the other after dinner — even though I can barely stay on my feet. Somehow, I still manage to cook dinner every night. It feels like an endurance test.

It's nice that he doesn't treat you like an invalid, someone says to me.

But I *am* an invalid.

I can't do anything.

Every morning when my alarm goes off I feel scared — scared to look at Marius, to speak to him, to hear his voice. I'm scared the mask will slip, scared I won't be able to fake it anymore. As usual, Marius will ask me to make him coffee. He asks me from bed, without even getting up. He only comes downstairs when the coffee is ready. It's a kind of ritual we have. Sometimes I find it sweet, other times asphyxiating.

I want to keep making him coffee, but it's starting to feel beyond me. I keep making it, pouring the water and sugar as quickly as possible so I can go straight back to bed, and huddle under the covers with the cats, and sink my head into the pillow. I talk about it with Eugenia, a yoga-teacher friend, over the phone *(I'm sorry, are you saying he can't make his own coffee?)* and as I do my voice contorts, my throat anticipating tears.

No, I want to keep doing it.

As long as I can still make him coffee, it isn't over.

Eugenia goes quiet. She's not used to hearing me like this. I've lost all sense of tact and decency.

Well, keep me posted, she says.

She hangs up.

She's embarrassed.

Did I scare her?

Now that the figure-ground relationship has fallen apart, fear has colonised everything. I'm inured to it.

Either I'll survive this or I won't. I might have a month left, or a year.

Either way, I have to keep moving forward as best I can.

Occasionally I feel like crying, so I do. I cry in the bathroom, in the street, on public transport. I don't care if people see me. I cry thinking about Marius, about what I'm doing to him, the pain I'm about to cause him. I cry thinking about the cats — no one will look after them as well as I do. I cry thinking about the days when I was free to waste my time figuring things out, experimenting, starting something and then abandoning it two days later, or an hour later, as though life were eternal. I cry at the idea that there's no way out, that I'm losing control of my mind and body. I cry, but crying doesn't make me feel any better; it's not liberating. My anguish is a gigantic insect vomiting its viscous bile. It envelops everything: my head, my mouth, my breath, my footsteps, my hope of making it to summer, of still being alive at the end of the year. It engulfs everything, swallows me. It comes in waves. As it ebbs I try to re-emerge, but every movement pulls me deeper underwater.

I make one last attempt. I write to my doctor at Sacco.

Hi, all good with the treatment, no side effects, but I'm still feeling unwell. It feels like I'm getting worse every day.

An hour later, he replies.

Your latest test result looks good; you're just a little low in vitamin D, which is very common in patients with HIV. So we can rule out organic causes. Your symptoms suggest you might be experiencing an anxious-depressive state, in which case psychological (or possibly psychiatric) support might be useful to help you overcome this phase.

He doesn't believe me.

He thinks I'm paranoid because of the diagnosis. But he's wrong. I've accepted the diagnosis. I've got HIV, but that's not a problem. If I weren't so unwell, I'd prove it.

But I'm an unreliable witness. What I say doesn't count for anything. Everyone projects their terror onto me. They interpret everything I do through the lens of their own fear.

You have HIV — you must be devastated.

You have HIV — no wonder you're not lucid.

I change tack.

I text my original doctor.

I want to have some tests done.

Different tests, new tests, further tests. Whatever I can get.

I want all of them.

Once they discovered I had HIV, the tests stopped. That was the end of it.

They were satisfied.

After all, one person can't have every illness in the world.

I quit

I quit liceo scientifico after four months.

September, October, November, December.

I drop out in January.

My Italian teacher convenes a meeting with my mother and tells her that, if I continue the way I'm going, she's sorry, but I'm going to have to repeat the year. I've failed every exam so far, written and oral.

But why? You've never struggled at school.

I don't know.

I don't understand.

I don't want to tell you.

I've stopped studying; I don't even open my textbooks. Books, study, everything to do with school is a reminder for me now. *Remember: you can't speak.* Letters, syllables, whole sentences I can't pronounce. My voice stuck in my throat. The laughter, the shame.

But in October, my sister, Tecla, was born.

And I fell in love.

She's small, tiny. Tegola, Tegolina, little bean, baby nose. I rename her — words are my way of appropriating things. I plant a forest of new names around the things I want to save. All day and all night, I help my mother look after my sister (half-sister? no, sister). I change her, apply Fissan moisturising cream, bathe her, put her little socks on, clear her nostrils

233

with saline drops, mix powdered milk, semolina, creamed rice, puréed meat, fish, fruit.

Is there something greater than love?

Devotion?

Her scent, her hands, she must want for nothing. Precious things are to be protected. Little pink and yellow rompers, the fanciest bottles and dummies. Towards the end of my mother's pregnancy, I was already buying things for the baby. I used — I still use — nonna's pocket money to expand my sister's wardrobe, to buy her special treats, and toys, and books for me to read to her or for her to read on her own when she gets older. I go to Fiordaliso and spend two or three hours in Chicco, the baby store, then roam the aisles of the hypermarket. If I can't afford what I want, I steal it. I learnt how to do it properly watching nonna and zia Tata. I'm not afraid of being arrested. I just have to be aware of my surroundings, and be on the lookout for plain-clothes security guards. Often they're very well hidden, posing as customers. Some of them are even women.

A newborn baby inevitably becomes the priority, sweeping everything else away. The rest can be sorted out later, or forgotten about.

Tecla's arrival is a distraction. And while we're distracted, I drop out of liceo scientifico.

To avoid having to repeat the year, I enrol in a different school: Liceo Artistico Hayez. My father takes me to school on the first day of second term, a February morning.

First three hours: drawing from life.

Subject: flowering sweet potato in a jar.

Mine turns out horribly. I feel like shit. The others have been drawing for months; they know how to manage proportions, lines, chiaroscuro. Take note for next time, the teacher tells me. But I can't shake the desire to run away, the sensation that I'm in the wrong place. It's not over yet. The next two hours are P.E. We're divided into boys and girls. Then we're grouped with all the other boys in the school — not just all of ninth grade, but also tenth, eleventh, twelfth. Am I supposed to play soccer and basketball against eighteen-year-olds?

No chance in hell.

Excuse me, prof, I don't feel well.

I make my father come and pick me up.

I may not be strong, but at least I can save myself from suffering. Even the smallest animals have their tactics in the fight for survival.

My first and last day at liceo artistico.

I drop out.

No, mamma, I don't want to go. I don't want to go to school anymore. I don't want to speak in front of people, read in front of people, expose myself, endure the fear and anxiety every morning. I've tried as hard as I can. Now my persistence has given way to obstinate refusal.

Never again.

What are you going to do, then?

I want to go to a vocational school. No words, no theory. I love studying, but it doesn't matter; I can survive without it. I'll give up books if it means the world stops demanding I recite words in front of other people. I've decided it's more important to feel safe than fulfilled. I need a school where I can be silent.

What am I? What do I want to be? I'll be whatever I can be. I'll pretend it's not an enormous sacrifice, a surrender. I browse the internet for ideas, searching, seeking.

This year's a write-off, mamma. I might as well take my time thinking about what I want to do.

Alright. Just make sure you choose something.

I could be a tattoo artist, a makeup artist, a beautician. Mamma is almost happy: something concrete, something she understands. Can you tattoo me? Wax my legs? Do my makeup?

But we can't afford it. I'd have to go to a private college.

A bolt of inspiration: an ad in the Yellow Pages. There's an esoteric college in Rozzano. In Rozzano — really? White and black magic, love spells, divination.

Mamma, can I go here?

How much is it?

Five million lire a year.

Are you out of your mind?

For months now I've been obsessed with the Tarot. I came across a little book on the Major Arcana in the bookshop at Fiordaliso, and I've been hooked ever since. In class, instead of studying for my exams and assignments, I studied cartomancy, astrology, telepathy, palmistry, pyromancy. I read the books of Rosemary Altea, the English medium who went on Mauricio Costanzo's show and could see all the audience members' dead relatives.

In the mornings and evenings — sometimes even late at night, until one or two in the morning — I watch the psychics on local tv. The ones with pay-per-call hotlines, reserved for people eighteen years and over. I start buying Tarot decks, both classic and modern. I order them online, too embarrassed to go into a shop. Who knows what kind of people frequent places like that? Runes, Tarot, the Sibyls Oraculum, the I Ching, the Book of Changes. I sit in the kitchen, at the table draped in the waxed linen tablecloth with the strawberry print (the tablecloth spoils the atmosphere, so I remove it), and hold consultations with imaginary clients. I take notes as they tell me about their problems.

Miriam 43 y/o Sagittarius, wants her ex back.

Luigi 53 y/o Taurus, asking about work situation of daughter Valeria 24 y/o Virgo.

I shuffle the cards — it feels so good to hold them in my hands, my mind absorbed by the task, everything else melting away — then lay them out. The three-card spread, the Celtic Cross. Past, present, future. Querent, quintessence card, synthesis card. I talk to myself, explaining, expounding. I interpret the spread and give the most balanced reading I can. I don't want to raise any false hopes. I'm sincere. Professional.

The High Priestess. The Emperor. The Tower. Judgement. I scrutinise the illustrations on the plasticised rectangles of card for the answers my clients are seeking.

No, I don't discuss health problems. You can go to the doctor for that.

Signora, please ask a more specific question.

The cards can only answer if they're asked correctly.

My mother thinks I'm going out of my mind. When nonna Lidia comes over to help with my sister, mamma tells her how I spend all day in front of the tv with my Tarot cards. As soon as mamma goes into another room, nonna asks me whether I think she should play two or three numbers on the lotto this week. Alex is the same — he asks me to analyse his dreams using the *Smorfia Napoletana*, a book that helps convert the language of dreams into winning lotto numbers.

I learn the names of all the tv psychics. All stage names, naturally: Stella, Sibyl, Cleo. One of them lives in Rozzano; mamma says she used to be a 'lady of the night'. I learn the different ways they read the spreads, what kinds of cards they use, where they work, how much they charge. I keep accumulating Tarot decks until I have a whole shoebox full. I get them mailed to me from a shop in San Marino — it has the biggest range in the country, the newest stock. Tarot of Marseille: 35,000 lire. La Vera Sibilla: 15,000 lire. Osho Zen Tarot, 32,000 lire. How many decks is too many?

I don't have enough money — what will I do when the mail arrives?

I think about it all day. I'm thinking about it right now, today, Sunday, even though I have to go to nonna Nuccia's for lunch. All my relatives will be there. Papà will be there. I haven't seen him in a long time. Six months? A little less.

I don't know how, but we wind up talking about mamma.

The usual accusations. I defend her, I get worked up.

Your mother is always so angry with Robby. Why? What has she ever done for you? She's always going on about child support, but how does she actually spend all that money your father sends her? I doubt she spends it all on you.

I don't know. Maybe they're right.

But mamma is mamma.

As a systems-and-family therapist will put it to me in twenty years' time: we all need something to cling to.

I go home. Two of mamma's friends are over for dinner. I don't feel well.

I'm not hungry, mamma.

Go and lie down for a bit.

When I get into my mother's bed — she's still using the quilt cover she and Tino bought — I start trembling. Like the shivers you get when you have a fever. But worse.

Mamma, can you come here for a minute?

I'm shaking. Am I having a fit? The bed dances with me. I'm all convulsion, all tremor. My mother picks up the phone and calls my father: Roberto, Jonathan is sick. Come, we're taking him to the hospital.

I was sleeping, says papà.

I have the morning shift tomorrow. I can't, sorry.

Mamma and I go without him, accompanied by mamma's friends.

I talk nonstop in the car.

About what? About everything. I don't remember.

Keep him talking, let him vent.

In the emergency room, with the tranquilising drip inserted into my arm, mamma tells me she'll pay for the Tarot cards that are on their way from San Marino.

Really? The whole 60,000 lire?

Yes.

Just relax now.

A pilgrimage

A pilgrimage, from hospital to hospital.

A procession without worshippers.

Not just on foot: public transport is allowed.

No villagers watching on, no children holding my hands in adoration. I go alone, at the beginning of spring, carrying my little plastic folder of referrals. Prescriptions, decision numbers. Pink pathology exemption card. Expiry? Unlimited, unfortunately, says the employee at the local health department on Viale Doria as he hands it back to me.

I've asked my doctor for every test I can think of. I have to rule out every single illness I've read about on the internet, one by one. This is my one mission, my one job. I'm desperate for another diagnosis. Please, let them find something. A lump, a blemish, an enlarged lymph node. Treat me, cure me, steep my body in drugs. Abdominal ultrasound, chest x-ray, MRI of the head: each test has its own set of rules to memorise.

Twelve-hour fast.

For this one you can just fast the morning of.

Any allergies?

Here's how you should prepare.

I convince Marius to come with me to Gaetano Pini Hospital for my neurological exam. I couldn't get an appointment anywhere else. The hospital is in Crocetta, opposite the little park dedicated to Oriana Fallaci. Marius is sceptical about all these extra tests, but I won't stop.

I'm unstoppable.

The usual process: waiting, reception, more waiting.

We're taken into a room on the ground floor. I give the neurologist my reasons for being there. I tell her about the weakness in my arm and hand. I tell her I have HIV, and immediately regret it. The moment I pronounce those three letters, her attention begins to wane. She stops looking. Like everyone else, she's already convinced the virus must be the cause.

The neurologist proceeds with the usual basic tests.

Reflexes. Strength.

Squeeze here. Follow my finger with your eyes.

Everything looks fine.

Nothing's wrong.

She cuts the appointment short.

Sits back down at her desk, prints a document dismissing my symptoms.

I ask her if there are any other tests we can do, to look deeper.

No, no. We're done. I've got a queue of patients waiting outside.

Next.

I can't help myself. If she won't say it, I will.

I'm worried it could be ALS, I tell her. Or a brain tumour. I fill the room with my self-diagnoses.

She snorts. She laughs in my face.

She gets up, walks me to the door.

Is it really nothing? But I can't even make it all the way back down the corridor. I have to stop, lean on Marius, rest every few steps. Is it really nothing? But my right arm is dying; I have to keep it hidden all day so I don't think about it, so I don't notice how different it feels. I need more tests. This illness is very good at concealing itself.

Eugenia gives me the number of a doctor friend who is both an infectious-disease specialist and an HIV activist.

His name is Massimo. Get in touch, ask him what he thinks.

I arrange to meet him at the hospital. Not for an appointment, *just a chat.* I describe my symptoms to him. He tries to play them down, he makes jokes. I insist. I hear the words coming out of my mouth, in front of this total stranger: I don't know what else to do. He replies: many diseases can't be detected in their early stages. Your general fatigue could mean nothing or it could mean everything. If the tests haven't found anything, then that's it. At least for now.

At least for now.

So I have to wait for a coup de grâce: a seizure, a blackout. The incontrovertible evidence everyone needs before they'll believe me. Marius included.

I spend the last of my savings on a private neurologist. I want a second opinion. The doctor is young. He says we can rule out ALS, because of my age. If anything, it could be multiple sclerosis, although that's also unlikely. Still, he doesn't dismiss me entirely. See? I'm not crazy.

He'd recommend an MRI, just to make sure.

Mainly because I'm HIV-positive.

Should I get a third opinion?

I write to the Centre of Neuromuscular Pathology.

Good evening, is it possible to make an appointment at your facility before receiving a definite diagnosis?

I'm sorry, I'm not sure what you mean. Please call the hotline.

I need a doctor who can see past my HIV diagnosis, someone

who isn't immediately duped by the virus.

What I don't realise is that this is how it will always be from now on. Any complaint I have, however minor — common cold, chest pain, dermatitis — will be viewed through the lens of my diagnosis. Every time I visit a doctor's clinic, or a hospital, or a specialist, the moment I say I have HIV, everything changes. The virus creates an aura of fear and respect around me. It demands caution, scrupulousness. It puts everyone on high alert. But none of it is about me. HIV is the star, the main event. They can't see past it. The best I can do is take advantage of their fear, and use it to get what I want.

Right now, what I want are more tests. But I want those tests to find something other than HIV.

Test upon test upon test. I continue my tour of Milan's medical clinics, even when it feels like my legs can no longer hold me up. Even after every last inch of my body has been mapped and inspected and converted into parameters. All that's left now is my brain. I want them to look inside my skull.

I text my doctor again.

Hi, are you able to request that I be hospitalised?

He doesn't answer immediately.

Ten minutes later he writes: Oh god. Call me.

He suggests I visit him so he can give me a referral for an MRI.

I go alone, no one comes with me. This is a showdown between me and my illness. My secret, private illness, invisible only because it's being masked by that other, all-too-public illness.

There are no available MRI appointments anywhere. My doctor marks the request as urgent, but even so, there's no guarantee I'll get in anytime soon. The only way, one receptionist advises me, might be to simply turn up at the hospital with your referral. They always keep a few spots free for emergencies.

The following morning, at seven, I drag myself out of bed to find a hospital that will take me. I try the Besta Institute, the Policlinico, the Igea health clinic on Via Marcona. One foot after the other, one step at a time. Surrounded by herds of students on their way to university. The weather is cold and misty. I feel like I might collapse at any moment. But no: I'm tougher than I'd like to be. That's always been my problem. I'm superficial, disconnected, foolish. My skin is iridescent. When my feelings manifest they are muffled, attenuated, as though they've been passed through a filter.

That's why you don't believe me. That's why no one takes me seriously.

In the small clinic where they finally agree to give me an MRI, I wait outside the examination room, opposite the nurses' desk.

A family is waiting next to me.

Family is important; families are there to support one another.

A couple with their twenty-something daughter. The mother is the one getting the scan. She looks about fifty, maybe younger. She has trouble walking; I don't think they'll be able to fix her. The daughter has to help her up. While the mother is inside, being immersed in the scanner's magnetic field, the daughter pulls out a textbook and starts studying. She underlines words in yellow highlighter. How can she concentrate in here?

How can she study for exams while her mother is dying?

I place my coat and backpack in the locker (*deposit all metallic objects*) as though I'm entering a museum. When it's time for me to go in, the two nurses — both kind, older women — ask me to change into a paper smock.

Take everything off and put this on.

They ask me to lie down on the bed that will soon disappear into the mechanical tunnel. They offer me headphones to help dull the sound of the magnets, then activate the automatic mechanism that will draw me into the machine's white orifice. They leave the room and I'm alone. A needle in my arm delivers contrast dye into my bloodstream.

Nonna Nuccia also had an MRI once. Years ago. I was only little at the time. She told me she felt unwell during it, and had to ask to be taken out of the tube. They had to take a break before resuming. I'm scared the same thing will happen to me. I'm scared I'll start to feel claustrophobic inside this tiny suffocating grotto. Trapped, unable to move. I'm scared the tattoo on my neck — a yud, my initial in Hebrew — will catch fire. The smallest letter of the alphabet, suspended in the air like an apostrophe; the fundamental building block of Creation. I heard tattoos can cause problems in MRI machines. Will my skin blister? Will I burst into flames? Is this the dress rehearsal for my cremation?

I close my eyes and allow the fear to flow over me, an evanescent river, independent now from its source.

I get used to the noise, the sounds.

Banging metal, gentle whistles.

I fall into a half sleep.

There's no discomfort I won't bear. But for what?

You're going through all this to give a name to what's consuming you, when you could simply wait and see. Let everything be revealed in the fullness of time.

Mamma defies him

Mamma defies him, provokes him.

This isn't the first time.

You know what he's like. Why don't you leave him alone?

Alex and my mother fight often, but tonight words aren't enough. Insults become screams, then smashed crockery. His hand raised to strike, hers to protect. Alex has lost control, like a dam bursting its banks — although maybe the banks were just an illusion.

They fight often, but tonight he wants to kill her.

It starts after dinner. My mother's boyfriend lifts the table with his hand and threatens to flip it over, dishes and all. Then, in the corridor, he lifts Tecla's pram in the air and slams it down. Once, twice, how many times? With all his manly force. The man of the house. He grabs mamma by the hair and throws her down as if she were a ragdoll, as if she were senseless flesh. I stand, frozen, as my mother's body becomes a shapeless mass, an object on which to unleash some external fury, some frustration that has nothing to do with her, that can't possibly have anything to do with her. How long does it go on? How many seconds?

All I can do is run away, find help.

I open the front door and let mamma's screams fill the stairwell.

The cries my mother makes as she's beaten, battered by the man she loves. Why? Because he can. I open the door and free her screams. I let them rise all the way up to the eighth floor. Listen! Listen, everyone! You all have to hear this son of a bitch kill my mother.

At least they'll know the truth — some small justice.

Make noise, get help, go outside. Someone somewhere will hear you. That's the rule I was taught, although I'm not sure when, or by whom.

He hasn't killed her.

Mamma gets up.

Alex retreats to the bedroom, slams the door. He slams it so hard it bounces back open. He slams it again, closing it this time.

What now?

Mamma is coming towards me. We're leaving; she's carrying the tuft of hair Alex ripped out of her head. She touches the bald spot, the little patch of white skin behind her ear.

Hair grows back. What's important is that it's over.

He's stopped.

Mamma picks up Tecla, who is crying — what did she see? what will she remember? — and the three of us go to our neighbour's apartment. Massimo, forty years old, one of the three children of the couple that lived here when I was living with my grandparents.

Close the door, close the door.

Tina, what the fuck happened?

Tina, you have to leave him.

Obviously, clearly, mamma will leave him. She can't possibly accept something like this.

He's an animal. An animal.

Carabinieri, police.

Zio Franco arrives.

Alex leaves. He goes to his mother's house.

Report him, mamma, you have to report him. Now, not later, when the memory of what happened has slipped into the swamp of the mind, the place where nightmares are kept, along with all those other things we forget in order to keep living.

A day passes. Two.

Alex texts. Alex calls.

He asks for forgiveness. *Give me another chance.*

Mamma, if he comes back I'm leaving.

I don't want to raise another child without a father, she says. I promised things would be different with your sister. Not like they were with you. Better, a better life.

Mamma, if he comes back I'm going away.

Where will you go?

Away.

Somewhere.

I'll move in with papà.

Three, five days max. Then I'll be back in Rozzano. My father is not a father; I can't live with him. My father was meant to be alone. I could go to my grandparents' house. With nonno Biagio. No, I can't. I don't want to. I have nowhere to go. I have to stay here. In Hyacinth Street.

Alex again. Alex returns.

They get back together.

It's confirmed: I count for nothing.

Alex moves back in. I have no say in the matter — it's my mother's house, not mine. But I can protest. A vow of silence. This is my condition, my decision. Mine and mine alone.

No communication.

I establish a new system that will last for years. Three, maybe four, I can't remember now. The only weapon I have against Alex is my silence. Acting as if he doesn't exist. Denying him any kind of relationship. *As far as I'm concerned, you're not here.* Sins against my mother are the only sins that cannot be forgiven. My silence is a game designed to save our lives, to grant us the protection my mother can't provide.

Rule 1: Never be in the same room. We eat separately. Mamma calls one of us to the table, then the other.

Rule 2: Never speak a word to him, under any circumstances.

Rule 3: Never look him in the eye. Never look at him at all. When he comes home from work and I'm home alone, I unlock the front door and walk away without opening it. No greeting, no acknowledgment. Like being welcomed by a ghost.

Rule 4: Indirect contact only, via a third party. I am permitted to employ the service of spies. Sounds ridiculous? All these protocols do feel a little unnatural.

Rule 5: Everyone must know. The more people who know, the better. *You explain to them why I'm acting this way. You tell them what happened.*

My reaction is also a reprimand: as long as I'm here, as long as I refuse to speak to him, as long as my system remains in place, there's no starting over.

We will remember what happened.

Who you are. What you did to her.

I no longer exist

I no longer exist.

I sleep all day.

Fourteen, fifteen hours at a time.

Spring 2016: hibernation.

It's been twenty-four hours since I got my MRI results. All they detected was a slight compression of the cervical vertebrae.

What did I tell you? There's nothing wrong with you.

No suspicious shapes or shadows. No scleroses, no tumours.

It makes no difference, though. ALS doesn't show up in MRI images. There are other tests for that. I've found a new one: electromyography. It checks for neuromuscular abnormalities. I have the appointment in my diary, but when the day comes I'm unable to leave the house. *Asthenia* — more new words for my vocabulary. I'll stay here, confined to my home, until my body has deteriorated enough to be taken to hospital in an ambulance. If only they would listen to me. What do I have to do to make them see I'm terminally ill?

Thanks to HIV, I'm not just sick, I'm also a liar. I am a well of useless, endlessly repeated words.

How are you?

Not good.

The same.

Nothing new.

Why do you keep asking me?

Elena and Gian visit. Two friends who work nearby — in a museum, or a gallery, I don't remember. I can barely make my way to the intercom to buzz them in. I push the button and sink back into the couch, my sanctuary. I'm happy they've come, but I don't think they can tell. I can hardly speak. I respond to their questions without lifting my head from the cushion.

Would you like a tea?

They make me one. I force it down.

My body is impervious to comfort; it denies me any sense of relief. I let them make the tea to create the illusion there's something they can do to help, so they won't feel like they've come in vain. But the moment Elena and Gian leave, I'll fall straight back into a catatonic stupor. Right side, left side, blanket, cats, then back to sleep. Sleep is the only remedy I've devised to keep the fear at bay.

Because they're my friends, I make an effort. *Up, up, the least you can do is sit up for ten minutes.* When I'm with people I switch back on, my eyes reopen. The simulation begins. The gaze of others is a temporary tonic. It restores a thin layer of decency.

But the moment it lifts, I regress.

I'm free to collapse, to withdraw, to extinguish my senses.

Geminis are like that. We're comedians, swindlers. Our smiles conceal private worlds of pain. Our planets are Mercury and Pluto, named for the god of thieves and the god of the underworld. In tricking others, we trick ourselves a little, too.

Marilyn Monroe and I have similar birth charts. We're both Gemini/Leo rising.

We also have the same blood type.

You have to go to school

You have to go to school.

Either that or you start looking for a job.

You have to do something, my mother says, rocking my sister to sleep in the kitchen. We've just finished dinner. First, the three of them together — like a real family. Then me, my mother watching as I eat.

When is this going to stop? she tries asking now and then, referring to my hostility towards the father of my sister.

I don't know.

Never.

When I move out.

Months pass, and finally I decide. In September I'll enrol in a professional training course. Cosmetology. I'll become a hair stylist *(you're going to be an artist when you grow up)*. In the meantime: Tarot and online chat rooms. I shut myself indoors. The apartment becomes my world. I have no friends. I don't need friends, I'll tell my first psychotherapist. To be perfectly honest, I don't even know what friends are.

Then, at fifteen, my coming out.

Without planning to, without even thinking about it, I tell my mother I like boys. A fact I'll have to reaffirm at eighteen. Still? she'll reply. I thought it was just a phase. My mother says the most predictable things. Phrases she's heard on tv, in the street. The familiarity is reassuring.

I come out to my mother not because I feel the need to confide in her, or be accepted by her, but because I've met a guy on the internet and I need permission to go out with him.

Permission? Sadly, yes. I'm almost never allowed out on my own.

We're on our way home from the park, pushing Tecla in the pram, when I tell her. When I try to tell her.

It's tiring, constantly having to summon the courage, the strength, to ask her for anything. Any little thing.

I've been chatting with someone online.

Someone?

It's a boy.

Ah.

Were you expecting me to say that?

I've always had my suspicions, she says, making a face that summarises the years of Barbie dolls, nail polish, Polly Pockets, Disney princesses. But then I changed my mind, after you got into those calendars.

Not long ago I started collecting the free calendars that come with the men's magazines at the kiosk. Nude actresses, tv presenters, showgirls. I hang them up inside my wardrobe. Like a trucker, says mamma. Mamma doesn't want them on the walls: when people come over they shouldn't have to look at that stuff.

My obsession with the calendars doesn't mean I like women. I like photos of women in the same way I like illustrations of Sailor Moon or Sheena, Queen of the Jungle. I like things that attract attention.

Especially if they're feminine.

Nonno Pier gave me my first computer when I was thirteen, shortly before he died. A gigantic grey box. In theory it was meant for schoolwork, but in practice I use it to further my sentimental education. All online. All virtual. Emotionally speaking, I'm a digital native. I've never chatted anyone up in real life. To this day, I've only ever found boys on the internet.

I'd be the perfect subject for a study on the Millennial heart. First we fall in love, then we meet in person.

At fifteen, I'm convinced love is downloadable — all you have to do is find the right profile. I'm a classic sufferer of love-at-first-click syndrome.

At eighteen, I'll be much the same. And at twenty-five.

I remember the shock of entering a chat room for the first time. The realisation that there's actually someone on the other side. Another human being, right now, at this very moment. And I can talk to them. It takes me a few days to work up the courage to write anything. No meet-ups at first, just a series of infinite conversations, body and heart activating in synchrony. *So this is desire.* I spend four, five, eight hours a day in front of the computer.

What are you doing on there?

Reading, researching. I lie, improvise.

My early teens are spent not out in the world — where would I go? — but on the internet. I meet people from all over Italy. My preferred chat sites — Gayromeo, Me2, Gay.it — are like supermarkets, with catalogues full of boys to choose from. I set the criteria, and the search engine selects the profiles.

Age? Twenty-five plus.

Height? He can't be shorter than me.

Hair? Brown or light brown.

Eyes? Blue or green.

Build? Muscular, or at least athletic.

Size: L, XL, XXL.

The motive for my coming out is a thirty-five-year-old from Monza. A thin man with an enormous nose. A dancer. We send each other text messages constantly.

Where are you now? Have you finished? What about now? What are you doing? Let me know when you get home. Why didn't you reply? Were you with someone else?

Now he's asked me on a date. He wants to meet me.

The word *gay* isn't even mentioned the first time I come out to my mother. Neither of us dare to say it.

My mother doesn't get upset. She's used to rolling with the punches; she has a high disaster threshold. Only a major calamity sets her off. To be fair, I've never heard her make a homophobic remark. I can't say the same about my father. I'll never officially come out to him. He'll receive the news second-hand, from nonna Nuccia, more than ten years later.

My mother doesn't get upset, but she says no. No, you can't go out with a man you've never met before. A fifteen-year-old boy can't go out with a thirty-five-year-old man he met on the internet. Neither of us makes a scene. The conversation unfolds quietly.

When my mother says no, she means it. Her decisions are stone-hard, lapidary. No explanations are offered. None are required. For her, raising a child is about exercising power, affirming supremacy.

Why not?

Because I say so.

Years later, I'll learn the term *ethical voluntarism*. Things are good or bad not in and of themselves, but because my mother wills them so. My mother is the measure of all things. My mother is God. Tina's Ten Commandments.

As I continue to use the chat rooms, more and more people invite me to meet up. Men. Older men in their thirties and forties. Some even older. When I tell them I'm a virgin they grow insistent. They can't wait to get their hands on me. They send me licking lips emojis. *Mmm*, they write, *say no more*, or *turn your webcam on, let me see*. They describe in meticulous detail all the things they want to do to me, to this body of mine that has never touched another human being.

Who says I need my mother's permission?

I start planning secret rendezvous.

I grow more comfortable with the idea of actually doing it.

Of bridging the virtual/real divide.

My first meetings are purely external. Public places. Words only, no bodies.

All good things take time.

Even before these early meet-ups, I go on a date with one of the psychics from tv. I'm fifteen. His name is Magic Max. As well as reading Tarot and performing ancient Egyptian rituals, he has a number of side projects. He once designed a Tarot deck inspired by the symbology of water, and he's known for organising esoteric soirées at which he debuts his original musical compositions. He writes Enya-esque Celtic ballads and sings them through a synthesiser. He records them, too, and sells the CDs to his guests.

I like Magic Max, but I don't know if he's gay. I try to find out. I text him and ask him on a date.

He doesn't reply straight away. He doesn't trust me.

He responds the next day.

How old are you?

Sixteen. (I'm rounding up.)

Does your mother know?

Yes, of course.

A lie.

I haven't mentioned this to anyone.

We meet in Milan, in an unfamiliar piazza chosen by him. When he arrives, when I see him, I want to disappear into thin air. That's not the Magic Max I know. Is he an impersonator? Is this a set-up? This man is a five-foot-two ex-bodybuilder ravaged by age and gravity, wearing a skin-tight fluoro-yellow synthetic T-shirt. His skin reminds me of Alex's — overbaked by UV rays. Pencilled-in eyebrows, blue-tinged teeth, thin moustache attached to artificially filled lips. This is not the man I know from the television.

But it's him. The tv lights don't just illuminate him — they remake him.

Pleasure to meet you, you can call me Massimiliano.

I want to go home.

We get into his car. I'm disorientated, I don't recognise any of the streets. We cross a bridge, drive past some fields. Where are we going? Is he planning to hurt me?

Shall we get something to eat?

Oh god, do I really have to sit through a whole meal with this guy?

We arrive at our destination and he parks the car. It's a place he always comes to, he says. Some Italian restaurant. The staff eye us as we walk to a table at the very back. How many boys has he taken here?

As we're waiting to be served, he starts talking. He explains the local professional landscape, the secrets behind psychic hotlines, the history of his refusal to collaborate with disgraced tv personality Wanna Marchi (he turned down an offer to join

her team a long time ago, intuiting that something was amiss
— she was later arrested for selling fictitious cures against 'black
magic' to impressionable old ladies). He warns me about the
many charlatans in his line of work. He's different, though, he
hastens to add. He's a serious practitioner.

I smile and nod until the pizza is finished.

I eat quickly, big mouthfuls.

The empty plate is a sign: the meal is over.

We get up, he pays, and we leave the restaurant. We get back
in the car.

His hand on my knee, a quick squeeze. Is he testing the
waters?

I don't want things to drift in the wrong direction. I have to
get out of here.

I rummage through the canvas messenger bag sitting at my
feet. I pretend I've received a text message.

Oh! Can I ask you to drop me at Brera? A friend of mine is
leaving tomorrow, and I really have to see him before he goes.

I hope we can meet up again, says Magic Max.

I smile without lifting my eyes from the screen.

Traffic lights, a curve in the road. Is it okay if I let you out
here?

He's actually stopping.

I jump out of the car.

Via Fiori Chiari, Via Fiori Oscuri — Street of the Light
Flowers, Street of the Dark Flowers. I disappear among the
knots of drinking revellers.

Clouds of smoke, a wild swell of voices.

The cobblestones under my feet feel like freedom.

20 April

20 April.

Today is the last day of my life.

My third appointment with the infectious-disease specialist is scheduled for ten thirty, but I won't make it.

I can't go. I can't stand. I can't walk.

Marius is sleeping next to me. I curl closer to him to escape the cold and the fear. I'm trembling, my legs are spasming. Epileptic fit? If I roll myself into a ball maybe it will pass. I've slept so much over the past week, but my tiredness never goes away. How many hours can a human being sleep for? I'm cold but I'm sweating. For three months now I've been waking up in a sweat-soaked T-shirt.

20 April, 2016. My rock bottom. I don't have HIV. Or rather, I don't *just* have HIV. Or rather, HIV is not the real problem. This morning I have an appointment at Sacco, and I absolutely have to be there. But I can't.

Mamma, no, I'm not going.

What will you do, then?

She'll come and get me, she says.

When?

Soon, I'll leave right away.

Mamma is coming to take you to the doctor.

I set an alarm. I have to get up. But I can't. I hold Marius to absorb some of his strength.

How are you feeling?

Bad.

Poor *iuby*.

The word for love in Romanian is *iubire*.

Even getting up to go to the bathroom is a struggle. I have to lean against the wall. Come on, hurry up and piss. Piss and go back to bed. Most mornings I relocate from the bed to the couch, and lie there all day. Like a carcass, like a used rag, like a deflated balloon. I'd like to do that today. But I can't. I have to go to the hospital. Even if there's no point. I have HIV, I've started treatment, but I know something else is wrong with me. I know it, I can feel it. I've known it the whole time, but no one believes me.

The alarm goes off; it's 20 April, written on my calendar are the words *appointment Sacco*. My mother has made up her mind: I'm coming to get you, we'll go together. You, me, Marius.

As few steps as possible, please.

Marius says: let's take a share car.

They do everything, they make all the decisions. I don't even try to intervene. Do what you want. I'll do whatever you tell me to do. It's useless anyway. I know I'll be dead in a matter of days. But I'll humour you — it's an important appointment. I don't want to disappoint my doctor.

I'm still in bed. I roll first onto one side, then the other.

It's almost time.

My mother messages me on WhatsApp.

Leaving now.

I can't even look at my phone; I can't move my fingers to the screen. Everything is too heavy. Six hundred kilos of smartphone. My body is a lump of lead carried on an origami skeleton. I put the phone on the ground, on the floor, hoping it never rings again. I hope my mother gets lost on her way here. I hope she gets stuck somewhere and has to turn around, or changes her mind and never leaves Rozzano. I hope she never reaches our street.

But here she is: my phone buzzes again.

Almost there.

How did she get here so fast? Did she fly? Mamma speeding through the sky, her old powers restored. Mamma finally revealing herself for what she's always been: a fairy, a goddess, a wonder woman.

She made it here in a split second — or maybe I fell back to sleep.

I turn around. Marius is still sleeping.

I hold him again. What should I do? I ask his body, because I can't say it with words. For two or three seconds, as I hold the only person I've ever said *I love you* to, my mind goes blank. Two or three seconds of peace. Then it starts up again, worse than before. Let go. I have to let you go. Let myself die, let my eyes close forever, in spite of how much I love you. I have to leave you here for some other boy to love. Let you get your life back, let you live the life you should be living at twenty-three. I imagine Marius planning my funeral. Where will you bury me?

Milan or Rozzano?

I'd like to be buried in the Cimitero Monumentale.

But then how will mamma and nonna Lidia come to see you? Do you really want to make them drive an hour and a half every time? You can't do that to them. Think about other people for once in your life.

I detach myself from Marius and return to my side of the

bed. To my minimalist crucifix. No arms, just black IKEA sheets. Yesterday I emailed my original doctor and the doctor at Sacco. I'm in a bad way and I want to be hospitalised, I told them. I threatened them.

I'm calling an ambulance. I'm calling the police.

I'm going to the emergency room.

Look after me, you pieces of shit.

Help me die properly.

The doctor at Sacco has already decided it's my head that's the problem. Just my head. I'm stressed, depressed, mentally ill. He won't prescribe any more tests; he has no intention of looking for any more physical maladies. We know what's wrong with you; we found it and we're treating it. Today he wants me to speak with a psychiatrist. He doesn't get it at all. I'm at a dead end. These people want me to die thinking I'm insane. They want me to think I'm making everything up because I'm so traumatised by my diagnosis.

I turn over in bed again. The muscles in my legs are twitching.

Stop it, *iuby*.

As if I'm doing it on purpose.

I can't get up, but I have to because my phone is ringing.

My mother is here.

I just got off the Metro.

There's no more time, I have to get to my feet.

Marius gets up: come on, we're late.

I try to get dressed, but all my movements collapse into one another.

Iuby, can you dress me? It's too hard.

Iuby, where are you? I can't put my shoes on.

Marius is typing into his phone, trying to find the closest share car.

Got one.

Fifty metres from here.

Walking downstairs I see myself from a distance, from above. I am pure spirit: I have already left my mortal body. I didn't think I'd be able to go down the steps on my own. I'm not used to the feeling of my head moving in space. I'm not used to space.

My mother is waiting for us at the intersection, on the footpath near the tram tracks. Cropped blonde hair, enormous black glasses. She's become more androgynous with age. No more high heels. Activewear more often than not. She is both woman and man, both mother and father. She's always been stronger than her men, her partners, her husbands.

She's trembling. My mother is afraid, even though she pretends she's not. She's used to crises, to being deployed. In fact, she relies on them. They're her antidepressant. But this time it's different — she could lose me. *He's my son; I'm calling him Jonathan.* A new battle, one nobody saw coming.

She wasn't too worried about my illness until a few days ago, when I texted her in the throes of one of my desperate early-morning awakenings. Lying in bed, not knowing what to do, I wrote: *I can't do this anymore. I want to throw myself out the window.* I was half asleep, I wasn't lucid. Did I really mean it? Yes. I've thought about it. I've wished it would all be over. I've felt defeated by the rigid, mathematical impossibility of getting better. I've done every test under the sun. I'm getting treatment, but nothing is changing. Until now I'd always managed to get through rough patches by imagining new possibilities, a better future. But now I'm out of alternatives.

I've thought about climbing onto the wooden windowsill in our bedroom. I've imagined what it would feel like to abandon myself to the free fall — only two storeys, but two enormous storeys. The apartments in this building have four-metre-high ceilings. To hit the asphalt head-first, re-splitting the fontanelles, or else face-first. No nonna Nuccia to hold me back this time, to prevent me from becoming pink jam on the footpath. The sound of my skull shattering like a vase, my nose smashed against the ground, like when zio Mario lost his grip on my wrists, and mamma and papà had to take me to hospital. This time, though, my nose will be flattened, mashed to a pulp — will my corpse have a face like a snake?

Yes, I've thought about killing myself.

Cutting my life short.

Because it's clear my story won't have a happy ending.

Ciao, mamma.

She's standing in a pool of light on the footpath of Viale Piave. The early spring sunshine is strong, but still only lukewarm. I wait beside my mother, on this April morning that doesn't actually exist for me. It's there, but I can't feel it.

Marius goes to collect the share car. He pulls up in a hurry: let's go. I lie down in the back, finally resting. Kids in the back, grown-ups in the front.

Always the littlest in the family.

My mother doesn't have a licence. Marius has to drive. He's barely driven in the city. He's used to the villages of Umbria: quiet streets, few cars. But this morning he does it without complaint. My mother decides, Marius acts, and I let myself be led. It takes a certain talent to avoid being an obstacle.

We're on a mission.

This morning we're trying out our respective superpowers: my mother's is will, Marius's is action, mine is forbearance. I'm fighting, too, although you wouldn't know it by looking at me. Reclined across the seat, back leaning against the door, legs extended.

All good, Johnny? my mother asks.

Yes — the answer she wants to hear.

The movements of the car are like an anaesthetic.

I drift in and out of sleep.

I never want to get out.

Marius uses the GPS: he's only been to Sacco once before, by public transport, but he has an excellent sense of direction. He'll be fine. He'll recognise the streets, the intersections, the buildings. He's so much younger than me, but sometimes he seems so grown up.

The sunlight invades everything. I'm warmed by the rays reaching to me through the back windows of this tiny red car humming across Milan, ferrying us almost to the city limits, on this life-or-death expedition no one but us knows about. Delivering us all the way to the hospital, the place where either you're reborn or you die.

It's 20 April, 2016.

The most important day of my life.

The day I'm rescued by my mother and my boyfriend.

You're not gay

You're not gay.

In the summer of 2000, everything falls apart.

I like boys, men, males. I've known that since Jaco, since I was six years old. It's not something I've ever had to come to terms with. The *when did you realise you were gay?* question doesn't apply to me. I never had a problem with the way I was made, even when other people did. But now — July, August, the heat of summer — I experience a kind of retroactive doubt. Like a turning point, but backwards. It happens in a split second, like a flash of lightning: I thought I was gay, but I was wrong. Now what?

Porto Garibaldi, Province of Ferrara, Residence-Park Emilio. Rows of bungalows, turbid mud-coloured water, high tide, low tide, the smell of seaweed. I've been coming here every summer since I was a baby, with nonna Lidia and nonno Biagio. This is the place where, one afternoon, on the path leading to our little cabin, sun low in the sky, I thought I saw a hummingbird sucking nectar from a flower. Impossible — what is this, South America? For years I imagined mermaids lived just beyond the rocks where nonna's sister-in-law, zia Rosetta, would go to gather mussels.

This year mamma and Tecla are with us.

Every day after lunch we put my sister down for a nap. Back and forth with the orange pram in the undercover parking lot, opposite the park's main entrance. Sometimes mamma rests, and

I go alone. In my memory, the fear and anxiety of that summer move to the rhythm of a pram rolling back and forth between two endless rows of cars sheltering from the Adriatic sun.

Go down to the beach for a while, everyone tells me.

Why are you inside all the time?

I spend my days sitting on the top bunk with my new Art Nouveau Tarot deck, my phone, and a book on the interpretation of dreams.

Enough with those damn cards, mammà shouts. You're obsessed.

I continue shuffling.

You're not what you thought you were.

Should I turn back? Renege? *Intrusive thoughts* (I won't learn that term until years later) unfurl like petals, invade my mind like weeds, feeding on my panic. I need to know. I need an answer. I need a way to circumscribe the self, to define what it is that I feel.

I want to be gay. I want to go back to the way I was.

Pages ripped from newspapers, magazines, erotic comics. Photos of muscular men in their underwear, photos of topless women. I gather all the material I can, and put myself to the test. Sex as an instrument of control. Do you like women? I thought I didn't, but what if I looked deeper? Beyond the superficial? Look closer: examine your feelings, the ideas you've formed about who and what you are.

Try masturbating to a photo of a woman — can you do it?

Can you get it up?

You're gay, but you don't mind tits. Hard nipples, swollen breasts. Would you lick them? What does that make you feel? Disgust? Indifference?

Could you ever love a woman, in the romantic sense?

Possibly. But sex is one thing, and love is another.

Gay or bisexual? There's no way of knowing definitively, no way of isolating the specific point on the spectrum where you reside. No unequivocal proof of your sexuality.

That's the problem, admit it. You don't know how to bear the weight of uncertainty.

This is my sole preoccupation, my one vital interest in the endless desert of this summer. My mood crashes — my first depressive episode, an expert would say. Or *would have said*. I haven't spoken to any experts about this.

Summer: one of the worst times of the year, as everyone knows.

I was wrong. I was wrong about myself, about the one thing I should know better than anything else. Without a fixed point to tether myself to, everything turns inside-out. There's no way to stop the flow. I'm afraid I won't make it to the other side. I'm afraid of hurting myself.

If I grab a rope, it snaps in my hands.

I look for a way out through writing. Nothing creative, just an outlet. Like opening a window before the gas fills the room and explodes. I put together a notebook of *almost poems* — I don't know anything about rhyme and metre, so they don't deserve official titles. Are these the words I would say if I had someone to talk to?

Actually, I do have someone to talk to. Or write to. His name is Riccardo, and he's a thirty-two-year-old aspiring politician. His dream is to make it all the way to the European Parliament. I've only seen one photo of him. I like him; he looks like an American footballer, like a nice guy. But he doesn't want to meet me. I have a boyfriend, he says. And you're underage.

I text Riccardo when I'm afraid of losing control, when I fear my head might be about to cause me serious harm.

Are you asleep? Richie, Riccardo, are you there? Don't abandon me.

My fingers type blindly in the dark, while everyone else is sleeping.

That summer — the summer I think I'm going crazy — Riccardo is my only friend.

Nothing gives me any pleasure.

Drama queen. Don't exaggerate. Adolescence is hard on everyone.

I don't ask for help. I do everything alone. I buy a book on Bach flower remedies and choose the ones I need. It's not easy: according to their descriptions, I could use pretty much any of them. I send my mother to the herbalist to buy them for me (I don't go into shops). I've chosen three remedies: White Chestnut, Gorse, and Cherry Plum. They heal unwanted thoughts, desperation, and the fear of losing control. In that order. I mix the solutions in a bottle with a little bit of whiskey (it works as a preservative). I place a precise number of drops under my tongue three or four times a day. It doesn't take much; according to my book, the flowers heal through vibration. They're not like conventional medicine.

My therapeutic ritual. I follow it with absolute dedication.

Deliver me from evil.

Never skip a dose, or the pangs you're feeling will intensify.

What's that stuff you're taking?

Vitamins, mamma. Supplements.

I hold on. I abide.

I count the drops as they fall under my tongue.

★

July, August, September. School goes back — I call it school, but really it's a hairdressing course. The only fallback I could find. I want to study, but my stutter has made it impossible. My new school is a Professional Training Centre on Via Pestalozzi, in Milan. Close to the Naviglio Grande.

Autumn is here — the conclusion of the fifth season, according to Chinese medicine. Relief, the lifting of burdens. I barely notice the friction easing, the force of gravity growing weaker.

I like boys. And if I don't — patience.

It's time to focus on my course.

Mamma buys me the big bag of materials I need. Brushes, combs, blow dryer, scissors, rollers, fake heads to practise on — beautiful doll's heads, like giant Barbies. One million lire. Mamma has to borrow money from nonno Biagio to pay for it.

Now make sure you go, she says. Don't make me waste my money.

Of course I'll go, mamma.

A new project; a new identity. I can't wait. I'm still a student, forever a student, but this time there'll be no more reading in front of the class, no more pronouncing words before a room full of eyes and ears.

When the course begins, my identity crisis takes a back seat. Take note: the mind is more dangerous than the real world. The worst problems are the ones you — artisan, carpenter, puppeteer — create for yourself. Shadow play. External problems are solvable; they can all be worked through, or side-stepped. But when the mind itself grows hostile, what do you do? Where do you turn? All that energy inside you needs to be released, shared, sent out into the world.

Otherwise it will turn on you.

Arm in arm

Arm in arm.

My mother walks me down the tree-lined paths leading from the carpark to the hospital.

Pietà in motion. A tiny protest march.

Marius isn't here; he's looking for a parking spot.

I'll let you out and find you later.

Who knows how long he'll take.

Will he arrive in time to say goodbye to me?

I've made a promise to myself: this time I won't take no for an answer. I'll force them to admit me.

Where do we go? my mother asks. Can't we take the shuttle?

No. The first time I came here, with Alessandro, we tried that. A small, shuddering carriage crowded with old people and sneezes. The shuttle takes a long, roundabout route to get to the infectious-diseases building. Getting on and off is a challenge — every stop is a test of endurance and agility, dodging plastered legs and wet coughs. I'd rather walk.

Will you make it?

I'll try.

One last push.

I draw momentum from my mother, borrowing the force of her body to propel my own.

Building 56.

This is it. We're here.

We descend the stairs and head past the reception desk towards the consulting rooms.

The room is the same as always.

All white, all blue.

Even the lights are irritating.

I abandon my body to the ultramarine faux-leather chair. It gives me no comfort. Need without reward. The best I can do is satisfy a simulacrum of desire.

Today of all days, my doctor isn't alone. He's joined by two young guys. They look about twenty-five, maybe twenty-seven. Students? Interns? At first I'm embarrassed to be seen like this — crumpled, mouldy, an absolute wreck — but soon I surrender.

So, Jonathan. How's it going?

He knows very well how it's going. My repetitive, nagging emails over the past few days have made it abundantly clear. I usually try to be easygoing in my interactions with others; I hate being a burden. But today I have to put everything on display, bring it all to the table. The cold, steel vivisection table. I might even have to exaggerate. It's the only play I have left, if I want to be taken seriously.

Not good, I reply.

I use the most serious tone of voice I can muster. I wish I could do more: throw myself on the floor, start convulsing, drooling. Look! I'm dying!

My doctor makes a face that is both arrogant and compassionate at the same time. Authority. The hierarchical pyramid. He knows what's going on; I don't. It doesn't matter how I feel. I'm just a poor, mentally ill patient. Raving, delirious. When I leave the room he'll tell the two students, the two interns: sometimes you'll get cases like these, people who've lost control. Be patient with them. They're fragile.

He examines me as usual, then reiterates his stance.

Physically, there's nothing wrong with you. Nothing extraneous to your infection, I mean.

Imposter. Drama queen. Lunatic.

You should speak with our psychiatrist, Doctor Nuvola.

She's in the building next door.

She's expecting you.

Consistency

Consistency: respect the choices you've made.

Finish what you started.

But I want to study — I miss books, I miss the way they make me feel.

I last nearly six months in the hairdressing course. I push through, I put my head down, I try to find meaning in the identical, repetitive actions required to master this profession. I learn how to straighten hair with a blow dryer, how to put rollers in. Who actually uses those? Only old ladies, these days. I learn how to give a rudimentary manicure — a useful skill to have — and use a curling iron. I practise at home on my mother, while my sister is sleeping. Coils of red hair, mamma's head enormous, full of ringlets. Duchess, vamp, princess Sissi.

Doesn't she look gorgeous, nonna?

She looks ridiculous, *par' 'na scem'*.

You're good at makeup, one of the teachers tells me. You should study makeup artistry. Doing makeup is a bit like painting, so it feels familiar. I used to add makeup to the faces of the women I drew: powdered pencil for eyeshadow and blush, red marker for lipstick, black pen for eyeliner. I practised on my dolls, too, when I lived with my grandparents.

I make an effort, but the practical lessons are so boring. I throw myself into the theory, lessons on chemistry and biology that don't actually count for anything at the end of the course. I pore over the photocopies on skin allergies and follicles and hair bulbs. I draw precise miniature diagrams in my notebook — *this is a hairdressing course, not a medical degree.* I study despite the fact that no one else seems to care, despite the fact that there's absolutely no point.

When I ask questions, my classmates laugh at me. *You talk like a book, no one understands you, talk normally.* This isn't a school; this is a pipeline to the workforce. Apprenticeship, job offer, contract, pay cheque: these are the things that matter. And I'm not the slightest bit interested in them.

If I want to be invisible, I'm in the wrong place.

I start my apprenticeship at the nicest salon I know, the one in Via Margherita, where Tino used to take me to get my hair cut. I choose the salon. I decide. I refuse to go to one of the places affiliated with the training centre. I want to work in the salon where Tino and I would sometimes cross paths with tv celebrities: Paola Barale, or the Cuccarini dancers. If I have to be a hairdresser, at least let me work in the nicest place possible. I want to be centrestage, in the spotlight. But hairdressers belong backstage, where the lights don't reach. I don't know how to do anything, so I just wash people's hair — too hot? too cold? — and sweep the floor, collecting piles of freshly cut locks.

Don't lean against the wall, it's a bad look.

What did I tell you?

But there's no one here (trying to defend myself).

I don't care, go and find something to do.

The bathroom is flooded, a broken pipe, I have to mop it up. *With those rags — yes, the ones in the bucket. And get a move on, it's busy out there.* Cinderella, servant. Isaura the Slave Girl, my nonna Nuccia would say. I survive a week, two weeks, then

I make my escape. Without warning. Escapology is a recently acquired skill, but now I've started I can't stop. I go out for my lunch break and don't come back. The owners of the salon call my mother at home.

Signora, hi. Your son went for lunch a few hours ago and we haven't seen him since. Do you know where he might be?

No, my mother doesn't know anything.

Maybe a dizzy spell, a panic attack.

She calls me: where are you?

Mamma, I don't want to go back there.

So don't. Just come home.

I try changing salons. My mother's hairdresser in Rozzano, near the town square. All women.

Hi, here's your uniform: white shirt, rubber clogs.

One day, two days.

I quit that one, too.

Mamma, I want to go back to school. Normal school. I want to study. But first: a psychologist. I need help. I want to get better before I go back. I thought I had it all figured out — hide, burrow down, bury yourself so you won't be exposed. But it's not that easy; you can't just flick a switch and change who you are. I stutter, yes, but I still want to study. I don't want to do anything else. I can't do anything else.

And who's going to pay for this psychologist? mamma says.

You and nonna Nuccia can go halves.

I already asked papà. He says he hasn't got any money.

At fifteen, I attend my first psychology session. It's at a subsidised cooperative in Viale Monte Nero. My aim is not to stop stuttering — I still stutter to this day, even though people claim not to notice — but to learn how to avoid being paralysed by fear. Or, in technical terms, to learn 'how to overcome my anxiety disorder through systematic desensitisation'. My cognitive behavioural therapist is young. Tall, thin, with light-brown hair and extremely blue eyes. He also works at the San Vittore prison. Do I have a crush on him? Something like that. I either hate men or I fall in love with them.

We talk about my stuttering, and not much else. That's how cognitive behavioural therapy works: focus on the symptoms, on resolving those. The symptoms are the priority. Everything else — family, dreams, memories — is background information. I wonder: will the underlying causes simply resurface later, in another form, via new channels?

That doesn't matter right now. What matters is finding a way to manage my panic.

To go back to school. To do what I want to do.

For example, I don't tell my therapist I like boys. I don't tell him I use chat rooms. Whenever our discussions verge on the emotional — *have you ever been in love?* — I change the subject. I'm embarrassed. My mother is the only person I've told, and I haven't spoken with her about it since.

Don't ask, don't tell.

He sets me tasks, exercises, tests. He makes me compile a kind of logbook, a chart that I keep folded up in my wallet and complete throughout the week. The columns read, in order: situation / how do I feel / what is the worst-case scenario / what is the best-case scenario / how will I approach it. Every time my stutter tries to sabotage me, I have to stop and fill in the columns. I pin the moment down with words. You're not broken; your problems can be identified, named, circumscribed, managed. Even when the words don't come, I learn to recognise that I'm not about to die. I learn not to let my feelings invade everything. Like an animal with an open wound, my meditation teacher will put it, years later. You grew up in a state of alarm.

Tasks, tests, exercises. My therapy involves deliberately exposing myself to the situations that scare me the most: answering the telephone, going into a shop and buying bread, asking someone on the street for the time. Whenever something inside me resists — *no, run away* — I reaffirm my goal: I want to go back to school. I want to study.

It works.

I enrol in liceo artistico (again?), but this time I choose a school with a stronger focus on theory.

Role-play: before going back, the psychologist wants me to practise with him.

Now go outside, and when you come back in, pretend you have to present yourself to the class.

Name, surname, where you're from.

I'm Jonathan Bazzi, I'm from Rozzano, I've chosen liceo artistico because I don't know what I want to do with my life. I'm interested in a lot of different things. But I don't think you can learn everything from books.

The fear of not being able to speak will never leave me completely.

Soon after I return to school, my appointments come to an end.

Jonathan, your mother and I agree that, considering your progress and your family's economic situation (even though most of the fee is covered, mamma can't wait for the bills to stop coming), this is a good time to finish up our sessions. Please reach out if there's anything at all you need. Break a leg.

2001: the fall of the Twin Towers.

I walk through the front gates of Liceo Artistico Umberto Boccioni, Piazzale Arduino, Milan.

Two years late. Right on time.

I'll be the smartest kid here.

The best student in the whole school.

A kind of short, wide cottage

A kind of short, wide cottage.

Immersed in foliage. Slightly raised, sitting on an artificial hill surrounded by gardens.

The psychiatry building at Sacco looks like a Los Angeles rehab facility. Veranda, rocking chairs, fountain, plants. People smoking in their dressing-gowns. Girls interrupted: is this real, or am I imagining it?

So this is where I'll live (for how long? a month? a year?). I'll feel nothing. My mind fogged by sedatives. Sleeping Beauty goes to rehab.

Marius arrives, and we all head inside together. Marius, my mother, and I. The three of us in a line. I wish I were well enough to savour this image, to pause it forever in my memory. A narrow corridor. Consulting rooms, noticeboards with flyers advertising workshops, activities, children's services, helplines. The world of psychological distress is familiar to me. A place where people look after the parts of themselves that are broken, the same parts that are broken inside me.

A guy who looks like the caretaker tells us Doctor Nuvola hasn't arrived yet. We wait outside her office.

Are you hungry?

No.

Leaning against the wall, clinging to it. Waiting for yet another pointless meeting.

Footsteps. Coming towards us from the glass door.

Is this her?

An undulating figure enveloped in yellow floral fabric. She is large, obese, holding a daily planner and manila folders to her chest. She's eating something: lollies? chocolate? Bulimia triggers — an eating disorder is the last thing I need right now. In my head I'd imagined a cold, sylphlike woman with a grey bob and cat-eye glasses. A shaman of the mind, a turtleneck-clad existentialist. Instead, my doctor looks like a preschool teacher with a nervous eating habit. Chaotic, cheerful, happy. Is this really going to work?

Are you Bassi?

Bazzi.

My mistake, I must have written it down wrong.

We're off to a good start.

We walk into her office and sit down, the three of us facing her. She sits behind her desk, surrounded by piles of books and rows of binders. A familiar constellation: systems therapy, psychodrama. No. This scene is new. This is my scene. The doctor asks me to tell her about myself. Not just how I am right now. Tell me your story, she says. To understand where you're at today, I need to understand where you've come from.

I talk for an hour and a half.

Maybe two.

I dredge up recollections, exhume old bones. With the anxious vehicle of my words I guide her through the landscape of my life events, from childhood to the present day. I am biographer, geologist, Sherpa. I show the doctor the peaks and troughs (mostly the troughs) of my mind. Marius and my mother are sitting right beside me. My tongue loosens. Something warms up inside me as

I speak. Things resurface. I focus on the memories that have led me to therapy in the past: the stuttering, the intrusive thoughts. Then my recent fears: the internet searches, the sensation in my right arm, the endless tests and doctor's appointments to try to get to the bottom of what is happening to me.

It's like this every time I talk to someone about all the things I've lived through alone.

I was raised by substitutes. Brought up by proxies. Faced with the shattered remains of their love, my parents prioritised moving on: finding another man, other women. Having another baby. Starting again. Re-attempting failed projects. They had to leave me behind. Is a three-year-old child really that cumbersome?

Alone I am restless, a worrier, but under the gaze of others I become a soldier. Rigorous, punctual, precise. My personality is inverted. My self-destructive impulses are transfigured. I can turn water into ether, I can read people's thoughts. I multiply the loaves and the fish. My nature is desperately, irremediably social.

Radically self-centred.

My egoism is a plea for help.

Please, help me stay in the world. Don't let me disappear.

In Doctor Nuvola's office, the words come easily. As though I'd prepared this monologue ahead of time.

I'm a river that's overflowing. I can't stop.

Every so often my mother intervenes, but the overwhelming voice that resounds in that room is mine. No hesitation. No filter. No armour. I tell the doctor everything, because I know the only way I'll get anything out of this misguided meeting (I'm still convinced the problem is in my body, not my head) is if I put everything on the table. If I'm completely transparent. Naked. If

I allow the doctor's intuition to penetrate everywhere, even the places I can't see, and take hold of whatever it needs to make a diagnosis.

Your doctor signalled depression as a possible diagnosis, she says. But considering what you've told me today, I don't think you're depressed. Or rather, I think you have mild depressive tendencies, but that these are fed by a severe anxiety disorder.

Anxiety? Just anxiety?

So my symptoms are imaginary? It's all in my head?

Somatisation: the stories I invent for myself manifest themselves physically. I'm a magician.

Doctor Nuvola prescribes two different medications. *These should fix you right up*. Psychiatrists are famous for rushing into things.

The first is an anxiolytic: think of it like aspirin. It should provide short-term relief of your symptoms. The second is a serotonin regulator: think of this like an antibiotic, working on the underlying causes, getting to the root of the problem. You can self-regulate with the anxiolytic — I'd suggest ten to fifteen drops three times a day. But you can increase or decrease the dose as needed. In the event of a crisis, you could use it as an emergency treatment. The other one has to be taken once a day for at least two years. It's important to keep taking it, even after you start to feel better. You have to complete the cycle.

Let's speak again in two weeks, she concludes. I won't be able to see you next time; I have too many patients. But give me a call, and I'll assign you to a colleague from the ward.

I'm not being hospitalised, then. I have to go home. Again. This time grasping to the thin hope, the ridiculous hope, that these two drugs will make some kind of difference. Am I really meant to believe anxiety meds will fix whatever's wrong with my body?

We leave and make our way back to the car.

Alex has come to pick us up.

He and my mother got married the year I met Marius.

The ceremony was held at the Rozzano cultural centre. I hugged my mother afterwards, and felt our story come to an end. It was raining rice — how could I not cry? Mamma, you did it. Things weren't always perfect, but at least now you finally have a family.

The sun is high. The air is warmer.

In the square in front of the hospital I take off my hoodie. Initiative, movement. A reaction.

T-shirt, sunshine, an inkling of an appetite. I feel both optimistic and utterly defeated at the same time.

You're all wrong. But I hope the same can be said for me.

Bombarded with chemicals: antiretrovirals for the HIV, antidepressants for the anxiety.

There's nothing left of the person I used to be.

Perfect is the enemy of good

Perfect is the enemy of good, my P.E. teacher writes.

Even though I've been studying for a week — twenty pages of notes, does that seem excessive? — I've decided I will not be taking the theory test tomorrow. I don't feel prepared. I've already texted my teacher (we all have his number; he acts like we're his friends). I have to make sure I get a perfect ten, like the last two times.

Even in P.E.?

Even in P.E.

I'm the best because I have to be, not because it just happens that way. There's no alternative. All the teachers love me — do you have any idea how many privileges that earns you? I have the highest average in the school. I've never received less than an eight out of ten, much less a fail. No one comes close to rivalling me.

But it's not competition that drives me. It's the fear of losing everything, again.

I have to be the best, even if it means not sleeping at night. If necessary, I set my alarm for two or three in the morning. Once I got up at one thirty to study for a philosophy test. I study in the bathroom, the only room in the house where I can have the light on without waking everyone up. I pace from the toilet to the basin, from the basin to the toilet, surrounded on all sides by the red and white tiles Tino had installed. Our apartment is tiny, a little cubbyhole. Mamma and Alex watch tv in one room — *we're entitled to a bit of down time after work, are we not?* — while I skulk around in search of somewhere I can concentrate.

I go over my notes in the bathroom, but I draw in the kitchen. Anatomical studies, acrylic on canvas, geometric designs.

I can do whatever I want, as long as I don't bother anyone. *You're not the only one who lives here, you know.* As long as I don't get in the way of anyone's football matches, or cartoons, or romantic comedies.

I'm the best student in my school, but at home no one cares. In some families study is considered an obstacle, a mistake. It doesn't count for anything in the real world. It's not a serious pastime. Study is for parasites and malingerers. Work, earning a pay cheque — that's the real commitment. The only possible goal. You're better off getting a job. The sooner the better. Any job will do.

When I get home, the aura I've cultivated for myself at school vanishes. It's worth nothing. It blinks out like a neon sign the moment I set foot in Rozzano. You did what you had to do, my mother says. But the powers I've acquired are useless here. At best, they might come in handy for answering questions on Gerry Scotti's quiz show, or if someone needs help composing an email or letter for some bureaucratic purpose. The other kids in our neighbourhood are rewarded for promotions, or for passing high school. Not me. No one recognises any of my achievements. But that's how it should be. School is *my* thing, school is about *me*. I do it for myself and no one else.

When I'm preparing for an oral exam, each page of notes (papers stained with sweat, creased by my anxious hands) is read aloud dozens of times, until I've learnt every single word by heart. Until my voice is hoarse, until my throat constricts and the muscles in my shoulders are tense.

Stiff neck — time for some painkillers.

The words lose all meaning. They are only rhythm, only sound.

This is a tournament. I study with my whole body. I am an athlete.

When it's too noisy at home — laughter, yelling, talk shows — I go over my notes in the park. I walk in circles, notebook in hand, orating about art history, or Italian literature. My mother comes looking for me. She's afraid of the parks in Rozzano. What happened to her when she was little? What happened to you in the park, mamma?

Again. One more time. An entire afternoon, an entire day, an entire night of repetition. It's never enough. If I get everything perfect, every last conjugation and article, then I'll barely stutter. No one will even notice. If I pronounce every sentence exactly the way the teacher does (mimic, chameleon), then everything will be okay.

It will never happen, but if I were to get a five out of ten I'd drop out.

Shut up, what the fuck are you talking about?

Just watch me.

The literature teacher, Menna — a devotee of D'Annunzio and every other fascist, reactionary intellectual — has a reputation for being tough. He's never given anyone more than eight out of ten. But I win him over. I charm even him. First, I manage to squeeze a nine out of him. Then, in twelfth grade, he gives me a ten. I'm the talk of the school. *That's the kid who got a ten from Menna.*

People stop me in the corridor.

Congratulations — how did you do it?

I can't explain it; I'm simply me.

I'm beyond imitation.

This was my destiny.

I have to protect my coveted position. I never lend out my notes (if anyone asks to borrow them I lie, say I forgot my notebook, or I've already given them to someone else, sorry) because my notes are impeccable. I transcribe every word, note down every pause.

I don't want to share them — take your own. The words inside this notebook are all I have.

Nothing will change after I leave high school. At university, too — studying first Philosophy, then Fine Arts at the Accademia di Brera, then Human Communication Sciences, then Philosophy again — I'll settle for nothing less than perfect. Thirty out of thirty, margins overflowing with praise. I'll receive just two lesser grades in my time: a twenty-eight and a twenty-nine. Two affronts, two stains on my character. Marks of shame. I wish I could erase them — can I give them back?

I won't accept anything below the highest possible grade.

In high school I develop strange methods to avert disaster, especially when it comes to oral exams. I stop masturbating for days, sometimes even weeks, before an exam. I'm worried that if I masturbate, God will punish me by making me stutter, and everything will fall apart.

Zero, fail, drop out.

Find a job.

Now that I've been given a second chance, I do everything I can to avoid catastrophe.

Don't touch yourself. Just study.

God doesn't like it. God is always watching.

God? Yes — some kind of generic god. Not necessarily the Catholic God.

I study eight, ten, twelve hours a day. All that matters is study. If you excel at study you'll be loved (or envied) by everyone.

One by one, I abandon all other commitments, hobbies, passions. I stop taking singing lessons, throw out all my Tarot cards and runes and astrology books. I must have no distractions. I must do nothing but prepare for my tests, go over my notes, work on my drawings and assignments. My classmates call me selfish, self-centred, up myself. I end up believing them. Why does nobody suspect that the reason I force this punishing regime on myself — the reason I never allow myself to put a foot wrong — might be because, in reality, I feel worthless? If I were confident, if I had self-worth, I'd feel safe. I'd know my path. I wouldn't come undone at the thought of a nine out of ten. I wouldn't need to stand on a pedestal in order to breathe.

My teachers use me as an example: a highly evolved young intellectual. Look at Bazzi, they say. Does he look like a nerd? Does he look like he spends all day studying? No — he has his methods. He knows how to make time work for him.

They're wrong. I'm easily distracted. I have a terrible memory. My grades are the product of obsession, mania. I'm driven by a sense of urgency, by a fear of being challenged. It takes days of repetition for anything to stick in my mind — I'm quick to grasp things, but they're easily displaced. Remembering concepts and definitions requires effort, persistence, brute force. I have to destroy my voice, my body, my soul.

I like being at school, though. For the first time in my life.

My class is almost all girls — there are only four boys, plus me — and a number of us fall under the LGBTQ+ umbrella. This is Milan. Queer is cool. Some of my classmates are lesbians for a semester. Strictly hetero students (not counting the straight kids who are still deciding) are in the minority. We all hang out after school. I even start going out in the evenings. My first tastes of *social life*. I spend almost all my time in Milan. I only return to Rozzano when absolutely necessary. To sleep, and to study.

My mother doesn't like it. She wants to restrain me, limit my freedom. Keep me where she can see me. Over the summer she refuses to share her season Metro pass, and won't give me money for public transport. She's constantly imagining worst-case scenarios: muggings, fights, hate crimes. For her, leaving the house after dark is inconceivable. But in winter it gets dark at four in the afternoon.

I soon realise that her fear is a leash I have to remove.

The arguments start.

How long do I have to keep living here?

Simona and Dario are the classmates I get along with best.

Simona is from Buccinasco, Dario is from Corsico. The far south-western periphery. My neck of the woods.

Simona and Dario like each other, although neither of them is single.

Simona, who will eventually become my best friend, has been obsessed with a boy from her home town for months. She met him at the youth centre, a kind of secular church she goes to every day after school. The boy's name is Marco. He plays the guitar and sings, an anachronistic Kurt Cobain from the hinterlands of Milan. They were together for a few months, then he dumped her. To be with someone else, reportedly, or out of guilt for being with someone else. But Simona is determined to win him back. (Eventually, she will. They'll be together for twelve or so years, then she'll dump him. Revenge served ice-cold).

Dario is a perpetually stoned writer who spends his afternoons making electronic music instead of studying. Simona and I take turns giving him our homework. Dario has already failed one year of high school — he'll never graduate. He's with Vale, short for Valentina. Red bob (or is it orange?), two years older than him. Vale doesn't talk to little kids like us.

Apart from my mother, Dario and Simona are the first people in the world I come out to.

And I do it for the best possible reason.

His name is Ernesto.

My mother starts coming every day

My mother starts coming every day.

My nurse, my sitter. Warden of my body.

One week becomes two, then three.

April concludes. May arrives.

Mamma, how long will you keep coming?

Marius often works during the day. If she didn't come, I'd spend most of my time alone. Impossible: how would I manage?

My mother is afraid. Is she worried I'll starve? Hurt myself? She takes time off work, uses up all her sick leave. She arrives at nine or ten in the morning and stays until the afternoon. We sit together on the couch and watch tv. My body outstretched, empty of any desire to do anything, to be anything, to go anywhere. I've lost all enthusiasm, all interest in living, everything that once stood between her and me. My mother has put her life on hold to sit here beside me. Mother and son, alone on an island of time and space, completely severed from the rest of the world and from everything that has ever been.

Mamma, don't you take your shoes off inside?

How long can you stay today?

Her visits are momentary parentheses. Exceptional events due to force majeure.

I wish my mother would stay forever.

I make her watch re-runs of cooking programs and infomercials all day. When I'm alone I watch videos of Italian

YouTubers. Marius says they're all losers, that Italian YouTubers are just pathetic imitations of American YouTubers, but I don't care. I'm just looking for a distraction, something to pluck me briefly from the pit of fear in which I usually reside. Over the years, we learn what kind of activities work best for us in our hours of need. Our own personal crisis-management rituals. It helps to have a ready-made structure to erect around bad omens, or bouts of paralysis, or moments of collapse.

I still drift in and out of sleep, but less than before.

Mamma doesn't like it.

No more sleeping, you'll go senile.

Every day she makes me have a shower, get dressed, go outside. If it were up to me I'd go downstairs in my pyjamas, but she won't hear of it. Appearances are everything.

At least one lap around the building, she says. But once we're outside, we always do more. From Porta Venezia we walk to Lima, the next Metro station, halfway down Corso Buenos Aires. If he's home, Marius comes, too.

See, you can do it.

For my mother, those five-hundred metres are proof that my mind is the only obstacle to my recovery. The doctors were right: there's nothing wrong with my body at all. What I don't tell her is that these daily walks cost every ounce of energy I can summon. That from the moment we leave the apartment, I'm counting the steps until we can turn around and I can lie back down on the couch.

I do it for you.

Anything to please others.

My mother mainly comes over to feed me. She arrives bearing packets of pasta and fresh vegetables. Mamma, are you shopping for two households now? She cooks meals using the cheapest ingredients: fusilli and zucchini, rice and lentils, potato minestra, discounted soy cutlets with salad. I eat quickly, take my medication (the drops and tablet Doctor Nuvola prescribed) and make my way back to the couch.

My mother watches over me, she takes care of me.

Mamma is always there in an emergency.

She makes sure I take my medication, but not too much.

How many drops? Let me see.

When I was unwell, she says, when I was depressed after your father and I separated, I was the same. I couldn't do anything, I couldn't even stand up. They gave me this stuff then, too — she gestures towards the little bottle of medicine and the blister pack of tablets lying on the table. They help, but it has to come from you.

You have to be the one to decide you want to get better.

For my mother, everything comes down to willpower. There's nothing wrong with you — it's all in your head. Mind over matter. Where there's a will, there's a way. Reaction and defence.

If you let yourself go, it's all over.

You'll never get better.

I pretend to agree with her — or rather, I refrain from disagreeing with her — but I know she's wrong. It's not up to me. There's nothing I can do. I will never change my mind about this. My illness is physical, material, nested deep in my organs. My mind has nothing to do with it. My mother is projecting her experiences onto me. She's hoping this is just the same thing she went through. She wants me to take after her. *The only ones who can really hurt us are ourselves.*

I don't know if she's told anyone in our family about me. She might have told zia Tata. She wouldn't have said anything to her parents — they don't even know I'm gay. *Jonathan has HIV.* They'd drop dead, they'd have a heart attack. What lie must she have told them? That I'm depressed? Our family is fluent in the language of depression — no one would be shocked by that.

On the other side of the family, at least, word has spread. Nonna Nuccia knows. And not only her.

I find out nonna Nuccia has told my father.

I should have called him myself. Officially, his diagnosis is much worse than mine. Leukaemia is far more dangerous than HIV, these days. There's no comparison.

But I didn't call him.

I waited. I waited for him to reach out. To see if he would.

And, to my surprise, he does. My father messages me on WhatsApp.

Can I call you?

He calls, he makes an effort, he tries to fix the broken connection between us. He does the right thing. He does what you'd expect a father to do; blood of my blood. He calls and asks how I am, and updates me on his illness. He has chronic leukaemia, which means there's a chance it can be managed with medication. If not, they'll have to consider a bone marrow transplant. Look for a donor. Not me, obviously. Contaminated biological material.

We just have to be patient, he says. Keep fighting.

Who is we?

Me and him, father and son — we're the same now. Only now, thirty years later.

It's clear that his interest in me is an echo of his self-interest.

This is the worst thing you've ever done to me. The worst thing we've ever done to ourselves. I feel as much sorrow over your illness as I would over the illness of a stranger.

To be unmoved by the idea of the death of the father.

To be unmoved by the idea of the death of the son.

The importance of being Ernesto

The importance of being Ernesto.

Ernie. Ernesto. My cherub, my angel.

I need to share my elation with someone. My joy, but also my desperation. The pain that engulfs me in waves and makes me bury my head in my arms on my school desk, enclosing myself in darkness so as not to see or feel anything. I think about it for days, weeks, before I finally tell Dario and Simona.

So, what's up?

I like someone.

His name is Ernesto.

Ernesto, right, says Dario. He's in Vale's class.

Ernesto is only one year older than me, but he's two grades ahead of me in school. Ernesto: my first love. *I always thought my first love was eternal, my first heartbreak inconsolable*, wrote Jeanne Hersch, the Swiss philosopher. I copy the sentence into my diary.

They say your first love is the prototype, the model for all future loves.

Mine wears a maroon jumper — I buy an identical one from the vintage shop in Ticinese (do you want Ernesto, or do you want to be Ernesto?) — and jeans on his short legs (he's slightly duck-footed). I like short guys. Not too short, though. He has watery eyes like an abandoned cat — blessed be the eyes of Ernesto. I'm in love with him all through ninth and tenth grade. I feel like I've been punched in the head every time I see him in the corridor. I start running, my heart somersaulting in my chest, expanding, transcending my body to fill the entire school, filling every classroom, every floor of Liceo Artistico Umberto Boccioni, then exploding out and rising up, thousands of kilometres into the sky. It watches us all from the edge of the atmosphere, my heart in orbit, and sounds an alarm, a warning for humanity: this boy is in love, be gentle with him. He deserves all the kindness in the universe.

I observe Ernesto carefully, looking for signs of affection. There: when he was checking the noticeboard in the hallway, he looked at me.

I don't think he did, says Simona.

He did, out of the corner of his eye.

He likes me, I can tell. Ernesto the artist, the Egon Schiele fan. Ernesto's drawings are the best in the school. He has a huge future ahead of him — you don't have to be an art critic or a gallerist to see that. He's obsessed with Giacomo Casanova (the sex addict?) and owls. Ernesto's father was a painter, but he died. Ernesto wants to be just like him; he wants to be the reincarnation of his dead father. My first love has so much pain inside him. It's okay — I'm here now. I will be the salve for Ernesto's broken heart.

I can't wait any longer. I decide to act. I write him a letter and send it to his home. (How did you get his address? I stole it from his file at reception.) He lives near Bande Nere Metro station. I go there, to gaze upon the house of my beloved. A small brown building — no, sand-coloured. It's hard to believe such an unremarkable place is capable of holding all that light.

I send the letter. No response.

I ask Dario for help.

Valentina can talk to Ernesto; she's in his class. I wonder how it feels to sit next to a deity. Vale can ask him if he's received the letter.

I'll let you know, Dario says.

Dario meets me in the courtyard next to the gymnasium.

Good news?

No. Ernesto likes girls.

I feel myself sinking into the centre of the earth.

But he says he wants to reply to your letter.

He won't reply. Not ever.

My feelings (imagine if all the wonders of the world were collected in a single place, then you might feel something like a muted version of the effect Ernesto has on me) mean nothing to him. They don't even merit a response. Not a note, not a text message, nothing. Not even a go fuck yourself.

First lesson of love: what feels like a magnitude-eight earthquake to you may very well go unnoticed by everyone else.

But I don't give up. Ernesto will love me. He can't be straight; he must be confused. He's probably scared to admit he's attracted to a boy. It happens. It could happen — not to me, of course, but to him. The synchronicities of love are unfathomable; the paths of Cupid are infinite.

What I feel is strong enough for the two of us. My love can fill both our chests. Jonathan and Ernesto: we were meant to be. Don't worry, I'll do everything.

If you were to ask me if I'd rather live to eighty without Ernesto or be with him for one year and then die, I wouldn't hesitate.

Do you hear yourself? We should record you, Dario and Simona tell me.

Stalker. Groupie. Pest. For at least three years I send Ernesto gifts and messages on his birthday. 15 July: the festival of Venus. Each year I'm met with silence. Nothing, no reaction.

Maybe you're scaring him?

He might report you.

Then: five, six years after I sent that first letter to his house, Ernesto gets in touch. I'm twenty-two or twenty-three. We get a coffee in the café at the Accademia di Brera. He wants advice on how to exhibit some of his recent drawings — unsettling subjects drawn in pen, visual records of hallucinations, deliriums. Is Ernesto taking drugs?

His eyes are even more beautiful now than they were before.

You know me, he says (is this actually happening?). How do you think I should organise them?

I don't know what to say — I improvise an answer.

I'm hypnotised. I've dreamt of you without meeting you. I've swallowed you whole. What would I know about exhibiting your drawings? Drawings that, even today, I would devour like an unholy Eucharist. The body of Ernesto, amen.

After that, nothing. Silence for the next two, three, four years. Ernesto goes away, he leaves Milan.

Depression, sadness, lack of inspiration. He wasn't drawing anymore. Milan was destroying him — do you know that, or are you imagining it? He moves to Trentino, high up in the mountains. He starts drawing comics, illustrating the songs of De André and De Gregori. Van Gogh, the bipolar genius, replaces Schiele as his muse. I follow his art account on social media. Is Ernesto famous now?

He deserves fame, and more. This is only the beginning.

I knew it, I saw it before anyone else. Already at sixteen I was a dowsing rod, a talent scout. My problem was that I took my job too personally. *I've only ever been able to love men when they're soft and weak and sweet,* Alda Merini wrote somewhere. I'm the same: I can only love boys (boys, not men) when they're melancholic, crumpled, sweet-eyed, borderline vagabonds. Failures? Would-be suicides? My love is all spirit, all light, all desire — I've never dreamt of having sex with Ernesto.

The erotic life of the saints has its own rules.

What would common people know?

Cashew nut biscotti

Cashew nut biscotti. Kneaded and baked on an afternoon in early May. For the first time in a long time I feel capable of leaving the house on my own, doing the shopping, coming home to prepare something. Benedetta Parodi has inspired me — she has given me the strength to follow her example. The desire to imitate her has gradually accumulated over months of watching re-runs of her cooking shows. She's become my greatest motivation. I copy every last detail: the presentation of the ingredients, the execution of the recipe, the exhibition of the final result. A batch of irregular, sand-coloured biscuits covered in pieces of slightly burnt dried fruit. My way of celebrating the fact that I'm not dead, that Marius and I might yet survive everything I've put us through.

I do the shopping at the supermarket underneath our apartment. I carry my bounty back up the stairs and lay everything out on the table. I mix the ingredients, then cook the biscotti in the oven. I let them cool on a paper bag, one of the ones our loaves of bread come in, then I photograph them. I post them on Instagram. Caption: *Pamela's Bakery.*

I start seeing friends again, and replying to group chats I'd muted, annoyed by all the meet-ups and projects floating past me, untouchable.

How are you?

Boh. Up and down. Still resting a lot.

Francesco and I are having coffee at the café in the street behind my apartment.

That's okay, he says. That's normal.

Sending down roots, nourishing my body, taking care of myself and others. Have I finally stopped sabotaging my survival instincts? I still spend a lot of time on the couch. Rhythm, habits — when I feel a little less weak I make an effort, I go out. Not for long: a few minutes, half an hour tops. Sometimes I regret it. In a burst of optimism, I take a photo of a flower: orange, veined with black. Before posting it I place a giant textbox over the image and write: *Thank you, Proserpina*. I'm afraid it's too good to be true, but the desire to believe surpasses even my anguish. It prevails over every bad omen.

At the end of the month, I receive a message.

It's from Giuliano, one of the first people who ever published my writing. I worked for him between 2014 and 2015, writing articles for his website about Italian history and religion and folklore. Saints, martyrs, processions, legends, folk tales. They were published in English: I'd write the pieces in Italian, he'd have them translated, and the next day they'd be online. Not much of me remained, in terms of language or style, but it was a start. The website eventually shut down. Now Giuliano mostly works on PR campaigns for fashion brands. But towards the end of May 2016, there's news.

I've been appointed editor. Would you like to join the masthead?

The magazine is well known, famous even — Italy's first online LGBT periodical. I've been offered a chance to write, to pay the rent and buy my groceries with money earnt doing a job I actually enjoy. Potentiality/actuality. The chance to become what I am, to manifest my vocation. Okay, great, amazing. But why did this have to happen right now? I've been waiting for an opportunity like this for years, and now that it's here I can't take it. How am I supposed to get up every morning and go to work? How am I meant to prioritise a project over my body? I've been on the couch for five months. I've grown accustomed to being motionless.

I don't reply.

I take my time.

I'm a champion at ghosting. I was left hanging for years, and now I do the same thing to others. I'm scared that if I take the job, I won't be able to keep up the facade. I'm scared I won't be able to turn up every day and fake it in front of an office full of strangers (how many?) who have no idea what's happened to me, what's happening to me, what might happen to me.

Two days later, Giuliano messages me again.

Marius and I are having breakfast, listening to Beyoncé. Marius is cradling the coffee I prepared for him. Without too much effort, it's true. But stagnation is almost as bad as relapse. Marius has been playing Beyoncé's new album on repeat. Does it bother me? The question never arises. He simply does what he wants — it's the Romanian way — and only stops if someone explicitly asks him to.

So, are you in or not? Giuliano writes. I need to know if I can count on you.

Yeah, sorry, I've had the flu (I lie). Let's meet up.

Tomorrow?

So soon?

It's now or never.

I'll be there in half an hour

I'll be there in half an hour, max.

I turn off the computer and go into the bathroom to get ready.

Inside and out.

I want you clean.

My mother, ever the ball-breaker, appears in the doorway.

Where are you going?

For a walk, I won't be long.

If it's too late at night, she protests. It's no use — I go out anyway. I sneak out if I have to. I'm a hurricane, a storm, an eruption: there's no stopping me. Alex never gets involved. Around the age of nineteen I start speaking to him again *(please, Jonathan, at least for your sister's sake)* but our interactions are governed by certain rules.

My mother doesn't want me to go out, so I wait for her to go to the bathroom then I make a mad dash for the tram stop. My hands tremble, freezing, as I wait for this guy to arrive. I wish he were already here, so I wouldn't have to endure this waiting.

How much longer?

A quarter of an hour.

And now?

Five minutes.

It's always like this when I make plans to have sex with someone: a cocktail of fear and yearning. Panic attacks — although I don't know that yet. I haven't yet understood what's happening to me. I still think it's normal to be overwhelmed by fear whenever I'm about to go to bed (or couch, floor, back seat, field, basement, park, garage, barn, store room of a shop) with a total stranger. I think it's normal for my legs to buckle underneath me, my mouth to feel dry, my heart to race. I feel like I'm about to pass out. Everything has to happen immediately. They have to come and pick me up, no more than one or two tram stops from where I live. I never go to their place if it means delaying the moment of truth. The slow drip is agony. Anxiety, denial, shortness of breath. I have to meet them in the heat of the moment. If it weren't an emergency, I would never do this. It's not like me. I'm different. I'm better than that.

Okay, half an hour. No weaselling out of it this time, the guy writes.

Yeah, yeah.

What if I stand him up? What if I just stay home and stop replying?

If you feel that way, why are you even doing this?

Me against myself; desire and repulsion in the same body. I both want and do not want to be humiliated, overpowered, violated.

Whore.

I want you to insult me.

I'm also scared because I know sex is dangerous. You can get sick. Be careful, set clear boundaries. No, I don't do bareback. Condom or nothing.

You can usually tell when someone is sick, anyway. It's something I sense, rather than consciously think. The sick ones are always more brazen, more reluctant to use protection. They have nothing to lose. Some even like infecting others. An eye for an eye.

I'm so scared of getting sick that I can't even bring myself to get tested.

One day I will, I tell myself.

But I never do.

Still — I'm careful. I don't do anything stupid.

I'm split, broken.

Torn between good and evil, between the boys I fall in love with and the men I seek out for casual sex. The former are angels, the latter minotaurs. This is how I'll phrase it to my psychologist, years later. I'll make a collage to explain myself better: two clusters of bodies representing my bipolar relationship with sexuality. On the right, young men with blond beards, beautiful eyes, mouths, hands, angelic faces haloed by stars and blooms of light. This is love. On the left, a dark-red background, men with their backs to the camera, faceless flesh, muscle, feet, reptiles, darkness, anonymous fury.

Looking at it, the psychologist will say: this makes my stomach hurt.

I'm a man, and that's what men are like. They separate sex and love, right? Except, every time I have sex without love I regret it. There's a part of me that experiences sex only as violence, as theatre, as performance. Tops and bottoms, toxic masculinity, rape fantasies. Let yourself be dominated, fucked, defiled, while you dream of love, while you chase boys who don't want to be with you. Because you're not pretty enough, because you're too small, too hairy, because they're looking for something you're not, something you can't give them.

The questions I ask to bring myself to the point of no return: do you fuck hard? how hard?

I broke his bed.

I broke his arsehole.

The more explicit, the better. Sex as aggression.

I'm reliving the porn I watch on the internet.

As if I were a spectator. As if I were on the outside looking in.

The boys I like, on the other hand, don't make me think about sex at all. Ernesto and the others are like painted saints, ethereal figures, little holy spirits to be caressed or, at most, kissed (*go on, give baby Jesus a kiss*). I *can* still do it; I can still go to bed with them and enjoy it — of course I enjoy it. But that's not what it's really about, that's never the point.

A first kiss is something to be savoured. My first time isn't.

Daniele is thirty, I'm eighteen. He works as a sales assistant at a Spanish fashion designer's shop off Corso Como. We kiss at his place, in Pasquetta. My mother helps me prepare a packed lunch to take to his apartment. I choose the dishes, we make them, then one by one we transfer them to Tupperware containers. Carpaccio with rocket. Torta salata. Mini toasts. Sitting on his bed, Daniele teaches me how to kiss. Never swirl your tongue around. Don't open your mouth too wide. I develop a serious crush — I think I'm in love with him. But two weeks later, he disappears.

You're too shy, he says. You feel closed off.

Then, when I'm almost nineteen, my first sexual encounter. I meet the guy online. We chat, we meet up. He's in his mid-forties and works at Malpensa airport. I know nothing else about him, not even his name. We meet once, then we never see each other again. We use a condom for everything. We don't go all the way — just foreplay, heavy petting. My first contact with another man's genitals.

Sit on my face.

Take me in your mouth.

The taste of latex, the smell of intimate wash. The sudden, nauseating closeness of a body I haven't chosen. When I go home I feel horrible. Bath, then bed. But I can't sleep: I disgust myself. It's not a thought, it's a feeling. The disgust is corporal, cellular. I can barely stand to be inside this skin that still reeks of what I've done. What I had done to me. No matter how many times I wash — lather, massage, rinse, repeat — I can't seem to scrub off the feeling of his saliva on my skin. Old man's spit, cigarette and alcohol breath. I feel them on me all the time, day and night. It makes me want to vomit.

In my notebook I write: I am dirty. I've let myself be contaminated. Artist, top of the class, the most special creature in the world, and now? You've ruined yourself. You let old men fuck you.

I think: I bet I've got AIDS now. This is how people get sick.

Sex with strangers — don't do it unless you're willing to take the risks.

I don't want to, but my libido makes me do it. Or is it my anxiety?

Is there a difference?

Adolescence: my hormones are in the driver's seat.

Two months later, my first complete sexual experience. Mattia (probably not his real name). Forty-two, forty-three? Ugly, exceptionally ugly. Huge horse teeth. Stupid, ignorant. They'll all be like this. If we're going to have sex — just sex — then I can't be attracted to them. If I like them, if I find them beautiful or even just cute, then I instantly fall in love with them. I won't even make plans to meet up unless they promise to love me back. Forever. Before we can go to bed together, I need their word: I like you, I love you, I'd do anything for you. Usually I disappear before we even meet, though. I can't bear to look at them.

My first time with Mattia happens in his car, at night, in a cornfield near Linate. I'm scared someone will appear through the leaves of corn.

Did you lock the car?

Of course I locked it, what do you take me for?

It's over quickly. He goes in and comes straight out. He annoys me. I have no reason to tolerate him. I'll see him a few more times over the years, but each encounter will be the same: quick, hasty, ridiculous. Each time, I'll feel a little sick afterwards.

Each time, Mattia will pick me up from the same place *(half an hour, usual spot?)* and we'll go to the same tiny studio apartment he'll insist isn't his. Whose is it, then? The story changes each time. It's my brother's. It belongs to a friend. To a colleague who's away on holiday — really? How long has he been away? All I know is we can't go in together. I go in first, then Mattia comes in ten minutes later. In the meantime, I have to get undressed and wait for him in the bathtub. He pisses on me *(fuck I'm busting, I drank two bottles of water for this)* then we move to the single bed in the middle of the apartment. Condom on. He spreads me open. He enters me. I can't stand it, I can never stand it while it's happening, I only ever want it before it happens.

I come immediately and say, that's it, get out.

He gets angry: *next time I'm tying you up.*

We have to organise a gangbang, he says.

I know a couple of guys.

Mattia is an ugly, obscene loser. That's why I chose him. But the trick only works beforehand, when I'm excited. Afterwards, when we're in his car, driving back to Rozzano, I can't even look at him. If he asks me a question, I reply with monosyllables. I hate him. I hate the shitty house music pulsing out of his car speakers. You absolute fucking moron. God, you're so fucking ugly. I chew gum to get rid of the taste.

His face, his mannerisms, his voice: Mattia is the amalgam of everything I despise.

But he has a big dick, he goes to the gym, he showers, and he's always available. He always makes time to see me, even if he's already been with two other guys that day.

Do I only enjoy sex as ambush, punishment, danger?

Do I only like sex when it's not really sex?

The casual hook-ups continue, but they don't happen often. Every three or four months. As infrequently as possible. Sex erases me, makes me disappear. It takes me away from everything I usually am, everything I'm trying to be. If I should be studying, I don't study. If I should be drawing, I don't draw. I don't read, I don't go out, I cancel all my appointments. I spend hour after hour trawling the internet, looking for the right guy.

Eighteen, nineteen, twenty years old. How many people have you been with now?

Thirty?

Fifty?

More?

As I get older, I realise some people can sleep with twenty or thirty strangers in a month.

As I get older, I realise some people can fuck without remorse.

Can I even remember all the people I've been with up to now?

There's the hairy Freemason I meet up with every time I get

drunk. The rent boy in Piazza Trento who says: *you wanted a boyfriend, now you've got one.* The manager of the big publishing group, who's been with his partner for ten years. The Vatican expert (he's also an aristocrat, a prince, so he says) who wants to take me to saunas where you get naked and do it in front of everyone. The diminutive firefighter I meet up with for threesomes (they snort coke first, I just smoke a bit of weed). The Filipino guy I give head to on a camping mattress in an attic. The sixty-year-old man who makes me go to his place at seven in the morning but can't get it up. The guy with the toupee I meet up with while his wife is at work. The ugly-as-sin worker at the self-service restaurant, who pays me a hundred euros for a blowjob. Then there are all the others whose names and faces I don't remember, the ones my memory has reduced to a situation, a place, a detail.

The separation of sex and beauty.

It's not always possible.

Eric, dyed blond hair, slim, slender. Small, hard muscles. I like him. More than that: his face excites me. He lives somewhere in Brianza. I take the train to his place in the evenings, after he's finished work. He's a salesperson in an electronics store. He says he made a porno when he was younger — I call bullshit. I want him to be my boyfriend. But he has other plans.

The only thing he likes about me is my age.

Whenever I spend the night at his place (it only happens two, three times in total) he walks me back to the station the next morning, after breakfast. I take the Cadorna-line train back to Milan. I know he won't call me. I never know how long it will be before I hear from him again. I feel empty, gutted, like a fish being eviscerated in the kitchen sink. Still alive. The same physical, animal pain I feel every time a boy I'm seeing fails to reply to my text messages straight away.

Until they openly declare their interest, I'm incapable of doing anything.

I can't study. I shut myself indoors.

Give it time, don't be like that.

You have to be patient.

I scare them all away. If I like a boy, he has to tell me he likes me back within a day. Two days, max.

The law of sentimental gravity: the closer two bodies get to one another, the greater the emotional attraction. And I feel it intensely. If they're near me — in the same room, at the same table in a café — I can't tear myself away. If I'm forced to move, it feels like my bones are being ripped out of my body. It takes several days for them to grow back. Until they do, every last organ in my body — stomach, pancreas, liver, spleen — is completely exposed. You try going to class, listening to the professor, taking notes under those conditions.

Marco, Antonio, Armando, Filippo, Andrea, Luigi. Each time, my heart swells for nothing. None of them like me enough. We go out once or twice, I ask for commitment, they vacillate. I insist, fantasy souring to fury.

Hey, are you there?

Reply, arsehole.

If I call, they don't answer their phones.

They vanish, they never text me again.

I go back to having sex with monsters.

Distraction, excitement, then disgust.

I've only been having sex for two years and already I wish someone would exterminate my libido. Chemical castration, like they do to paedophiles. I wish someone would sterilise me. Cut off my balls (I still need my penis).

Is there a tablet I can take?

If there were a drug that would extinguish my sex drive, now, at twenty years of age, I'd take it.

A brand-new life. Safe, pristine.

Uncontaminated.

The medication has stopped working

The medication has stopped working.

My father is sick again.

His leukocyte values are through the roof, and going up.

They'd warned him: sometimes this happens.

They change his medication. He's scared the new drug won't work either. He starts experiencing every possible side effect, all the ones listed in the product information. He loses his appetite, continues to lose weight. The pain in his side persists. Punishment, surely, for everything he's done to me. He's convinced this is the end.

Like me, he's encouraged to visit a psychiatrist.

He refuses.

I don't need a shrink, I'm not crazy.

I'm getting married next week, will you come?

Another wedding. His fourth.

I understand the emotional instability, but why does he always feel the need to get married?

Giulia is from Naples, like my mother — a return to his origins. She's only five or six years older than me. She sells mozzarella at her brother's shop, which is right underneath the police station on Via Chopin. That's where they met.

She and my father are getting married, and he calls to invite me five days before the ceremony.

We only decided at the last minute, you see.

A lie: the wedding has been planned for months.

It's being held at an open-air agritourism venue near Pavia. My father spares no expense. For him, each time is like the first. The young, fresh-faced groom; my father and his fantasies. An American-style ceremony, drowning in frothy white flowers. Weddings are like a magic spell he keeps repeating, in the hope that this time it might work.

He's got some nerve, my mother says.

Everyone is sceptical — family members, acquaintances. *Let's hope it lasts this time.*

My father is only fifty-three. Leukaemia permitting, he can probably squeeze two or three more marriages into his lifetime.

If it were up to him, he wouldn't have invited me. He wouldn't have even mentioned it. Giulia was behind it. She grew up without a father — or rather, with a father she barely knew — and she projects her experience onto the failed relationship between her future husband and his son. How these sensitive, intelligent women end up with an emotionally manipulative serial cheater like my father is beyond me.

Marius comes with me to the wedding.

My father has respected our relationship from the beginning. At the end of the day, he's a hopeless romantic. Love has always been the driving force in his life. It's just that he doesn't know how to make it last. *I can't help it, after a while I just get bored.* I wonder how much he hates being the person he is.

At his wedding, my father is visibly moved. He cries during his speech. He's marrying the woman who has helped him through these difficult last months, who has stayed by his side despite having no idea what the future holds for him. In the end, everything will be fine. The new medication will work, and my father will be out of danger. Although there's no such thing as a life-expectancy guarantee. From one moment to the next this new drug could stop working, and everything could change.

My condition also improves, gradually.

I don't notice it happening.

I go to the editorial office every day. There are three of us: me, Alessio, and Giuliano. Plus the occasional collaborator. The responsibilities of the new job redirect my attention from my illness. We cover the legalisation of civil unions, then the Orlando nightclub shooting, then Brexit. It almost never stops — we continue working from home after hours, even on weekends. We broadcast livestreams of the Milano Pride parade from our phones. We editorialise on different topics: bioethics, gay icons, fashion. We publish interviews with prominent community members. We revive a website that, until recently, had been on the brink of death. I relish the feeling of working as part of a team, of uniting to achieve an objective. I immerse myself in an extraordinary flow. I only snap out of it occasionally, to realise that I'm no longer thinking about what might happen to me.

My body has returned to its rightful place.

It no longer devours my thoughts.

Was it the anti-anxiety medication? The new job? The sunshine, the warmth of spring?

May, June, July. Summer arrives, and I am alive. I never thought I'd live through the winter. The fever and exhaustion and fear are over. I hope. I've been returned to the world, rebirthed. Born again. I can get back to the existence I led before January. I can think clearly again. I say things like: next week, at the end of the year, in a month's time, in three months' time. My life feels like a mosaic that has been dismantled and reassembled into a more beautiful version of itself. The new design is brighter, more brilliant.

It's hard to know how to celebrate the greatest good in the world.

How do you mark the moment in which you realise you still have a future?

First, by shaking off everything that has happened.

I don't call Sacco to make another psychiatry appointment. Irresponsible, crazy. I wean myself off the drugs on my own. Slowly, of course — I read on the internet that you're not supposed to stop taking them suddenly. A few drops of the anxiolytic every now and then. I reduce the dose of the tablets to a half, then a quarter.

Within two weeks, I'm off them completely.

Everything back to normal, everything more or less back to the way it was before.

Was I bluffing?

Was I just looking for a pretext, an excuse to put on a show?

HIV as catalyst, the body as arena, as amphitheatre. My stage. Feeling something and *believing* you feel something are indistinguishable processes. The all-powerful brain. No physical perception without emotional inflection.

I'll never truly understand what happened to me.

The education of the body

The education of the body.

Self-taught.

Twenty, twenty-two, twenty-six years old. Yoga offers me another path towards healing. My shame diminishes. I stop using sex as a way to annihilate myself.

I practise the most intense style of yoga, the most physical. Ashtanga. The most misunderstood, the most undervalued, the most ridiculed. Sweating, tying the body in knots: proper circus stuff. They say Ashtanga is the style you choose if you want to get into acrobatics. I choose it because it's the least rhetorical form of yoga. A complete absence of words. Two, two and a half hours of effort and concentration. Binds, inversions, backbends. Excessive, extreme — violent? The discipline of air and fire, breath and release. Like chemotherapy: exhaust the body to encourage its rebirth.

At twelve or thirteen I'm already obsessed: I buy books on Ashtanga yoga and imitate the poses I see in the photos. I won't start practising seriously, though, until the end of high school, inspired by Madonna's transformation during her *Ray of Light* period. Her toned, veiny arms. I want arms like that. In a film with Rupert Everett she even plays an Ashtanga yoga teacher. I watch the teaching scenes on repeat, watch her flow from one pose to the next. Spirituality on display. I'm transfixed. Madonna is my new mother figure, the priestess of the new-age order I aspire to belong to.

I start practising at the end of high school and continue for years. At first I attend a weekly class held in the gym of one of the primary schools in Rozzano Vecchio. Everyone else is over fifty. They come after work, they're tired, sleepy. They puff and snore and fart. They can't perform ninety per cent of the positions demonstrated by the teacher. With my perfectly erect shoulderstand, I become the star pupil. A few months later, I start trying out all the yoga studios I can find in Milan. I experiment with all the different styles, and when I hit on the one preferred by the Queen of Pop I fall in love. Long sequences of poses, each one more complicated than the next.

First series, second series, third series — like levels in a computer game.

Westerners like it because it's challenging, because it tests the limits of the body. I like it because it makes me the child prodigy of the Milan yoga circuit.

Thanks to my natural flexibility, within the space of two years I can access poses no one else would even attempt.

I practise yoga in order to be revered. The same motivation that drove me to study so hard in high school.

I astound people: look at me with both legs behind my head! I could fit into a little box, like a contortionist. But as I master each impressive pose — handstands, arm balances, defying the laws of nature — something in me begins to transform. My body mutates. It hardens, grows stronger, thicker.

From the outside I look masculine, manly.

On the inside I feel new, different.

On earth as in heaven, in body as in mind.

I start meeting up with guys from chat rooms again. If I don't like them, I simply tell them I'm not interested. I'm no longer easy prey for monsters. I learn to say no, to protect my boundaries.

My own personal sexual revolution.

I also learn to be patient when I am interested in someone. I try not to overwhelm the boys I like with my anxious demands for commitment. I give them time — I give them space. A respectful distance for a person I know nothing about.

When I'm about twenty-eight, Facebook brings all the boys who once ghosted me back into my orbit. The ones who ignored my texts ten years ago, who stopped answering their phones. At first I'm convinced I must still like them. See? Everything works out in the end; everything comes full circle.

But actually, no. I don't like them anymore.

I wasn't waiting for them at all.

For me it's yoga that changes everything, but it could just as well have been dance, or a martial art, or swimming, or rock climbing. Some people try, foolishly, to gain control through food — either drowning themselves in it or depriving themselves of it. The power of the body over the mind. I enact physical metaphors like counter-spells. I make things happen on the yoga mat that I hope to manifest elsewhere. The inverse also occurs: emotional responses are incorporated into the body, psychological legacies clothed in flesh.

The pursuit of growth via the path of intuition.

Find a process to follow, some sort of method. A framework. Familiarise yourself with the techniques and rhythms and structures mastered by your instructors. Those impersonal mothers and fathers who, through the repetition of certain fundamental gestures, teach you how to live more lightly in the world.

Learn to put hinges on your rib cage, so you can choose how wide to open it. Make a wire skeleton for your soft clay body, so it doesn't collapse onto the first person who comes along.

Sprezzatura, Cristina Campo called it. A certain joyful impenetrability; the music of an interior grace.

With light heart, with light hands / life to take, life to leave.

This is something I can't change

This is something I can't change.

I have HIV. I am HIV-positive.

I'm one of them.

I don't know what I want to be anymore — a cyclical refrain of mine. I don't know who I am, I've never known. My whole life until now has been a relentless attempt at becoming something, at assuming some form, embodying some identity. Singer, painter, journalist, aspiring university professor, philosopher. I've thrown myself into countless passions, most of them short-lived: yoga, kung fu, literature, guitar, music theory and solfeggio, meditation, classical dance, feminism, Judaism, Buddhism, animalism, esotericism. Magnificent, for a time, then tedious. Sooner or later, every identity I try to assume ends in failure. Rejected, dismissed — I quickly move on to the next thing. This isn't it, either. I have to be something else.

Now, finally, I'm satisfied.

I have something firm, an unalterable quality to show to the world. Something I can't shake off.

Instead of a diploma, I have a medical report. I have the results of a blood test. My training takes place at a hospital. I provide biological material for research. My doctor is my tutor. He sets specific tasks for me to complete, thrilling goals for me to reach. We work together to keep me alive and in the best possible condition. We collaborate to keep the treatment working, to limit the side effects. To prevent my liver from being poisoned, my bones from growing brittle, my kidneys from succumbing to the toxic medicine.

I look forward to our appointments.

Men are also capable of looking after ourselves. Men can also be trusted.

HIV-positive: an identity chosen for me by my body. I can decide to recognise and accept it, or deny and ignore it, but, regardless of my decision, the identity remains. It's very patient; it doesn't mind waiting for me.

I have HIV. I am HIV-positive. What does that mean? Do I scare you? Do I disgust you? It doesn't matter what you think. I don't care. I've been unwittingly drafted into the army of the impure. The plague-ridden. Carriers of a special breed of evil.

Branded. Stigma. Shame?

Come autumn 2016, I feel nothing.

Whenever I think about it, a sense of unreality invades me. I don't feel angry, or embarrassed. I have HIV — all that means is I have to see my doctor a lot, and do lots of tests. Like millions of other people in the world, for all kinds of reasons.

Everything else is extrinsic. Put there by you, by us.

September, October, November. As time passes, I identify less and less with my illness. I don't feel represented by this shadowy presence — octopus, cephalopod, medusa — that has stalked me since adolescence and now, finally, has me in its clutches, dragging behind it a host of interpretations and reactions that have nothing to do with me.

HIV belongs, above all, to the world.

It says more about you than it does about me.

It is layer upon layer of overlapping gazes.

HIV has its own history, its own traditions, of which I am only marginally aware. Destinies, statistics, organisations, clinical cases, media stories. A long sequence of narratives that predate me, that I know very little about.

And at the same time, HIV is *inside* me. It travels through me, uses my body, and I observe this invasion from the outside. I am a spectator. It's easy to feel a sense of emptiness, of alienation. If I want to take ownership of this new identity, if I want to reach an embodied understanding of who or what I am, it might be wise to seek out people who have already been through this process, or who are going through it at the same time as me. Find support groups, summits. There's one held in Bologna every year: three days of sharing and workshops, like a yoga retreat. Perhaps I can come to terms with the reality of my condition via the experiences of others.

Stand in a circle, see myself reflected back at me.

If I want to take ownership of this, it might be wise to talk about it.

But to whom?

To everyone?

Knowing I have HIV makes me want to do something about it. Act, take control. I don't want to feel powerless. I don't want to submit — I'm only interested in things I can learn from. Maybe I could write about it. Take advantage of my privilege as an unashamed HIV-positive person. Rename what has happened to me, tame it with words, so as to see it more clearly. Use my diagnosis to speak life into what has been kept quiet. Imbue it with meaning, instead of leaving it to rot in the closet of shame.

I want to stay with the pain and chip away at it with words, so that it might grow a little smaller.

There's also the fact that I can't stand the idea of feeling cowed, constrained.

Invisibility forces us into a kind of second-class existence. Secrets inhibit our movement.

I haven't done anything wrong. We haven't done anything wrong. Those who think otherwise are simply trying to protect themselves at our expense: it's a kind of exorcism, an ancient apotropaic ritual.

Say it, speak it, let it be known — also because nothing in this world ever truly stays hidden.

I've already informed my family members, my friends, everyone I wanted to tell. But who's to say whether those people will keep it to themselves? I know what the gay community in Milan is like. I've seen it at its worst. Prejudice — including serophobia — is fuelled by rumours. People love to gossip. Word would get out eventually. Over the years, my friends have told me about mutual acquaintances who contracted the virus. They didn't ask the person's permission before sharing that information; they told me without their knowledge. What was divulged in confidence became the basis for an endless series of conjectures, not all of them respectful. It became an excuse to nurse fantasies, to indulge preconceptions, to justify and explain character traits, flaws, behaviours. To pity, to belittle.

Even today, in gay chat rooms and dating apps, alongside specifications like 'masc4masc' and 'no fats no femmes', people clarify: 'I'm clean UB2'.

I can't stand the thought of having to guess who knows and who doesn't.

I want to take the reins while I still can.

Let the light in — lay everything bare.

★

1 December, 2016. I write a short article, practically a declaration. The only one who could have stopped me is Marius, and he doesn't. I ask him if he has a problem with it. He thinks about it for a second, then says no. My friends, on the other hand, urge me not to do it. They're gripped by a fear that doesn't touch me.

Are you sure?

Give it some thought.

Is it really necessary?

Once you've done this, there's no turning back. No matter what you do in the future — even if they're big, important things — you'll always be remembered for this. They'll always put the same words next to your name: *Jonathan Bazzi, HIV-positive author.*

Doesn't that thought frighten me?

Is that really what I want?

My HIV diagnosis is an incontrovertible fact. Like it or not, it's one of my many physical attributes. One hundred and seventy centimetres tall, brown eyes, brown hair (what's left of it), plentiful body hair, shoe size 43, speech disfluency, inguinal hernia (which may have disappeared of its own accord — *impossible*, the doctors said, *we'll have to operate*), left mandibular canine disturbed by wisdom tooth (my whole mouth askew), nasal septum bulging slightly on one side, myopic, mild intolerance to alcohol (if I have more than one drink my skin goes all blotchy), HIV-positive.

So?

HIV is an objective physical condition. It's not something you choose. In reality, the virus says nothing about me. It says nothing about the person who carries it. HIV is always the same. It doesn't discriminate. If anything, what counts is the way someone bears their diagnosis, how they decide or manage to navigate it. Have you ever thought about that? Do you even give a shit?

I have decided to identify myself, to tell my story rather than leaving it to the imagination.

Truth is the weapon I've armed myself with.

Camaraderie is the answer I've chosen.

When you learn you have HIV, you feel like you're the only one in the world.

Shot with a silencer. Screaming underwater.

A dark cloud, an executioner's hood, a code of silence.

Because no one else talks about it, you feel like it's just you. That's not the case: I discover this by rejecting the tradition of shame and discretion.

The article comes out and my inbox is flooded with messages. They continue to pour in for days, weeks. They continue even now. Expressions of appreciation, mostly, but not exclusively. I have supporters, but I also have haters. I am both paladin and scapegoat. Many of the people who write to me are HIV-positive. Men and women. Minors, people my age, elderly people. Homosexuals, heterosexuals, bisexuals. People I know, but that I didn't know were HIV-positive. Online and real-world friends, acquaintances collected over the years — at university, through yoga. Strangers who follow me on Facebook. But also doctors, healthcare workers, infectious-disease specialists.

I discover that my new psychologist has HIV.

I bump into him one afternoon at Sacco. He's there for his

regular check-up. I'm there for a vaccination — one of the many routine procedures recommended for HIV-positive people. We cross paths in the corridor, between consulting rooms. I say nothing. If he wants to, he'll acknowledge me. And he does.

This is why I was so calm when you told me, he says.

He has it. So many people have it. But no one knows, no one thinks about it. The thought isn't there to comfort you when you receive your diagnosis. It can't be.

HIV-positive people are everywhere; they are a silent, invisible multitude. And they're watching you. They are your friends, your past and future lovers, your trusted experts. Their bodies are no longer public exhibits, forcing them to reveal themselves and risk being pilloried, lynched. Their faces betray no signs of sickness. They are unidentifiable. They look healthy, beautiful, gorgeous: the kind of boys I would fall in love with on social media.

Fact: HIV-positive people who are undergoing treatment and have a negligible viral load cannot transmit the virus.

Fact: as research advances, fewer and fewer active ingredients are required for successful treatment; less medication means fewer side effects.

Fact: within the next year or two, new drugs will be available that only need to be taken once a month, or perhaps even once every two months.

This is the reality of HIV today. Despite this, people living with the condition are still subjected to a toxic blend of invisibility and guilt. There's no way out of it.

I wish I was as strong as you.

Maybe I will be, one day. Who knows?

I think you're amazing, so brave. We have so much respect for you.

The messages I read are full of praise and gratitude. But these people are speaking about the world, about themselves and others, not about me. Their descriptions don't fit me — courage isn't the word for what I have. What happened to me happened spontaneously. I simply felt the urge to share, to write a post or walk into a room, to look at you and say *I have HIV*, and to accept the small consequences in your faces. Your expressions, your gestures. Your words, your silence.

Megalomaniacal, egocentric, arrogant: the people who accuse me of exhibitionism are, in fact, telling me that I should have done the usual. I should have hidden away.

Removal, omission. Leave everything as it is.

From December on, different reactions begin to accumulate.

Some people write to me in the throes of anxiety. They describe a risky sexual relationship, or what they think might be early symptoms, and ask me to assess the likelihood that they've contracted the virus. As if I were some kind of clairvoyant. They want me to be their online HIV test.

Most of them are very young, but some are older.

I'm the only resource their fear can tolerate.

I try reassuring them: I'm sure you're absolutely fine, but you should get tested anyway. They persist, accuse me of providing false comfort. Messages brimming with unwarranted alarm — most of the situations they describe aren't even vaguely risky. They write to me in an attempt to expel the terror from their hearts. And I remind them that, even if they do have it, they will survive. It's not like I'm typing from the grave.

Other kinds of messages appear.

A friend of mine writes: now I understand why you vanished

a few months ago.

A friar tells me I have disobeyed Christ.

Some write to tell me they can't accept their diagnosis; others, that they're afraid of being alone forever.

My boyfriend left me when he found out.

Everyone I knew is gone.

I know that feeling well. The feeling of looking down from the window. The little bit of courage I possess might have been the only thing that kept me from the edge.

I found out on the day of the solar eclipse.

Jonathan, this diagnosis has knocked everything out of balance for me. Things were already intense, but now they're worse. Everything feels amplified — problems, beauty, possibility, imminent catastrophe.

I've disassociated from everything. And from myself.

I hope I'll be able to put myself back together one day.

Confessions, confidences. Protected by the filter of social media, they feel safe to talk about themselves. To tell their stories — so many stories.

Like the story of Antonio, from Benevento: rejected by his family for being gay, he didn't discover he had the virus until it had already progressed to AIDS. The doctors tried their best to save him. In 2017, not long after he writes to me, Antonio will die. He'll try until the very end to get in touch with his mother. It will be no use — he won't get to say goodbye.

After the publication of my article, I have a number of real-world encounters with people who now know. An old high school teacher. Yoga acquaintances. Classmates at the university where, almost a year after the diagnosis, I resume my studies. A bearhug from a friend: fuchsia locks blooming from platinum-blonde roots. She hugs me in spite of my sweaty body (infected sweat, HIV-positive sweat). You can't catch it through sweat — she knows that too, surely — but the thought rises in me all the same. Isn't she worried about getting so close? Isn't she scared of me? Disgusted by me?

Everyone I run into now has a different tone of voice when they ask me how I am, their faces expectant, itching to broach the topic.

They rarely do.

Declaring my diagnosis to the world also rolls out a red carpet for anyone who wants to hurt me.

I'm exposed, uncovered. *You're not protecting yourself.*

In the summer of 2017, a new app comes out that lets you send anonymous messages to your contacts. I download it, and after the usual questions (how I caught it, if have any regrets) it begins. Within a couple of days the messages start flooding in, one after the other.

Why would you publicise that you've got HIV?

Slut.

So you act all intellectual then you get AIDS. If you were actually smart you wouldn't get sick, skeleton boy.

Getting people to pity you won't make you healthy.

Maximum respect, but I don't understand why you take so much pride in being sick.

Ask the Lord for forgiveness.

When you're about to come do you at least pull out for your boyfriend's sake? It must be so scary for him.

No offence, but you really do look like someone who would have AIDS.

What you think is solidarity is actually commiseration.

AIDS fag.

So will you post on Facebook when you transition from HIV to AIDS? Will you have a party?

Do you remember the one time we went out together and I told you you'd be lost without me? Looks like I was right.

The temptation of anonymity is irresistible. They want to wound me, but they fail. Their repertoire is predictable, banal, clichéd. They all miss the target. Not one of the spears they throw at me comes close to hitting a vital organ. By refusing to stay silent, I've made myself transparent. My skin is like air; I can vanish completely if I need to. Words — fierce or gentle — go right through me.

My body retains only a trace of them as they pass through.

I display their trajectories like scars.

Like offerings, sent back out into the world.

Beyond

Beyond the window: office buildings, factories, billboards.

The overpass, the A4 motorway stretching west to Turin and east to Trieste.

The tram is taking me back home from the hospital, along Viale Certosa. People embark and disembark: old people huffing and glancing around the carriage, a mother wearing a hijab, asking someone to help her with the pram. Two schoolgirls sharing a single pair of earbuds. Patients, like me, on their way home from Sacco, having done whatever the day required of them.

I'm always in a good mood when I go to the hospital.

Sometimes even euphoric.

Returning to the place where I thought it was all going to end.

An initiation rite that now I repeat, reclaim.

This morning I got the usual tests. At first I had them done every two months. Now it's every three or four, because everything is going well. The virus has been suppressed. Undetectable viral load. Mission accomplished. For now — forever? While I was at the hospital I also stocked up on my medication. The special tablets I take at ten o'clock every night. You can only get them from the hospital pharmacy; they're not sold commercially.

The trip to Sacco is never-ending. The tram ride alone takes up half the morning. Today, the view of the hospital complex shrouded in mist made the journey seem even more like an infinite plunge into the void.

I don't know if we're even in Milan anymore.

There are easier options. I could go to the San Raffaele centre instead, which I'm told is excellent, and is much closer to home. But while my doctor is here, I wouldn't dream of it. I didn't choose this place, but now Sacco has become a kind of mirror, like all things that hold firm despite the vicissitudes of will. Despite the shifting humours, the ebbs and flows of energy, the effects and affects of mood enhancers. It sits on the periphery, like everything else that doesn't matter or has been pushed away. The landscape declares as much: here, there is only space for what is real.

Sickness is sickness, you can see it with your own eyes. Wellness, too.

In the end, isn't fear always an attempt to keep something hidden?

Sacco doesn't look like a hospital, exactly. It's an enormous complex broken up into small and large buildings, each separated by streets, gardens, and rows of trees. A village, a town. A housing project. A bit like Rozzano.

That place where I was a foreign body. An intruder.

Where I grew up on the sidelines, against the wind.

In Rozzano I had to learn to reject other people's interpretations of the world. My natural deviation from their values ended up working to my advantage. I developed basic survival tactics early on in life — one benefit of being marginalised at such a young age.

I was born in Rozzano, but I don't know how to fight. I stutter. I like boys.

I have HIV, but I'm not the kind of patient who simply acknowledges it and adapts. Who can turn their diagnosis into a secret that only grows bigger in the dark.

As a kid in Rozzano, I didn't know what I was doing. I instinctively followed the veins of gold in the tunnels. I kept my sights on what I thought was beautiful. I played alone, I read books — small acts of resistance. Slowly, I began to float away. Even when I didn't seem to be, I was elsewhere.

If today I am no longer too bothered by people's estimations of me, perhaps it's because of where I grew up. Rozzano: both my poison and my antidote. In the face of prejudice, do you raise the stakes or do you keep your head down? Even the walls have ears. Air your dirty laundry wherever you feel safe.

When it comes down to it, isn't the measure of a person determined above all by their reaction to circumstances, facts, and experiences beyond their control? We are living systems, always capable of rearranging our situation.

I grew up surrounded by the cement boxes of public-housing towers but existing in a kind of inter-space, breathing from a different air bubble. I have known the silent rootlessness, the emptiness of unbelonging. I got used to the idea that I should be ashamed of what I am, and I understood that the poisonous pact can be broken by speaking out. By exposing the script, reading the unspoken rules out loud. By inhabiting the space of exclusion in my own way — introducing a bug into the system, and watching to see what happens.

Will I get hurt?

Is it worth it?

If I refuse to play my part, the space of exile might become a space of protection.

Out of place then, out of place now. I refuse to quietly bear the stigma of my illness.

In Rozzano I practised singing a higher note.

A wrong note?

I won't close my mouth now.

I'll keep trying until I hit the right chord.

The various hospital wards are housed in separate buildings scattered among the greenery. Mine is the furthest from the entrance. Almost every time I go to Sacco, I get lost. I don't have a good sense of direction, and the streets all intersect, like paths in a garden maze. Each time I walk through the gate I make a conscious effort — pay attention, you know this place. But after a while, a very short while, I give up. I rely on the few details that look familiar, the tiny clues that appear around me.

Building 56.

The infectious-diseases building is always full of people, especially in the mornings, when blood tests are taken. The building has a vintage vibe, dishevelled and stiff at the same time. Both brazen and reserved, private and ostentatious. The patients are a motley crew. There are the veterans, the worn-out survivors. Then there are newbies, the recently diagnosed. The ones who were late to the party, like me. Who caught the virus after it was no longer fashionable. There are people who have lived fabulous, reckless lives, and others for whom half an hour of carelessness was enough. The full spectrum of existences, from the most extreme to the most banal. Stories that remain unspoken, left to the imagination. Because, above all, these mornings at Building 56 are about collective discretion — privacy, restraint, the desire to blend in.

Glances stolen from the corners of eyes. Little ploys to try to conceal the obvious.

Some are stoic, dignified, standing tall and averting their eyes. Others hide, slipping bottles of tablets into their bags with the dexterity of magicians, as if their situation weren't already crystal clear to everyone around them. Some flirt, trying even now to pick up, to get laid. Some rush to get everything over with as quickly as possible. Some gaze into the distance with glazed eyes.

I have already declared my diagnosis to the entire world, so I shouldn't have a problem with being seen here. But it's hard not to feel observed (judged?) in a room full of silent faces. Everything seems to be hanging in the air. There is always the temptation to withdraw, to erase what has been. It's hard not to notice the expression of the cashier when I hand her my pathology exemption card, that little pink missive that says, in no uncertain terms: *no, I'm not just here for the HIV test.*

Is it compassion? Disapproval?

Indifference?

The ritual is always the same: wait, co-pay desk, delivery of the prescription, tests, consultation with the doctor.

In the toilet cubicle I redistribute my urine samples into the correct vials — the nurses are always messing up the test codes. I feel like an alchemist, pouring piss from one tube into another. I'm re-enacting the iconography of Temperance, the Major Arcana card that, in most Tarot decks, depicts an angel decanting a mysterious liquid: holy water, primordial soup, elixir of life. The card of patience, of regeneration, of restoring equilibrium.

I am preparing my bodily fluids for examination. My body is invested with new meaning. I am part of history, now. Samples of my blood have been frozen for a number of national research projects. Small red icicles sitting in a laboratory freezer somewhere. Another project, in collaboration with the hospital's psychology department, analysed my urine samples over the course of a year to monitor my cortisone levels — my mood hormones. They're trying to get funding for a free psychological support service.

2016–2019.

I've been in treatment for three years now.

I take one tablet a day.

Just one.

It's pale pink, the size of a sugared almond. A lolly to be swallowed whole.

Apparently, pale pink is the oldest biological colour in the world. Scientists recently discovered traces of fossilised chlorophyll in ancient shale rock from a long-disappeared ocean, located in what is now Mauritania. The pigment is a soft pink, tinged with yellow. The colour of the oldest known life form.

Antiretroviral medications like the ones I take prevent the virus from replicating, until it is undetectable. In other words, until the instruments of modern medicine are no longer able to pick up any traces of it. That doesn't mean the virus has disappeared completely.

We know it's still there, because if I were to stop taking my big pink sugared almond tablets, it would start replicating again. The drugs keep it subdued, corralled into a few corners of the body. They call them *sanctuary sites* — hidden viral reservoirs, places the drugs can't quite reach. Small occupied territories from which the virus continues to wage its slow war. My body knows they are there: chronic low-level inflammation is a permanent symptom of HIV.

I decide not to look into the long-term effects of this inflammation.

Each time I go to the hospital, I write a little diary entry on the tram ride home. It's become a habit. I'm lucky: everything is going well. Writing about my experience, sharing it with others, is also my way of reorienting myself. I lose my way, sometimes, thinking about all the people who have been taken away by this virus. People exactly like me. I could have been one of them. I *am* one of them. What differentiates us is something beyond my control — it has nothing to do with me. It is the research, the hard work of hundreds and thousands of women and men I will never meet. I am my mother's son, but now I am also the son of medicine — medicine gave me my diagnosis, medicine gave me these pale pink tablets that force the microscopic invader into hiding. Send it fleeing, like my cats when I turn on the vacuum cleaner.

The virus is a dumb beast that's afraid of the colour pink. A bit like the boys in Rozzano.

As the tram is re-entering the city, my phone rings.

It's Marius. He asks if I want him to grab anything for dinner on the way home.

What do you feel like?

I don't know — you?

Wait, today's the nineteenth.

Our anniversary.

Shall we go to the Lebanese place?

Okay.

Ah, *iuby*, if you go home first, would you please bring my tablet?

My pink tablet has to be taken at the same time every day. It's important. If I miss one, or if I take it at the wrong time, the virus could develop a resistance. It could take advantage of even a slight lapse in the supply of active ingredients in my system, and start replicating again. It wouldn't be the end of the world if this happened, but it would mean I'd have to change medications. The technical term is *treatment failure*. And since each drug — there are several on the market nowadays — has its own set of potential side effects, it's best to err on the side of caution.

I've never forgotten to take my tablet. A few times I took it an hour or two late, and the guilt lasted for days.

Once the initial adjustment period was over, taking the tablet became an automatic gesture, one I might even repeat unconsciously. I've had to take certain precautions: I bought a cheap plastic tablet organiser with a compartment for every day of the week. Every Monday morning I fill it: seven pink tablets, sitting in a row. It makes things easier.

I also set a daily alarm on my phone. I made Marius set one, too. If we're apart at ten o'clock in the evening, he texts me. He knows I get distracted easily — sometimes my thoughts overlap, with no respect for order of importance. I remember we're out of oat milk, but I forget a brilliant idea I had about an essay I just finished. I remember trivial details, but I don't remember the cats have no kibble until the shops are already closed.

Did you take it?

Iuby, your tablet.

Don't forget to take your tablet.

The synchronised alarms on our phones are a bridge between us. Wherever we are, whatever we're doing, it brings us back to one another. It re-tunes our connection. If Marius doesn't text me a reminder, I know it means he's still working, or maybe he's at after-work drinks and he's had a few too many. Sometimes I overthink it: he's forgotten about me, he doesn't care.

Does the wound of the unloved ever fully heal?

If we're out for dinner when the time comes to take my tablet, I hesitate. Despite my convictions, despite the fact that I've made a conscious decision to reject the compulsions of prejudice, I don't like taking it in front of everyone. I don't want the people at the table next to us to see, or the waiters, or the hostess roaming around dispensing polite smiles. Single, naked gestures are more insidious than official statements. Declaring my illness is, above all, a way of protecting myself, of preventing anyone from *discovering* it while I'm sitting in front of them, vulnerable. Maybe it's not unlike refusing to read aloud, or preceding the act of reading with a theatrical confession: please excuse my stutter, I have no idea how this is going to come out.

Our friends have grown more comfortable with my treatment. Mirella, Alessandro, Simona. If we're out together at ten o'clock, they remind me themselves — sometimes they even joke about it. The veil of embarrassment has lifted. Their expressions, their tones of voice have changed.

At the Lebanese restaurant, I try not to think about the possibly spying eyes of our neighbours. I imagine I'm drawing a magic circle around myself. Inside the circle are my friends, my allies. Outside the circle are the judgements of other people. I push through the cloud of fear that orbits me.

At least this way everyone will know the truth.

Rewriting the rules — what is permitted, what is taboo — takes courage.

I fill up my water glass.

I reach into my jacket pocket.

It's not in the right-hand pocket. The left, then?

I find the tissue it's wrapped up in.

I remove it.
Open my palm.
Pale pink on white tablecloth.
No one takes any notice.

Acknowledgements

Thank you to Matteo B. Bianchi for lighting the fuse, to Tiziana Triana and Lavinia Azzone for making it all possible, to Viola Di Grado for the sense of structure and for curbing my wild proliferations of thought, to Teresa Ciabatti for tying up loose ends and for sending words and counsel from the eye of the storm, to Elisa Seitzinger for her miracle remedies, to Rosa Matteucci for the constant inspiration, to Giuliano Federico for fishing me out of my stupor all those years ago (and for the laptop I wrote this book on), to Francesca Genti for urging me to take this project seriously, to Gaja Cenciarelli for her warmth and contagious joy, to Andrea Zandomeneghi for telling me that, if it had been up to him, he would have published my writing that time, and to Federico Campagna, who I was sure didn't know I existed.

And thank you to Marius, Blueberry, and Mashed Potatoes, for the unimaginable.